THE COMPANION GUIDE TO
The Coast of
North-East England

Uniform with this volume

The Coast of South-West England

In preparation

The Coast of South-East England
The Coast of East Anglia and the Thames Estuary

THE COMPANION GUIDE TO

The Coast of

North-East England

John Seymour

COLLINS
ST JAMES'S PLACE, LONDON

William Collins Sons & Co Ltd
London · Glasgow · Sydney · Auckland
Toronto · Johannesburg

First published 1974
Reprinted 1975
© John Seymour 1974
ISBN 0 00 219051 6
Set in Monotype Baskerville
Made and Printed in Great Britain by
William Collins Sons & Co Ltd Glasgow

Contents

❧

Illustrations

❦

CHAPTER I

The Border to Berwick-upon-Tweed

.❧

THE East Coast of England starts from Scotland at a farm called **Marshall Meadows**. The railway runs close to the high sandstone cliffs, and British Railways signal the imaginary borderline by an elaborate sign welcoming Englishmen to Scotland and Scotsmen the other way.

On the narrow strip of land between the railway line and the cliff-edge is a little caravan site, perhaps the pleasantest on the whole of the East Coast. From here the sandstone cliffs fall 180 feet quite vertically to the beach, and the traveller might think it quite impossible to descend short of lowering himself down on a rope. Such a course is unnecessary. Just behind the little cottage perched on the cliff-edge (now 'ablutions' for caravanners and also a 'summer cottage', but once used by salmon netters) is a strange little dell. If you clamber down into it you will find the mouth of a large tunnel, or inclined shaft, driven steeply down into the sandstone. It is perhaps a hundred yards long or more, and fairly steep, but you will not slip because the sandstone is rough and doesn't get slippery even when worn, or wet. Down at the bottom there is a strange sort of masonry and concrete dock, perched on some sundered cliff, from which you can clamber down to the beach below. There is a rope to help you do this. It is not a descent for the infirm or the ultra-timid, but perfectly easy for any ordinarily nimble person.

And it is well worth going down, for Marshall Meadows Bay is a most beautiful place, one of the most delectable pieces of coast in Britain. A splendid little bay, sheltered from all the winds except the East, with the vertical sandstone cliffs all around and a little waterfall at one point falling straight to the beach below. There is sand in the bay itself, but to the south of it, at low water, are revealed large areas of flattish sandstone slab. These are indented with hundreds of small and large rock pools abounding with life; and here and there are perfectly formed pot holes, rounded and smooth, with the rounded stones which had caused them inside.

There are places where the softer shale which underlies the sand-stone has been cut away by the sea and the cliff has foundered: huge

9

chunks have been carved away, in places exhibiting plateaux at the top complete with grass and trees and inaccessible except to seagulls, stock doves and mountaineers.

There are caves, and at one point, at **St John's Haven** (which would only be a haven to the hard-pressed mariner indeed) there is a remarkable cave with a curtain of fresh water falling down across its mouth. Here an anchorite could live well provided for, for stock doves nest in high ledges inside, oystercatchers, turnstones, redshanks and curlews hop about on the rocks outside, shellfish abound, and the cave has a great store of driftwood for the holy man's fire. The cave is an uncanny red, which a good hermit would no doubt attribute to miraculous causes, but which is in fact due to a marine lichen, *Xanthoria parietina*. It would be an uncomfortable cell at high spring tide in an on-shore gale, and our hermit would have to clamber high up among the stock doves' nests to avoid being washed away.

And let the non-anchorite beware too, while on this splendid and dramatic stretch of shore, for there are plenty of places where he could be cut off by the rising tide. He would then either have to swim for it or climb a vertical cliff. On a rising tide do not get too far away either from one of the few places where you could scramble up, or from the tunnel mouth. The passage south, anyway, is stopped at any but the lowest tide by the Needle's Eye, a most spectacular arch of rock.

The tunnel, naturally, is reputed to have been made by smugglers, but it would have been well-equipped smugglers indeed to have driven such a hefty winze through the rock. It was in fact made by an improving squire in the early nineteenth century. He wanted access to the beach below, for he established a salmon fishery down there, and wanted to haul seaweed up (for fertiliser) and lower stone down from a small quarry which he had. Keels could have been beached in the little bay and loaded with stone from the small wharf. There were two sets of rails in the tunnel, and one truck went down while the other came up: both operated by a waterwheel driven by a small stream. The squire built a small dam about a mile inland, to store water for the wheel.

Berwick-upon-Tweed is that rare survival: a perfectly walled town. Except where a hole has been bashed for the passage of the A1 it is completely surrounded by a wall, pierced by gates, and for much of its length it is of a period and pattern which makes it unique in Europe. Besides being of enormous antiquarian interest,

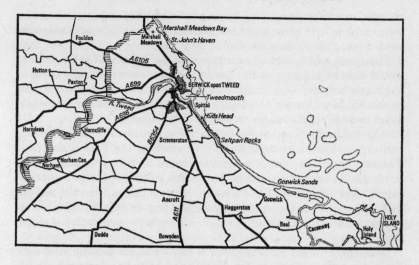

and a notable tourist attraction, this wall gives the town a quite extraordinary beauty and charm.

Part of Northumbria (as Edinburgh was) in Anglo-Saxon times, Berwick was annexed by that brand new country, Scotland, when King Malcolm II took Lothian from Northumbria at the battle of Carham in 1018, thus establishing the River Tweed as the boundary between England and Scotland. David I established Berwick as one of his four royal boroughs (the others being Roxburgh, Edinburgh and Stirling), and encouraged the trade of the town by bringing in Flemish craftsmen, founding a Cistercian nunnery, and possibly beginning the building of the castle. Under Scottish rule the town flourished, for as part of Scotland it was an important place and the nearest port in the country to the Continent. To the English Berwick could only have one importance: as an advanced base against Scotland. In 1172 Richard de Lucy and Humphrey de Bohun made a raid against the Scots, captured the town and laid it in ashes. King William the Lion was captured at Alnwick, and then released after the Treaty of Falaise in 1174, after having done homage to Henry II of England and surrendering Berwick to English rule. Richard *Coeur de Lion* handed it back again for the payment of 10,000 marks: his lion's heart being set on the Holy Land and not the wild kingdom to the north. English preoccupation with the Crusades and with the subjugation of the French caused them to leave the Scots in peace, but in 1216 the Scottish king, Alexander II, made the mistake of coming south and besieging Norham Castle. King John raised the siege and on the 15th January of the same year stormed Berwick, took it, and, according to the *Melrose Chronicle*, inflicted inhuman torments on the inhabitants, both men and women. After raiding into the north he came back to the town and personally set fire to it, thrusting with his own hand a lighted torch into the thatched roof of the house wherein he had lodged for the night *contra morum regum indecenter* – according to the *Chronicon de Mailros*.

The town reverted to the Scots, however, and in 1266 a Franciscan monk of Carlisle was able to compare (in the *Chronicle of Lanercost*) Berwick with Alexandria, in that it had the sea for its wealth and water for its walls. It was the greatest port in Scotland: nearly every Scottish abbey had its town house in Berwick, and in 1286, the last year of the reign of Alexander III, the town paid £2190 into the exchequer of Scotland, being the customs revenue from the export of wool and hides. This was equal to a quarter of the customs revenue for the whole of England. The town 'took rank with Ghent and Rotterdam and was almost the rival of London'.

But under Edward I the English turned their attention from harrying the French to conquering the Scots and the Welsh, and in 1292 Edward held his court in Berwick (the assembly of the States of England and Scotland) and there gave judgment between John de Baliol and Robert de Bruce, or Brus, as to who should be King of Scotland, in favour of de Baliol. Later, when Edward was in France, he was informed that an insurrection had broken out in Scotland, and he ordered an army to assemble at Newcastle on 25th March 1296, supported by a fleet of a hundred sail. He led the army across the Tweed at Coldstream on 28th March and was at the walls of Berwick on the 30th. He stormed the town, took it and slaughtered most of the inhabitants. The town never recovered. From being the biggest merchant city of Scotland and a port of international importance, it dwindled to a place of little commercial account, although it remained an important military fortification.

It was, for the English, the key to Scotland. The most practicable road to Edinburgh was along the coast (the A1 goes that way now), and Berwick commanded the narrow coastal strip between a spur of the Lammermuir Hills and the sea from its eminently fortifiable position. Further, it was a fortified port, and an English army wishing to invade Scotland, or wishing to defend England from Scottish attack, could be supplied easily by sea.

Edward, having subjugated Scotland, summoned a parliament to assemble at Berwick to settle the fate of the kingdom that he had conquered, and it was at this time that he ordered the building of what are still known as the 'Edwardian Walls'.

In 1297 the Scots were back again, this time under Wallace. But alas, in 1305 Wallace was captured, hung, drawn and quartered, and his top left quarter was brought to Berwick and exposed for the edification of the populace in what is now called Wallace Green. In 1306 the Countess of Buchan, who had crowned Bruce at Scone, was captured and kept in an iron cage at Berwick for four years, after which she was handed over into the custody of the Friars of Mount Carmel in Berwick who kept her until 1313.

But the Scots were not beaten yet. In 1314 they had taken Stirling Castle from the English king, and in June of that year Edward II assembled a large army at Berwick-upon-Tweed to go and take it back again. This vast host rode north one fine day in grand chivalric array to be smashed to pieces at Bannockburn. Edward II escaped with his life by taking to the sea in a fishing boat and thus returned to Berwick a defeated king.

Two years later Robert Bruce besieged the town, to such effect that the garrison were reduced to eating dead horses and even less savoury objects. On the night of 10th January 1316 Bruce tried an escalade but was defeated by the moon being too bright. But on 28th March 1318 he tried again and succeeded, and in Berwick he assembled many of his parliaments. Next year the English attacked the town with a big fleet and an army, and a huge siege engine called 'The Sow' which the Scots countered with another monstrous device called 'The Crab'. The attack failed, and the Scots continued in Berwick. Under their rule the trade of the town revived and the place became prosperous again. Near the Bell Tower can still be seen some of the defences raised by Robert Bruce during his occupation.

But the English could not rest while Berwick remained Scottish, and on 4th April 1333 a large English army arrived at the walls, equipped with the latest in siege engines made at Cawood in Yorkshire. It was during this siege that the son of the Scottish governor of the town, Thomas Setton, was handed over to the English as a hostage and later, when his father Sir Alexander refused to surrender, was hanged in view of his father, who stood impotent on the ramparts. A Scottish army under Archibald Douglas tried to raise the siege and met the English army at Halidon Hill (which is a couple of miles to the north-west of the town). Here the weapon which the English were developing, and which was to prove so invincible at Crecy and Agincourt – the long bow and the armour-piercing arrow – prevailed, and the Scottish army was shot to pieces. Berwick surrendered. Next year Edward III spent Easter in the town and was entertained with a grand jousting tournament between English and Scottish knights, during which much blood was spilled. The Scots recaptured the town at least four times after this, and by 1482, when Berwick-upon-Tweed was finally ceded to the English after a long siege, the town had changed hands thirteen times since the Scottish William had given it to the English as part of his ransom – which must have been very trying for the ordinary people of the town. Surely no town in Britain has seen so many violent times.

The English have kept the town from that time, although it is the wrong side of the Tweed, which is so obviously the natural frontier between the two countries. The townspeople may well strike the southerner as being more Scots than English, and of course the very county to which Berwick has given its name is a Scottish county. If Scotland ever regains independence it would be a handsome gesture if the town which is so obviously part of Scotland were handed back again.

Berwick was always looked upon as a separate dominion of the English crown until 1746, when the *Wales and Berwick Act* was passed. This declared that 'in all cases when the kingdom of England . . . shall be mentioned in any act of Parliament the same . . . shall be deemed to comprehend and include the Dominion of Wales and Town of Berwick-upon-Tweed'. But even as late as the Crimean War Berwick was mentioned separately in the declaration of war but was *not* mentioned in the subsequent declaration of peace, so it is sometimes said that Berwick is still at war with Russia.

But – to the ramparts. It is obvious that a town, on the wrong side of a wide river and bang up against the frontier of a hostile country, would have to be heavily fortified. Berwick was against the Scots what Calais was against the French: the ultimate outpost. The walls, built in the reigns of the first and second Edwards with nineteen fighting towers with timber platforms, were patched up and repaired from time to time, but by the time of the Tudors they were somewhat obsolete. The development of the cannon had made an entirely different sort of fortification necessary.

Henry VIII's engineers, realising how vulnerable the medieval walls were to cannon, built a circular tower on which cannon might be mounted, at the most northerly point (the north-east corner). He also tried to bring the old castle up to date with a gun tower. Other small round gun towers were added to the town walls and under his successor, Edward VI, a beginning was made with an elaborate citadel on high ground to the east of the town, cutting the walls. This was never completed and very little is left of it. But it was after the fall of Calais under Mary in 1558 that it was realised that a major effort had to be made to bring the fortifications into the gunpowder age.

The engineer Sir Richard Lee was sent north, equipped with the latest Italian ideas on fortification, and so well was his work carried out that Berwick-upon-Tweed could be defended today against quite a heavy attack by modern weapons: and in the last two wars, in fact, guns have been mounted on the Elizabethan bastions.

Because of the great expense of the necessary earthwork the perimeter had to be shortened, and the whole of the northern part of the town was excluded and abandoned as a fortification. It was planned, also, thus to abandon Lower Town, in the south of Berwick. Five great bastions were built at corners of the new ramparts, and a sixth, facing the river at the south-west corner, was planned but never started. No doubt it was considered that the medieval walls along the river, strengthened and supplied with gun platforms, would be a sufficient makeshift.

Before we start out on our tour of the ramparts it will be as well to consider the art of fortification as it had been developed in Italy in the Renaissance, and as it came to a culmination in far-away Berwick. Firstly, a stone wall was quite ineffective against cannon fire. So only the base of the rampart could be faced with stone, and this base was protected against gunfire by the fact that there was a ditch in front of it, and only a gun dragged right to the edge of the ditch could be brought to bear on the masonry. A gun thus dragged would come under intolerable fire from cannon mounted on the ramparts. The stone wall at the base of the rampart was necessary, though, to prevent enemy infantry from scaling the earthen rampart.

No obstacle, however, is effective unless covered by fire, and the scarp or stone face of the rampart down in the ditch, was covered by guns mounted in recesses called flankers which were protected completely from the fire of the enemy by the protruding bastions. The guns in these flankers were invulnerable, at least until the development of the mortar as an effective weapon, and they could take any enemy attack on the curtain wall by infantry in enfilade – i.e. by shooting along the line of the enemy.

Meanwhile, high up on the earthen bastions themselves, heavy guns fired out at the enemy, and an infantry attack on any bastion was enfiladed by fire from the two bastions on each side of it. In the highest form of this kind of fortress, the very land outside the fortification was landscaped to suit the defenders. Cleared of all obstruction it was carefully shaped to follow the trajectory of a cannon ball, so that such a ball fired from a rampart would travel parallel with the ground, at about the height of a man's chest, for much of its trajectory: 'grazing fire' as it was called. It was the intention thus to shape the 'killing ground' at Berwick, but this was never carried out. The development can be seen at its perfection at Jaffna, in Ceylon.

Further, high up on the bastions, *cavaliers* were raised: higher mounds of earth, flat-topped, from which long-range cannon could command the country for a long distance in front of the fortification, harassing any enemy build-up of forces, or knocking out their artillery from a superior height.

The Elizabethan ramparts of Berwick were never put to the test, but surely the best proof of the effectiveness of a fortification is that no enemy should see the point of attacking it, and this was probably the case with Berwick. With French help, the Scots were quite ready and willing to attack England in Elizabethan times, and the fact that they did not do so might well have been because they realised that they could never have overcome the defences of Berwick, and without Berwick they would have had no hope of seriously incommoding the English.

Approaching the town from the north, as we do in our coastwise peregrination, we come first to some earthworks at Spades Mire, of which nobody seems to know the origin or use. Further south is Lord's Mount, built under Henry VIII, and near it the Bell Tower, an octagonal tower with four storeys, probably Elizabethan on Edwardian foundations. We are now on the medieval, or Edwardian (Edward I and Edward II), north wall, and can follow this from Lord's Mount south-east until we come to the great ditch of the Elizabethan ramparts, at the corner bastion known as the Brass Bastion. We may here turn right and walk along the wide ditch, still outside the walls, past the next bastion which is called Cumberland, as far as Scotsgate. From here we can get an attacker's eye view of the fortifications at their strongest point, and can enter the town. It is here, indeed, that the Great North Road passes through. Inside the Gate we find stairs leading up to the top of the ramparts, where we can turn right and go back, with a defender's eye view this time, to the top of Cumberland Bastion.

Here we can see very clearly the whole plan of the fortification. We can look down, on both sides, into the recessed flankers, and see how their guns could rake the ditch in front of the wall. We can see

BERWICK-ON-TWEED: *Above*, the old Border Bridge; *below*, the sea wall seen from the battlements.

The nave of Lindisfarne Priory, Holy Island.

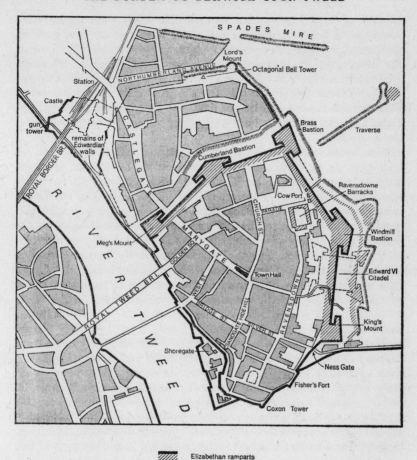

```
        Elizabethan ramparts
        Medieval walls
        Earthworks
```

the embrasures in the grassy bank on the first level of the bastion itself, and see how the cannon here once protected the bastions: Meg's Mount on one side and Brass on the other. And above all is the cavalier: simply a higher bank still, with embrasures in the grassy parapet pointing towards Scotland. The cavaliers, and also the top part of the earthworks of the curtain walls, were added in the seventeenth century.

The flankers have gun-ports in the stone walls that cut off the mouths of these recesses, but at one time there were upper gun-decks too, of heavy timber, so that there were two levels of guns in these small recesses. Any enemy caught anywhere along the face of the curtain wall in between two bastions would have a very short life indeed. Access to the flankers was by tunnel through the curtain wall, and these tunnels are still there, but locked: the key to one in Cumberland Bastion can be got from the custodian of the fortifications, who can generally be found either about the ramparts or in the Barracks.

Cumberland Bastion is of course named after the victor of Culloden. As we walk on towards the sea we come back to Brass Bastion, named from a brass cannon once mounted on it. Brass never had upper timber gun-decks to its flankers, and the latter were roofed over at their backs with arches in order to widen the 'gorge', or 'throat', of the bastion, and provide a continuous sentry path (a short length of which still remains to be seen over the rear of the west flanker). From the most northerly corner of Brass Bastion the remains of an earthen wall strike out across the ditch. This was intended to be a dam, and there were to be several more round the ramparts, with the object of retaining water in the ditch to turn it into a moat. Stretching towards the sea from Brass, across the open land of Magdalen Fields (now be-golfed) is an earthwork which was a traverse of 1564, intended to prevent an enemy from working south between the town and the sea. South we cross over Cow Port, the town's only surviving Elizabethan gateway, though the gate itself is mid-eighteenth century. We would be well advised to clamber down and have a look at it. Up on the wall again we keep on south to Windmill Bastion, which has gun mountings of nineteenth century and 1914–18 War on it, and from Windmill we observe, seaward, other grassy banks and mounds which are all that is left of a rough bastion thrown up in a hurry in 1545 (at least this is what it may have been) and also the ill-conceived Edward VI Citadel. Looking townwards from the wall south of Windmill we see the splendid little Magazine, built in 1749, and proof against the nastiest of early mortar bombs. (It was the mortar and the howitzer, and later the aerial bomb, which finally rendered the town wall quite out of date.)

Further south is King's Mount, a demi-bastion, on which I have picked fine mushrooms. From here we get a good view along the pier and down on the warehouses on Pier Road.

From King's Mount the intention had been to take the ramparts more or less straight across the town, on a ridge of high ground, to

Meg's Mount, the most westerly corner, thus abandoning Lower
Town to any enemy who might happen along. In any case Lower
Town would have been quite indefensible from artillery south of the
river. But this was never carried out: patently the river itself, with
the medieval wall along it, almost completely rebuilt in the eighteenth century, was deemed a sufficient defence. On Fisher's Fort, an
eighteenth-century battery position, stands a gun captured in the
Crimean War (the fine collection of guns that the town had before
was boiled down for scrap at the beginning of the 1939–45 War).
Further is Coxon Tower, a watch tower, and beyond this a long
eighteenth-century battery and a road leading to Palace Green
down which we can see the nice Doric *Main Guard House*, once
positioned at Scotsgate but removed in 1815 and rebuilt here. It is a
typical accommodation for a Quarter Guard, with a room for
officers, another for other ranks, and a black hole for offenders
against King's Regulations. Back on the ramparts we have a
marvellous walk along the Quay Walls, with the river on one side
of us and the splendid eighteenth- and early nineteenth-century
houses on the other. Alas some are falling into decay, and if they
are allowed to go some of the beauty of this most beautiful of towns
will die. The ghosts of the burghers of Berwick will face a heavy
charge from posterity if they spare that lick of paint, new panes of
glass and new roof tiles now. As it is, some of them are complacently
abetting the Ministry of Transport in its foul plans to bust yet another
hole in those marvellous ramparts – for a quite transitory purpose –
the town will be by-passed in ten years' time and render this proposed new gap for a road redundant. Could brutal philistinism go
further?

We carry on, past the lovely and still eminently useful bridge of
1613–20, across the horrible Royal Tweed Bridge of 1928 (main
span 361½ feet) and thence up three great ramps to Meg's Mount,
another demi-bastion, named after Roaring Meg, one of her erst-
while cannon. A few yards further brings us to Scotsgate again,
and we have completed the circuit of the ramparts: a walk that
would have delighted My Uncle Toby and his Corporal Trim, and
can scarcely fail to delight even the most unmilitary-minded of us
today. In the British Isles, only Londonderry has anything to compare with it.

If we are indefatigable we can climb down the steep ramps again
to the river bank and follow the very decayed remains of the
Edwardian walls to where they strike inland again, and then go on
along the river walk (delightful) and under Robert Stephenson's

stupendous Royal Border Bridge, which has carried the railway since its completion in 1850 and compares with even the magnificent Pontcysyllte Aqueduct which carries the canal across the Dee. We then come to the tattered remains of Berwick's ancient castle. Robert Stephenson quite simply blew this up to make room for his railway station, saying that this was the final Act of Union between Scotland and England. Would that he could have made some less vandalistic gesture.

Down the river is a round gun tower of Henry VIII, in which we can see the emerging need to make better embrasures and larger fighting platforms for the large cannon that were beginning to dominate warfare. Running very steeply up the hillside from this is the White Wall, which was to block enemy infiltration along the river. Behind this are Breakneck Steps, and as we mount these we must be careful to see that they belie their name. Down behind this is Castle Dene Park: the sort of municipal garden beloved of town councillors. Up on top is what was once a mighty medieval castle and is now a railway station, and a large hotel with a fine view. Of the castle (in which Edward I decided the crown of Scotland in favour of de Baliol) there is little to see. Although left so far outside the main defences by the Elizabethans, they still intended to defend it and work was done on it as late as 1600. In the eighteenth century it suffered from the old trick of turning an ancient monument into a stone quarry, and the arrogant Victorians completed the work. And now we have examined about all there is to examine of the defences of this fortified town.

For most of my information regarding these defences, besides my own observation, I have relied on the most excellent Ministry of Works Official guide book *The Fortifications of Berwick-upon-Tweed*, written by Mr. Iain Macivor.

CHAPTER 2

Berwick-upon-Tweed to Holy Island

❧

THERE is plenty to see within the ramparts, and a week in Berwick would not be too long to see it. The pleasantest thing to do is just to wander around, apparently aimlessly, and savour the flavour of the place. Any town within walls is apt to have that jumbled look which is so attractive, but surprisingly there are plenty of good open spaces too in Berwick, the most pleasant being the several areas of well-tended allotments, a fine example being just behind King's Mount. Here, though, is a saddening sight: Lion's House, the most imposing private house in Berwick and certainly the building with the finest view, being sacked by vandals because the money, or the will, isn't there to keep it in repair. Palace Green and the little roads that lead from it are charming. The Barracks, behind Windmill Bastion, (Ravensdowne Barracks) must at all events be visited. These were designed in 1717 after the 1715 Rebellion had necessitated the billeting of a lot of troops in the town. It is said that the design was influenced by Sir John Vanbrugh, and as that painter and architect was much in Northumberland after 1718, when he was building Seaton Delaval Hall, this is most probably true. It is a fine block of buildings, and must look almost exactly the same now as it did in the eighteenth century. It was for many years the depot of the King's Own Borderers, now the King's Own Scottish Borderers. This regiment was formed in March 1689 'by beat of drum', in Edinburgh, and since then has had a history that reads like some fantastic world tour. There is hardly a campaign in which the British were engaged in their process of making, retaining, and thereafter abandoning, the greatest empire this planet has seen that the 'Kosbies' were not in. Their regimental museum is still at the Barracks and is well worth a visit. The small part of their regimental silver that is displayed gives an indication of the sumptuousness and display of an officer's mess in palmier days. Don't miss that fabulous silver ram's head, which was used as a perambulating snuff box! A short history of the regiment is available in the museum.

Holy Trinity Church, in Wallace Green, was one of the only two churches built in England during the Commonwealth period, when people were more concerned with knocking down than in building such edifices. Cromwell, when he came through Berwick to the Battle of Dunbar, ordered that it should not have a tower, and the two rather incongruous polygonal turrets at the west end are nineteenth-century, as is the chancel (1885). The building is interesting, a cross between the classical and a kind of Gothic, with Tuscan columns and round arches inside, a rather beautiful flat sweeping arch to a north chapel, and a reredos by Lutyens. Originally there were galleries to the north and south and even one to the east (to prevent 'East worship'). It was built in the time of Colonel George Fenwick, the Parliamentary governor of Berwick, by a London mason John Young.

From the west front of the church the windows of the Municipal Buildings can be seen, in which people were incarcerated while waiting for transportation to Australia. If you can get permission to visit these prison cells it is worth doing so, for they are interesting.

There is another prison that is well worth visiting, and that is the top storey of the Guild Hall. The Guild Hall is a noteworthy building, the 150-foot high spire of which can be seen from far away to the south, or at sea. It was built under Joseph Dodds, who saw to it that his name was placed over the door in great prominence, but designed by S. and J. Worral of London in 1750. To visit it you must apply to the Town Clerk's Department, and pay 5p, and to do so is well worth while. There is a fine council chamber, recently very well restored, a ring of bells of great interest above a most interesting belfry, with poems in it:

> Keep stroak of time and goe
> Not out or elles you forfeit out of
> Doubt for every fault a jugge of beer.

and:

> When mirth and pleasure is on the wing we ring
> At the departure of a soul we toll.

Dorothy Sayers mentions these bells in *The Nine Taylors*. Each bell has a name, and a history.

The top floor must on no account be missed by prison lovers. We feel here that the place is still in use: commodious whitewashed cells with enormously heavy doors, a grid of bars concealed below the wooden floors to prevent digging out (revealed in one place), comfortable special cells for richer clients, with fireplaces and other amenities, a well-appointed prison governor's chambers, a most interesting list of regulations for the efficient running of this place of confinement, and a pretty horrifying collection of instruments of 'correction': branding irons, staples in the wall for holding the client during floggings, metal back shields to protect the kidneys from laceration during this operation, other kidney-pads which were hollow to contain cold water to lessen the inflammation afterwards, a smooth stone for the floggee to bite on. There is one big cell for drunks, with a sloping plank bed with a drain at the bottom. This, and other cells, are embellished by the graffiti of prisoners. There are several ship drawings, including one of a Thames barge, leeboards sprit sail and all.

It is hard to find out much about the maritime history of Berwick-upon-Tweed. There was a whaling fleet, and whaling continued till 1843. William Leith's sail loft (now a tent works) on Quay Street was a try yard (a place for 'trying out' or melting out the oil from the blubber of whales), and there is a representation of harpoons on No. 1 Wellington Terrace. Berwick was also a big herring port, and very small boats used to sail with a cargo of salt herring from Berwick to the Baltic, sometimes with as few as two men aboard.

But the famous *genre* of craft of Berwick was the 'Berwick Smack'. This was not a smack in the generally accepted sense of a fishing boat, but was a very fast cutter employed in passenger trade and light carrying between Leith and London. These vessels had their heyday between 1750 and 1850. They were quite small, with fine lines, but had a cloud of sail: a huge mainsail with a boom extending far abaft the taffrail and frequently trailing in the water, a mighty fore-and-aft jack-yard topsail and staysails set out on a very long bowsprit. They were an extreme example of the attempt to make sailing vessels go very fast by crowding on a great area of sail. And they *were* fast, commonly making the voyage between Edinburgh and London in three days and nights. They were so good that they captured most of the passenger trade from Leith, but Leith struck back in the end by building identical vessels, which were still called 'Berwick Smacks' although they had nothing to do with Berwick. Besides passengers they carried much Tweed salmon (parboiled to make it keep and stored in tubs) and horses and cattle as deck cargo. The eight or ten passengers paid £1 10s. for a ticket First Class or £1 steerage, 10s. for children under seven, and 5s. for a dog.

The first cold draught to the Berwick Smacks was from a steamer *City of Edinburgh* which started trading in 1837, but the *Stately, Lively, Ann, Commerce, King William* and *Princess Charlotte* continued to hold their own, while their owners and directors held their convivial board meetings in the Old Hen and Chickens, near Sandgate (which still flourishes). In the 1840s the company tried two steamboats (*Manchester* and *Rapid*) but gave them up in 1860 in favour of three clipper schooners – the *Thames* (130 tons and built at Aberdeen) and the *Tweed* and the *Teviot*, both built in the local shipyard of A. B. Gowans. One of these sailed from Berwick and one from London every week, and they were very fine craft which sailed in any weather that would allow a tug to get them over the bar.

The company, now called the Berwick Shipping Company, owed so much of its trade to salmon that it bought up salmon fishery rights up and down the Tweed. For a long time it ran these fisheries at a loss, paid for by the profit of the ships, but after a time the tail began to wag the dog. The railway took the coastal trade away and the three schooners were put to the Mediterranean and Baltic trades, and finally taken out of service altogether. In 1872 the company's name was changed to Berwick Salmon Fisheries Limited, and it still trades, very profitably, under that name.

It is very difficult to get any information now about the shipping of Berwick. The little *Stately* and the *Lively* and their sisters seem to have vanished without trace. I have managed to find one picture which seems to be of a 'Berwick Smack' and it is owned by one of the brothers Cowe of William Cowe and Sons, 64 Bridge Street, who incidentally knows more about Berwick than anybody else, and whose firm makes the only genuine and original Berwick Cockles, which are a kind of sweet. There is a little book too, *Recollections* by 'Quaysider', which tells us a little about the Smack crews, though nothing about the Smacks.

There is very little maritime trade left to Berwick, once 'The Alexandria of the North'. A dwindling traffic of grain, fertiliser and timber comes in, some barley goes out. There is no industrial hinterland and only a small agricultural one, and Berwick fights hard to retain what little trade it has. As a fishing port too it has declined. Gone are the days when a hundred Scottish *Zulus* and *Fifies* and *Skaffies* used to take in the Tweed on their annual voyage south after the migratory herring, bringing in their wake an army of fisher lassies to gut the fish they caught. Mr Holmes, the fishmonger and merchant in Bridge Street, still smokes some kippers in huge kilns and many more salmon, but he will tell you of the days when his yard was filled with fisher lassies, and when his firm moved once a year to St Ives, for the kippering campaign there.

From 15th February to 14th September every year you can watch the salmon being caught in the Tweed. There are perhaps twenty-five licensed crews up and down the river (the Berwick Salmon Fisheries Ltd have eleven) and they fish as far up the river as Coldstream. There are generally seven men in a crew including the foreman. Each crew has a winch on shore, and a 'coble', which isn't a coble at all, but a flat-bottomed punt. They operate with shore-based seine nets, which they call 'weir-shot notes', each net about a hundred yards long made of seven-inch round mesh. One end of the net is held at the winch, the other taken out into the stream, round in a circle and back to the winch and then the whole is winched in until the fish are beached. A recent enactment by Parliament has given the present holders of the Tweed salmon rights, sole rights of the fishery from Holy Island north (nobody can catch salmon off the coast of Scotland anyway), and this has been likened to a licence to print their own five pound notes.

Before we leave Berwick we must not miss Fairmile's shipyard. Indeed we can scarcely avoid noticing it: if not with our eyes then with our ears. It huddles, hugger-mugger, on the narrow spit of land between the medieval wall and the River Tweed, on the site of an old wooden shipbuilding yard. Situated many miles from any other steel shipyard, and many miles from a steel plate works, it is hard to see why it exists there at all. All material has to be brought through the narrow streets of the town, and through Sandgate, and if vessels have to be delivered by land (as many do) they have to be manoeuvred with incredible skill round sharp street corners. And yet exist it does, and contributes much to Berwick's prosperity. It is a friendly little shipyard where men whistle and sing over the noise of plates being banged about, and here twenty-five Fair Isle Class trawlers have been built, and half a dozen 73-foot twin-screw yachts: over a hundred little steel ships in all and the business is still going strong where many another yard, one would have thought much better sited, has failed in these hard times for shipyards. Incongruously the yard's head office is at Cobham, in Surrey.

Regretfully leaving Berwick we cross the old bridge to **Tweedmouth**. Here we might do worse than quench our thirsts at the Thatch Inn, which has a history written up inside. Following the Tweed downstream we pass the little harbour basin, alas now seldom filled with shipping, the lifeboat station and little yacht club, a defunct bacon factory and a working chemical factory, and come to the open sea, **Spittal** and its sandy beach.

This is a pleasure resort, and there is fine sand for the children, Johnny's Bingo for their Mums, deck chairs for their Dads, and plenty of bed and breakfast places and one or two caravan sites to house them all ashore. We come to rocks and cliffs; and at Hud's Head a discoloured trickle of water dribbles from the cliff, and is found to be the end of an adit that once drained Tweedmouth's very own coalfield. There was a small coal mine at **Scremerston**, a mile inland, and Scremerston is now a dead mining village.

As we walk southwards sandy beach is replaced by long straight walls of sandstone rock running out into the sea, and we are forced up on to the cliff-top and find some old edifices crumbling half way up the cliff which were once brick kilns, and Seahouse, which was once the squire's mansion but is now let off into flats (for some reason or other all this coast belongs to Greenwich Hospital). The Saltpan Rocks, down below, are a great place for lobsters and codling, but are dangerous to swim or boat in. The cliff drops down to a sandy beach again and to long ranks of sand dunes inshore with marram grass planted on them, and further south we come to the inevitable golf course.

We may plod on south-eastwards, keeping to the straight sandy shore which seems to stretch for ever in front of us, and if it be low tide, we can get, after five or six miles of it, nearly to Holy Island. If the tide is rising we must be careful though, for it is easy to be cut off.

There are strange masts planted along the beach. These are components of the 'fixed engines' allowed by the owners of the salmon rights along this stretch: Messrs H. Barker and Sons Ltd, of Billingsgate. From these they are allowed to put out seine nets, and for their seaward work they are using these days rubber inflatable boats, which even if they capsize will not brain anybody, as might have done the big wooden surf punts used previously. But more and more they are turning from seine nets proper to nylon or Terylene drift nets, only *not* drift nets in the sense that they are allowed to drift with one man walking along the beach holding the end of a line from them. This man makes them legal: they are still 'fixed engines' and not 'drift nets'.

If we tire of walking down the straight sandy beach, it is interesting to cut inland and cross the Goswick Sands. This, of course, we can only do when the tide is low, for when it is high they are flooded; and we should also use our common sense so as not to get cut off by the inrushing tide. There are before us now many square miles of tidal sand and mud: a whole never-never world that is neither land nor water and is fascinating to explore. The lagoon that lies between the sea beach and **Goswick** is reminiscent (on a fine day) of the great lagoon that lies to the south of Walvis Bay in

South West Africa. The many posts in the sand were put there in 1940 to stop German aeroplanes landing.

A track leads south from Goswick, crosses a stream by a bridge (if we walk up the stream we come to Haggerston, where there is a big ornamental lake, a Victorian gothic folly and a huge caravan site) and if we follow the shore we come to Beal Point. A local story is that Beal got its name from the words bee hill, because the monks of Lindisfarne kept their bees there, but this I very much doubt.

Shortly we come to the Holy Island Causeway, and, if the tide permits, we can walk across this to Holy Island itself.

CHAPTER 3

Holy Island to Bamburgh

❧

HOLY ISLAND owes much of its great charm to its comparative inaccessibility, and it will be a sad day for the island when the causeway is even more easily passable than it is now. It is still possible to get stranded on it with a motor vehicle, for the most exposed part of it is a mile long and the tide comes in very quickly. In the middle there is a bridge under which the flood or the ebb sluices as through a breach in a dam, and there is a refuge tower there for the unwary or the unlucky. In fact, if you abstain from trying to cross from two hours before high tide and three and a half hours after, you will be quite safe.

The causeway reaches land at the sand dunes near **Snook Point**. If you walk north from here you will come to a little house, generally empty, and a building that looks rather like a church and which is said to have been connected with a coal boring, or mine, sunk in 1840. The monks of Lindisfarne, as Holy Island was once called, mined coal there from the earliest days, and it is said that they probably invented the fire grate, for one was mentioned in their records in 1362. In 1344 they used 57½ chaldrons of coal in the brewhouse, limekiln, hall, Prior's chamber, kitchen and infirmary. The Snook, this lovely stretch of sand dunes, was always used by the monks, and other lords of the island, as a rabbit warren, and there was a lime quarry on it, and a kiln.

Back on the causeway (the old Pilgrim's Way traversed the sands to the south of the present road) we cross another mile of floodable sand, and arrive at the village, or town as it was originally called, of **Holy Island**. A splendid little Northumbrian village it is too, with hardly an ugly building and many very beautiful ones, and the Northumberland Arms, the Iron Rails, the Crown and Anchor and the Castle Hotel are all there in case the crossing of the sands has given us a thirst.

Most of the men who live in this delightful place are fishermen, and highly prosperous ones too. The population is round about two hundred. Many of the houses take in guests, a great number of whom are very pleasant professional people who have come to the

28

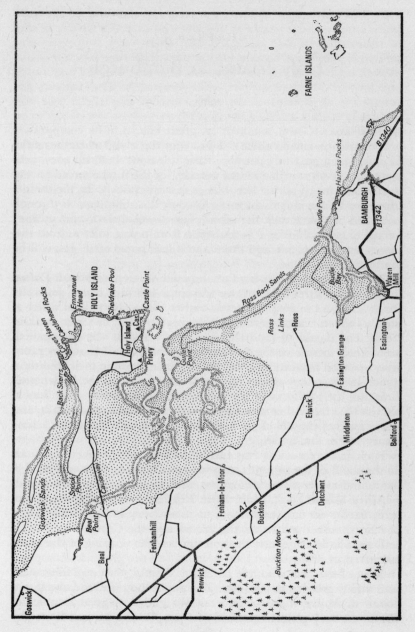

same place with their children for years. In the summer the little island carries a huge weight of trippers who come for the day in cars or charabancs (it was estimated that there were a quarter of a million in 1969), and because of this, the village itself is best seen out of peak holiday periods (the winter is of course the best time to see any part of the English coast), but fortunately these trippers are completely car-bound: on the most crowded day of the year you have only to walk a few hundred yards away from the village to be quite alone.

I suggest you walk north, along that track called the Straight Loaning, and past St Coomb's Farm. The flat land on each side completely belies the foolish map-maker (Speed) who wrote on the back of his map in 1610: 'The soile cannot bee rich, being rockie and full of stones and unfit for corn or tillage'. The soil looks very good; not at all rocky. In fact the monks grew wheat, oats, barley, flax, hemp, beans, onions and leeks. After a mile you will come to the dunes, among which tough little Aberdeen Angus cattle graze, and the track crossing these will bring you to the sea.

Coves Haven, which is where you will arrive, is one of the most delightful anchorages for a boat around the British coast, provided there is no hint of north or north-east in the wind. The little bay is deeply indented between the Back Skerrs Rocks on the west and the Castlehead Rocks on the east, seals and sea birds abound, there is some sandy beach among the limestone rocks, and in summer the water can be beautifully blue. Near Nessend there is a limestone quarry, whence a tramway once ran to carry the stone to Beblowe Crag (on the south-east of the island) where there was a kiln and a jetty to load burnt lime into ships. Walking east we come to Sandon Bay, equally beautiful, then, past the beacon on Emmanuel Head, south (where the limestone changes to sandstone, and where there were outcrops of a coal seam) and we follow a lovely rocky shore. At Sheldrake Pool are kelp pits, where seaweed used to be burned (for the manufacture of soap and glass), and we come, after a mile and a half, to Castle Point, near which **Lindisfarne Castle** stands on its vertically-sided rock, growing apparently right out of it, looking as nearly like a castle in a fairy tale as any castle could.

The castle is said to have been started by Prior Castell, of Durham, around 1500. Holy Island long belonged to the priors or bishops of Durham. But it was not until 1548 that the king sent engineers with a view to improving the fortification: the island possibly came to his notice when over 2,000 soldiers were landed there during Lord Hertford's raid against Scotland in 1543. Stone was used from the

Priory to build it. By 1559 there was a captain, two master gunners getting a shilling a day, a master's mate at 10d a day and twenty soldiers at 8d a day. After the union with Scotland the little fort was still garrisoned, and in 1639 had twenty-four men manning five iron guns and three brass ones, all commanded by a Captain Rugg, who will go down in history for the size and brilliance of his nose. Two observers noticed this. Brereton, in his *Journal*, wrote: 'in this island, in a dainty little fort, there lives Captain Rugg, Governor of the fort, who is as famous for his generous and free entertainment of strangers, as for his great bottle nose, which is the largest I have ever seen', and a Father Blakhal, after his ship took refuge from a storm in the haven in 1643, also met the gallant captain, and remarked that he was 'a notable good fellow, as his red nose full of pimples did testify'. He also noticed how the islanders fell upon their knees to pray to God when a ship was in danger of being wrecked on their island – not that He might save the souls of the mariners therein – but that He in His mercy might send her ashore so that they could loot her. Captain Rugg must have been a rollicking fellow, for he wrote a rhyming letter to King Charles I asking for his arrears of pay and subscribed himself: 'The great commander of the Cormorants,/The Geese and Ganders of these Hallowed lands.'

The castle was garrisoned until 1820, was then converted into a coastguard station, and thereafter became the headquarters of the Northumberland Artillery Volunteers. But it was in 1903 that the most astonishing transformation befell it. It was bought by Edward Hudson, the Editor of *Country Life*. A small army of workmen beset it and, to the plans of no less an architect than Sir Edwin Lutyens, they converted it into an eight-bedroomed house, which it still is. Filled with antique furniture, it is now owned by the National Trust and is open to the public from April to September for a charge of 10p.

On the shore by Rugg's Castle (as it should be called in honour of that jolly captain) is an old jetty, once the seaward terminus of the tramway that brought the limestone to the nearby kilns and the burnt lime to the ships. Then is the Ouse, a bay of mud (at low tide), with the Dancing Stone (or is it the Riding Stone?) which, when covered by the tide, tells us that we cannot get across the causeway. Over the Ouse are a number of strange black rounded objects, which are in fact the inverted remains of Holy Island's herring fleet.

Holy Island was one of the main ports of call of the mighty herring fleet that started from the East Coast of Scotland in the early summer and worked south along the coast, following the main

31

body of the herring, to end up in Great Yarmouth and Lowestoft in the late autumn. This fleet comprised drifters from all around the coasts of Britain, and outside them the Dutch *boms* salted and barrelled their herring aboard, not being allowed to land fish in the British ports. As the fleet worked south so did the army – the army of 'fisher girls': lassies from the north of Scotland or the islands, who travelled in their hundreds, slept where they could, worked from dawn to far into the night bending over the big vats gutting and salting and barrelling the 'Klondykers' as the salt herring were called and being paid so much a barrel. Nearly all the 'Klondykers' went to the Continent, to form a staple food for Poles and Latvians and the people of furthest Russia. In the 1860s it was said that a man could walk half a mile on upturned barrels during the herring voyage. As many as a hundred big luggers would crowd into the harbour. The islanders themselves owned thirty-six big herring boats, which must have been big for their day because it is also recorded that they also owned thirty-five forty-foot 'keels'. It is probably the 'keels' that we see today, upside down, sawn in half, with doors put in their bulkheads and serving as net and pot sheds for the fishermen of Holy Island.

For there are fishermen still and fishing, even more than tourism, is the mainstay of the island. There is a good fleet of open boats, and several larger decked ones, mostly engaged in lobster and crab fishing, with some salmon licences. The herrings of course have gone, and with them the herring fleets and the fisher girls. New and more effective methods of catching herring have destroyed the North Sea herring shoals completely, and the great East Coast 'herring voyage' is no more. In May 1854 a Dr George Johnson (who couldn't stand the smell of fish) wrote that Holy Island men used to stick a piece of candle to the back of a crab and shove this creature down a rabbit hole – to ferret out the rabbits!

We are now approaching the glory of Holy Island, and that which gives it its name: the ruin of **Lindisfarne Priory**. This might well be considered to be the most significant Christian site in England, for it was here that Christianity first arrived in a form that was to last among the English. The British, of course, or the people whom we should now call the Welsh, had long been Christians; the English of southern England were partially converted to the faith by the various missions sent by Pope Gregory. The Northumbrians were partially converted by Paulinus who gave the faith to their king Edwin in AD 625, but after Edwin was killed at the Battle of Haethfelth (near Doncaster) on 12th October 633 – by the combined

Above, Lindisfarne Castle; *below*, the Farne Islands, with the Inner Farne in the foreground with its lighthouse and the chapel and tower.

WILD LIFE ON THE FARNE ISLANDS: *Above*, guillemots on the Pinnacles; *below*, seals on the Brownsman.

armies of pagan Mercia and the Welsh under Cadwalla – Northumbria, and most of England, relapsed into paganism again. The Northumbrians rallied, however, under their King Oswald, and defeated Cadwalla at Denisesburn, and thereafter King Oswald decided to reintroduce Christianity into his kingdom, which he did by applying to the Irish, or Scots as they then were called, who had settled and built up a holy place at Iona, on the West Coast of Scotland. In 635, a monk named Aidan was dispatched from Iona to the court of Oswald at Bamburgh, and Aidan asked to be given Lindisfarne as his headquarters, for, being an island, it reminded him of his beloved Iona. And here he established his bishopric (for he was made a bishop) and his monastic house, and from here he converted, this time properly, the Northumbrian English to the Celtic branch of the Christian church. By every account he was a holy man, travelling humbly and on foot wherever he went, fearing not the powerful (Bede says of him: 'If wealthy people did wrong, he never kept silent out of respect or fear, but corrected them outspokenly'), and giving everything that came his way to the poor. Oswald was a fitting king for such a bishop, and Bede tells that when the king and Aidan were about to start eating at a banquet, and a servant came in to say that there were some poor people at the gate who were hungry, the king not only sent the food that he was about to eat to them, but even went so far as to break up the silver dish on which he was about to eat it and send the pieces to them too.

So Aidan, or Saint Aidan as he became, founded the abbey of Lindisfarne, and from 634 to 664 it was governed by the Celtic church: a purer, simpler and far less authoritarian rule, some might think, than the Roman one that replaced it after the Synod of Whitby of 664. After the latter's defeat of Celtic Christianity the Irish monks left Lindisfarne and retreated to Iona, and Lindisfarne became ruled directly by the Pope of Rome.

St Cuthbert was the most famous of the bishops after Aidan (see p. 55). He was a shepherd from the Lammermuir Hills who became a monk at Mailros (Old Melrose) Abbey, and who followed the abbot, Eata, to Hexham when that holy man was made bishop there, and afterwards himself became bishop of Lindisfarne in 685. Shortly after this he retired to the remote island of the Inner Farne, and when we get there ourselves we shall hear more of him.

On 7th June 793 the Danes came and murdered most of the monks and sacked the monastery, and in 875 the monks, led by their bishop Eardwulf (following the Celtic tradition the bishop of Lindisfarne was part of the monastery) decided to flee the island, which was in constant danger from the Danes, taking with them their most important relic: the body of St Cuthbert which had been buried next to the High Altar. They carried this about the country for seven years, giving rise to uncounted legends, settled at Chester-le-Street for 113 years, then in 995, moved to Durham, where they placed the remains of St Cuthbert, and which is now, therefore, the seat of the bishop who is the direct successor to St Aidan.

The ruins that we see on Holy Island today are of a cell of the Benedictine monastery of Durham, for under the Conqueror such a monastery was set up, and this new dependent priory established on the holy ruins on the island. It was at this time that the name Holy Island replaced that of Lindisfarne. From that time until it was dissolved in 1537, life was quiet and uneventful at the priory, as revealed by the very detailed monastic records which are preserved at Durham Cathedral.

All the building that we see now is post-Conquest, but do not miss the little museum at the gate, wherein are many pre-Conquest stones, including some which may be contemporary with St Cuthbert. There is one amazing eighth-century tombstone, with pagans in pleated kilts on one side advancing in battle array, and Christians on the other devoutly worshipping the cross, the sun and the moon depicted in the sky above. The priory church was begun before 1100 and completed within fifty years, although the nave walls were heightened in the fifteenth century and other alterations made. The church originally had an apse at the east end of the chancel, which is thought to have been pre-Conquest, but this is doubtful: the English soon came to prefer the square-ended chancel to the apsed one and most of their chancels were altered thus in early medieval times. Much of the church is left to see: the massive block of the west end, with a most primitive – almost Saxon-looking – arcade over the beautiful Norman doorway; much of the north aisle, and, miraculously, one of the diagonal ribs of the vaulting of the crossing: a slender and delicate arch with chevron mouldings famous as 'the rainbow arch' and the most impressive feature in a thousand paintings. The foundations of the monastic buildings are most interesting. They are well labelled by the Ministry of Works, and with the accompanying plan should be easy to follow. It will be seen that the priory was well fortified, for the Scots were never far away, and the priory records make several mentions of arms and ammunition. An excellent official guide book can be bought from the caretaker at the gate for 9p.

After seeing the priory, look at the parish church near by, for it

is very interesting (*malgré* the horrid Victorians of 1860). It is
mostly of late twelfth and early thirteenth century, although part of
the west front may be pre-Norman. Inside are stout piers of alternate
red and white stone. The three easternmost arches of the north
arcade are Norman, the fourth arch pointed Early English, as is the
south arcade. There is a good tombstone in the chancel, two
aumbries and near by the resting place of Sir William Reed who
died in 1604 and this truism is engraved on his stone, but in Latin:
'Against the power of death the garden has no remedy.' Newly
married girls are well advised to leap over the Petting Stone which is
outside the church at the east end. This will ensure happiness in
marriage.

The steep ridge of stone which guards the priory from the south,
and has a coastguard look-out on it, is called the Heugh, and, like
Beblowe Rock on which stands the castle, is part of the Great Whin
Sill which cuts like a wall across the north of England. The tiny
island with the cross on it is Hobthrush Island, or St Cuthbert's
Island, and here is the foundation of a chapel said to be that of St
Cuthbert himself, for that holy man spent much time meditating on
this rock before he took himself off to the Farnes.

But the glory of Holy Island is not to be seen there at all, but in
the British Museum. The Lindisfarne Gospels is one of the few
surviving works of fine Celtic English Christian art, and one of the
supreme treasures of the British Isles. It is written on vellum, and
consists of the four Gospels according to St Jerome's version, the
Eusebian Canons and two Epistles. There is something marvellously
satisfying about the illuminated pages at the beginning of each
Gospel, with their fantastic intricacy of interweaving designs. The
book is said to date from about 700, and was carried away by the
monks together with St Cuthbert's remains in 875. It was lost at
sea when the monks foolishly tried to make for Ireland, was miraculously recovered unharmed by the water, and almost as miraculously
escaped the Dissolution and came into the hands of Sir Robert
Cotton, whence it went to the British Museum. From it we can get
an idea of the refinement and high culture of the Northumbrians in
the Golden Age (the so-called Dark Ages), and we can possibly
reflect that there are few artists in this country who could achieve
anything like this today.

In our own secular age very little is made of what might well be,
for Christians, the holiest place in England: the beginning of
Christianity and a home and nursery of many saints. The Roman
Catholics have a house here, and every summer a tented camp for

boys from poor homes (nobody else is allowed to camp anywhere on the island – sleeping in a tent having apparently become a deadly sin in England), and the Anglican parson is currently trying to interest people in buying a house and starting some sort of Christian retreat.

But many more people go to the island for birds than for religion, and the sand and mud flats south of the island provide a paradise for both watchers and shooters of birds. Fulmar petrels and, alas, that deleterious bird the black-headed gull, both nest here (together with perhaps some fifty other species), countless waders: godwits, curlew, oystercatchers, turnstones, dunlin and knot in great numbers (if you see, in the winter time, what looks like a cloud flying along just above the shore – suddenly changing direction from time to time and yet keeping its shape – it will be either knot or dunlin). Eider ducks from the Farnes are frequently seen, three kinds of swans are sometimes there, and practically every marine and estuarial duck that we get in the British Isles. The Nature Conservancy controls part of the estuary but there is still plenty of it left for a man who likes a gun, and several of the Holy Islanders still keep punts. Others sink barrels into the sand, bale them out at low water, and sit in them, nearly freezing to death, to await the flight of mallard or wigeon or teal. For that most rugged of all sports, wildfowling, Holy Island is superb.

Whether you persuade a boatman to put you over the Harbour and land you on desolate Guile Point, or else go back the way you came and work round the shore, you will eventually come to that strange sandy promontory of the Ross Links, and on Ross Back Sands a footprint, if it is not overrun by the tide, may well last a month, so few people go there. It is one of the loneliest pieces of shore on the East Coast and long may it remain so. South of it is **Budle Bay**, where the Romans had their port of **Outchester**, and Spindlestone Heugh (the latter word pronounced *heuff* and meaning a crag) where lived the Laidley Worm (or loathsome serpent) celebrated in song and story. The Nature Conservancy has taken all this over, so much so that people who have lived there all their lives cannot go and shoot a duck, and the place simply teems with wildfowl. Waren Mill, up a creek up which schooners and barges used to go, is a very fine mill indeed, and one of the few independent malting houses left in England. The young miller, single-handed except for a lady who helps him by sweeping up, turns out eighty quarters of very fine malt a week, which goes to a brewery at Berwick to make very fine beer. But even he will no doubt be put out of business in due course by the mighty moguls who are flourishing on the contemporary Englishman's indifference to individuality or quality. Budle Bay, given over to the birds, was given a charter as a port by King Henry III: the hamlet at Waren Mill then being known as Warnmouth, and the port of Bamburgh. The walk around the bay, which is about five miles, is delightful, but do not try to wade across the narrow mouth unless you understand tidal waters. Several people have tried this and drowned.

At Budle Point, south of the mouth of the bay, we come to a golf course, and before we have finished our tour of the Northumberland coast we may well come to believe that the entire population of Northumberland spends its time hitting little balls about. Soon we come to Harkess Rocks, and a little automatic lighthouse, and there, before us, is **Bamburgh Castle** on its mighty rock.

Bamburgh itself is a most delightful village, although almost entirely given over nowadays to wealthy weekenders, commuters, and holiday-house owners. There is no fishing community, not much agricultural (although there is a very large and imposing Georgian farmhouse, still a farmhouse, next to the church – the vicarage is some way further west), and in fact not many original villagers at all.

The little place is overshadowed by the enormous castle: certainly the most impressive castle in England, and also by the memory of Grace Darling. To deal with the castle first (because it was there first): it is impressive chiefly because of its extraordinary position: like Beblowe on Holy Island (which I think ought to be called Rugg's Castle) it seems to grow straight out of an outcrop of the Great Whin Sill, and because its curtain wall surmounts vertical or nearly vertical basalt cliffs on all sides, it must have been, before the invention of artillery, quite impregnable. Neither sap, nor scaling ladder, nor siege tower nor siege engine could be used against it. The rock is a quarter of a mile long (and so is the castle) and 150 feet high, and in ancient times the sea lapped the bottom of it on the seaward side.

The almost legendary King Ida the Flamebearer is said to have founded his capital at Bamburgh in 547, and according to the Anglo-Saxon Chronicle he enclosed the place first by a hedge and then by a wall. His grandson Ethelfrith left the place to his wife, Bebba, and from her derives the name Bamburgh. King (later Saint) Oswald kept his court here, at which St Aidan was a frequent visitor, and after Oswald's death his head and right hand, both uncorrupted, were kept in the church as relics (St Aidan had

37

prophesied that this hand would not corrupt when the king used it for distributing his food to the poor). King Penda of Mercia, that most aggressive pagan king, twice besieged Bamburgh, and twice failed. His failure once was said to be due to the miraculous intervention of St Aidan. The latter was at that time in hermitage on the Farne Islands. He saw the smoke from great fires that Penda had lit along the wooden palisades about the town, and prayed to God for the wind to change, which it did, and the flames did not prevail.

Bamburgh in King Oswald's time was considered a great city, and it must indeed have been a centre of chivalry, religion and learning: it was the capital of Northumbria in her Golden Age. But Northumbria, along with the other English nations of the Heptarchy, disastrously declined (it almost seems as if too much religion sapped the martial vigour of the people – the Venerable Bede expressed a doubt at the end of his Ecclesiastical History that this might happen) and the Northumbrians could not even hold this marvellous fortress from the Danes: it was pillaged three times between 933 and 1015. King Oswald's head was stolen in the eighth century, his hand followed in the eleventh, and the church of Bamburgh thus lost its chief attraction for pilgrims. After the Conquest, when the Norman raiders carried death and devastation all over the North of England, it remained the only inhabited place. It came into its own again as a fortress when Robert de Mowbray, Earl of Northumberland, was besieged in it by King Rufus. Rufus, seeing he had no hope of storming it, built another castle beside it which he named *Malvoisin* and which he garrisoned and left. In due course de Mowbray rode forth, was captured by the Malvoisin force, which threatened to put out his eyes if his wife did not yield the castle. She did.

In the Wars of the Roses Bamburgh was mostly in the hands of the Yorkists, although Henry VI had it for a time, and lived there before the Battle of Towton. In the seventeenth century the castle was given to the Forster family by James I. The Forsters were a prominent and very wealthy Northumberland family the members of which, however, contrived to go bankrupt. Dorothy Forster was the most famous, and had a novel written about her by Sir Walter Besant. She rescued her brother, General Thomas, after he was imprisoned during the Jacobite rebellion of 1715. Her uncle, Ferdinand, was shot in the streets of Newcastle in 1701 by Sir John Fenwick.

After the fall of the Forsters the castle, now derelict, was bought by Lord Crewe, the Bishop of Durham and married to a Forster.

He died childless and left his estates to a charitable trust which he formed, called the Crewe Trust. It was said that this was the best thing he ever did in his life for one of the trustees, Archdeacon Sharp, did many very worthy things with the castle, establishing a school for girls in it, a refuge for shipwrecked mariners, a lighthouse and warning cannon to be fired in fog, a dispensary and infirmary, a mill to grind corn for poor people, and much else. Certainly no castle has ever been put to better use. All the range of buildings west of the Keep were built by the trustees. The next use the castle was put to was perhaps more debatable. The first Lord Armstrong, who made an enormous fortune out of armaments, bought it in 1894 and spent a quarter of a million pounds converting it into what it is today. A huge force of labourers and craftsmen invaded the place: two hundred carpenters and masons used to parade like soldiers with their tools before going off to work in the mornings, a number of blacksmiths were kept busy all day at their forges just sharpening tools. Lord Armstrong intended to turn the ancient capital of Northumbria into a fitting home for himself, but he died before it was finished. His son didn't like it and never lived there, and the present Lord Armstrong reserves part of the keep as a residence, which he comes to occasionally, and other apartments are let off to the wealthy and the famous. Presumably they don't mind the sightseers who are taken round in droves all summer: sometimes in parties of forty or fifty at a time.

We enter the castle by a steep and winding road which goes through a very fine barbican, under the Constable's Tower, and into the East Ward which, with the West Ward and the Inner Ward, measures eight acres. We can see which parts of the castle are old and which are new by the stone used: in fact most of the buildings except the keep are modern. Most of the stone for the original castle was quarried at North Sunderland and cut into blocks small enough to be carried by animals. Lord Armstrong's men used stone from Cumberland. The keep is a superb building, unusual in that its main door is on the ground floor, in what is generally considered the basement of a keep, instead of being up outside stairs and on the first floor. The reason possibly for this breach of security was the immense strength of the rock itself, rendering it unlikely that the keep would ever become the last resort. The keep is strong though, with walls eleven feet thick in places, and in it is a well (supposed to be of AD 774) which is 150 feet deep: an enormous distance for eighth-century well-sinkers to sink a shaft through the Whin Sill basalt and then through sandstone. But without the well, of course, the castle would have been useless. A wicked queen is said to live at the bottom of it in the form of a toad.

The King's Hall is a fabulous creation of the wealth of Lord Armstrong and the teak forests of Siam. It has in it a king's ransom of carved teak, and the King of Siam actually once came and had a look at it. In the many rooms of the castle there are portraits, including one of the Dorothy Forster that the novel is about, and there is a fine armoury, with a very good collection of muskets and early rifles. In 1970 digging is being started in the West Ward. Certainly there should be something to find in this fortress, once a city and a capital city at that, the history of which goes back over fourteen hundred years.

CHAPTER 4

Bamburgh to Seahouses

✤

HAVING looked our fill at this ruined castle, ruined first by neglect and then by restoration, we should visit the church, for it is one of the finest in Northumberland. It is called **St Aidan's**, and the saint is supposed to have died beside it, or at least beside the wood and thatch structure which preceded it and of which, of course, nothing remains, except, possibly, as we shall see, one beam. Nothing remains, certainly, of a Saxon stone church and the present structure is largely early thirteenth century. A memorial window in the north-west corner of the chancel depicts the saint's death, for it was outside this window that he is surmised to have died. Bede, in Chapter 17 of his Ecclesiastical History, tells us that he died in a tent which had been erected on the west side of the church, actually touching the building, and that when he breathed his last breath he was leaning against a wooden beam that buttressed the wall of the church. When, later, Penda the indefatigable pagan came and burned the church this beam refused to burn 'although in a most extraordinary way the flames licked through the very holes of the pins that secured it to the building', and so, when the church was built again (Bede says for the third time) the miraculous beam was set up inside as an object of worship. There is a beam now visible inside the church tower which is thought by some people to be this very beam.

This is a most splendid church. The nave is fine, Transitional and supposed to be of about 1190. The chancel is of about 1230, its lancet windows are original, and glazed with Flemish glass, and the whole structure is a masterpiece of Early English architecture. There is a lovely decorated squint, or hagioscope, south of the chancel arch; in the south wall of the chancel is a fine knight's effigy of about 1320 (we are told in the exceptionally good little church guide that we can buy for 7½p that his jupon bears the achievement *a bend lozengy cotised*), note the sedilia and piscina; on the north wall of the sanctuary hang the helmet, breastplate, sword and gauntlets of Ferdinand Forster, the very man who got shot by John Fenwick in the streets of Newcastle in 1701. We can read all about this

41

gentleman, and his heroic daughter Dorothy Forster, in Sir Walter Besant's historical novel *Dorothy Forster*. Forster remains were discovered when the crypt was reopened in July 1837. This crypt (entered from outside the church on the south side) is the most interesting part of the whole building and should not be missed on any account.

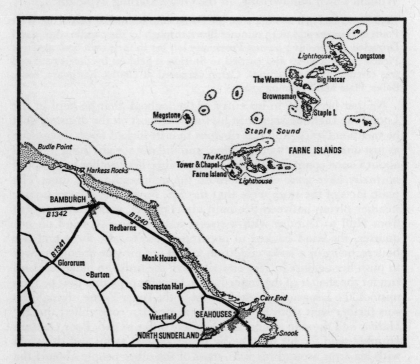

In the north aisle of the church is a moving effigy to Grace Darling, which was once outside the church under a canopy but the canopy was blown down in a gale. In the churchyard now there is a memorial to Grace, not over her grave for it was sited so as to be seen by passing ships at sea. It is splendidly Hindu in feeling.

But the best physical memorial to Grace Darling is her museum in the village, which the traveller must be urged on no account to miss: it should be seen if nothing else is. In the sternly masculine society of the nineteenth century in England, where saints were out of fashion, the Virgin Mary at a discount and even God wore an enormous beard, there was evidently a great unsatisfied craving among the people for a female object of veneration. Grace Darling provided just this: she took the place of a female saint in that Protestant male-dominated society.

Perhaps the best account of the wreck of the *Forfarshire* is in the letter to Trinity House reporting the incident by William Darling, Grace's father. The account may be read, as it was written in William's own handwriting, in the Grace Darling Museum:

1838 September 7th about 4 a.m. the Forfarshire steamboat struck the West Point of Harkers and in 15 minutes Brock through by the paddle wheels and Drowned 43 Persons 9 having Previously left her in their own boat and was Picked up by a sloop and carried to Shields. 9 held on by the Wreck and was rescued by the Darlings. Cargo consisted of Cloths, hardware, soap, Boiler Plate and Spinning gear.

Neither here, nor in his entry in the logbook that he kept in the Longstone Lighthouse, nor in his further report on the disaster, does he mention Grace, and it is obvious that he looked upon this rescue as just one of many, mere routine, and did not see anything unusual about Grace coming with him as crew since her brother who would normally have gone was ashore on the mainland at the time. The plain facts of the story were that the S.S. *Forfarshire*, a large luxury steamer plying between Scotland and London, was heading north from Hull to Dundee with a strong south-south-east wind on her quarter, the wind backed to north and rose to gale force and her boilers, being in a leaky condition, could not provide enough power to push her against it. Her captain gave the order to make sail and run for the shelter of the Inner Farne. It seems probable that he then mistook the Longstone Light for that of the Inner Farne, thought he was further west than he was, and he struck a rock called the Big Harcar and the ship almost immediately broke in two. Poor Captain Humble paid for his mistake by being washed away and drowned with his arms around his wife, most of the other people aboard the ship went with him, nine got away in a boat but twelve, including two children, managed to scramble on to the rock on which the ship had struck.

It was about four in the morning when Grace Darling, who was in the lighthouse with her father and mother, looked out of a window and saw the wreck, and it was two hours after this that survivors were seen. Grace and her father were convinced that no boat could put out from the mainland in that gale and so Grace took off all her petticoats and she and her father launched their coble (which they had hauled up and securely lashed during the night against the gale) and rowed her south for half a mile until they had some lee from the Clove Car and the Harcar and then pulled up-wind for a mile to the Big Harcar itself. Anyone who has ever rowed a coble of the size of the one the Darlings rowed will know that this must have tested them to the limits of endurance, and certainly William, by himself, would have had no hope of making up to windward at all. They found nine people left alive on the rock, the two children and one man having died of exposure. William managed to leap ashore leaving Grace to keep the boat off the rock with two oars, five people were got aboard the coble and William and such of the survivors as were sailors rowed back to the Longstone. The passengers were put ashore and Grace went with them to look after them, while William and two of the survivors made a return trip to the wreck to get the others. Half an hour after this a boat actually managed to get out from Seahouses, manned by amongst others Grace's brother, William Brooks Darling, too late to be of help. *Their* feat in rowing a boat five miles into the teeth of a northerly gale with no shelter from anything was remarkable, but after all such feats were performed all around our coasts in pre-motor days as a matter of routine.

It was some days before the public of England became aware of Grace Darling's existence. Then *The Times* printed a leader in which the question was asked: 'Is there in the whole field of history, or of fiction, even, one instance of female heroism to compare for one moment with this?'

It was as though some trigger was pulled which released some overwhelming pent-up emotion. The whole country went Grace Darling mad. Grace and her father had to sit for seven portraits in twelve days, and North Sunderland and Seahouses and Bamburgh became crowded out with portrait painters awaiting their turn, journalists, theatrical impresarios and people just wanting to look. A great nation-wide fund was raised, from which Grace herself refused to benefit in any way. Grace had countless offers to make stage appearances all of which she refused; supposed locks of her hair were sold all over the country, as were many tons of pieces of the dress she was alleged to have worn at the time of the rescue. Painters all over the country turned their attentions to the wildest and most improbable scenes of the wreck; poets, from Wordsworth down, celebrated the event in verse; books and articles were written about her, and she became the first ever great national heroine of England: to the English what Joan of Arc was to the French. And still, for every visitor to Bamburgh who goes there to pay his respects to St Aidan, I'll be surprised if there are not a hundred who go to offer

44

veneration to Grace Darling, and a better object of their veneration they could not find.

In the museum there is a mass of material relating to Grace and her family, of extremely strong period interest besides being of interest for its connection with Grace Darling, and not least is the original coble in which the rescue was performed. As evidence of how little the coble has altered since this one was built in 1830 I can relate that I had a coble built of just this size by Messrs Harrison Brothers of Amble in 1960, and it is the same in almost every respect as the one the Darlings rowed. In the last hundred and thirty years the coble has altered not one jot.

About the only people in England who were not in the least impressed by Grace's exploit, or the furore it produced, were Grace and her father themselves. Grace went on living quietly in the Longstone Lighthouse, her father did too and went on methodically recording the movement of fish and birds and ships and shipwrecks in his log, and Grace, who was twenty-two at the time of the rescue, died quietly of tuberculosis at the age of twenty-six. The one portrait of her in the museum which carries complete conviction is the one by H. Perlee Parker, and it shows her as a most strikingly beautiful woman, with every mark of a staunch and steadfast character about her face.

If we strike towards the sea again, through the wide range of sand dunes south of the castle perhaps, we will come to the reason for Bamburgh's popularity as a family holiday resort of the rich: a couple of miles of most magnificent sandy beach.

On the way along the coast to Seahouses is a nice group of buildings called Monk's House. This is on land which was granted in 1257 by Henry II to the monks then living on the Inner Farne, and on which they built a storehouse – a sort of shore base. Some years ago the present buildings included a pub, unfortunately now a pub no longer. It was called St Cuthbert's.

Seahouses started as a mere appendage of North Sunderland, but now the tail wags the dog. The two are in fact one large village, or small town, and a pleasanter place either to visit or to live in I cannot think of in England. It has a fine little artificial harbour, built in the 1880s and '90s, and a magnificent little fleet of fishing boats including ordinary decked boats with wheelhouses – 'keel boats' they are called on this coast – with nice names like *Children's Friend, Radiant Way, Faithful* and *Sovereign*. These are traditional motor fishing vessels such as one will find anywhere around the British coasts, built of wood, carvel planked, powerfully diesel engined, and lavishly equipped nowadays with echo sounders, Decca navigational instruments, radio receivers and transmitters and some even radar. These are not of course cobles. They are all a foot or two under sixty feet, for if they were over the skipper would have to have a 'ticket' and they would come under all sorts of other absurd regulations. They cost perhaps twenty or thirty thousand pounds these days, engines and all, and most of the electrical equipment is hired. Fishermen are going more and more in for such vessels, as the White Fish Authority gives generous grants and loans for the purchase of better fishing vessels.

Then there are three smaller decked vessels, used mostly for lobstering: the *Girl Dorothy*, *Favourite* and *John Wesley*.

But among these we notice half a dozen open boats of a kind seen nowhere else in the world except along this Northumbrian coast (and I am using the word Northumbria in its original sense, which includes Yorkshire) and these are the cobles. We have seen one in a glass case in Grace Darling's museum and a few at Holy Island and they are to be a recurring theme all the way up the coast (I have to use the seaman's term *up* meaning *south* on the East Coast, and *down* meaning *north* – because that is the way the tide flows) until we get to the Humber. And whether these vessels are ashore or afloat the connoisseur will appreciate their lovely lines and extraordinary fitness for the work they are called upon to do. The coble form, like that of most of the best working wooden boats of this world, was evolved, not designed. Nobody knows when this distinctive shape first appeared. We have seen that Grace Darling's coble was exactly the same as one built by a traditional coble builder in 1960, but the word coble was used right down the ages in Northumbria. The earliest form of it was used by Alred, who described himself as being 'an unworthy and most miserable priest'. He transcribed the Lindisfarne Gospels into the Northumbrian dialect in AD 950 (writing his translation between the lines) and used the word *cuople* to describe a boat in Matt. viii. 23. The word itself seems to be derived from the Celtic, and it is thought to have been brought to Northumbria by Aidan and his monks when they came from Celtic Iona. Is it not just as likely though that it was in use along this coast before the English came, by the original Celtic inhabitants? Certainly we can surmise away, because we shall never know.

The form of the boat, which makes it distinct from all others – although a very similar form was evolved in Japan to suit very similar conditions – is that of a clinker-built boat, i.e. with the planks

46

overlapping each other, with very wide strakes (planks) on heavy grown frames. (Frames mean ribs – and grown means that they were cut from crooked branches and not steam bent.) They were very deep and high and narrow-gutted in the bows but flattened out in an apparently miraculous manner forward of amidships so that the after part of the vessel is quite flat-bottomed. The forward part of the vessel has a distinct and quite deep keel. The after part has two 'draughts', in coble language: twin keels, iron shod. The rudder is narrow but extremely deep, and is unshipped before coming to land.

The purpose of this extraordinary hermaphrodite shape – that of a deep-keeled vessel forward and a flat-bottomed punt aft – is so that the coble can put off from, and come back to, open beaches, and at the same time keep the sea in practically any weather. The coble was evolved to work from the open beaches of Northumbria, and sail on one of the roughest and most treacherous seas in the world. She is launched bow-first – her high sharp prow meeting the breaking waves. She comes to land stern-first, her flat-bottomed aft protected by the iron-shod draughts coming first to the beach. Her deep fore-foot cuts into the sand and thus holds her head-on to the waves – which break harmlessly past those sharp high bows. A line from a winch or a tractor is then hooked on to her stern, and she is dragged out of her element stern-first. Owing to her marvellous ability to work from the open beach she is said to be 'boat and harbour in one'. Hundreds of cobles have been lost at sea, but it is claimed that not one has ever been lost in coming to land. The coble is said to be dangerous when running before a big sea, because a wave can get under that big raking transom and slew her round, or 'broach her to', when she will be swamped or overturned. Indeed in 1928 a big motor coble from Seahouses met this fate. But as an indication of their ability to keep the sea, thirty-foot sailing cobles used to sail in scores out to the Dogger Bank from Yorkshire beaches seventy or a hundred years ago, and Tyne pilots would sail to the Downs, off Kent, in open cobles to put pilots aboard incoming colliers – when the last pilot had found a berth a man and a boy would sail the open boat back to the Tyne. They did this winter and summer, and whenever possible they laid up under the sail thrown over a line, and cooked their food and warmed themselves over a charcoal brazier. And in 1962 a tiny coble (twenty foot long) was sailed and rowed from Amble, in Northumberland, to Skanor, in Sweden, crossing the North Sea in a force eight gale.

In the nineteenth century there were thousands of cobles along the 'coble coast', and every tiny village from the Scottish Border up to Skegness in Lincolnshire had a fleet of them. Very soon after the 1914–18 War the coblemen took to engines: they were twenty years ahead of the fishermen in the South of England in this, and the coble underwent a slight development: the deep forefoot became less deep, for this lateral resistance was not needed for sailing any more, the *floors*, or ribs that go across the flat bottom, became longer and the whole boat slightly fuller and beamier. As time went on cobles began to get bigger – and fewer. Between the wars fishing suffered from a decline. People were content with frozen cod from the deep-water fishing grounds and prime fresh fish from inshore waters went for very little: many men left the fishery and got jobs in factories or else went on the dole. During the Second World War nearly every fisherman was in the Navy or Merchant Service, but after that war fishing began to pick up. The fishing grounds, rested all during the war, were rich in fish, the White Fish Authority was set up by the Government to help fishermen financially to buy boats and, with increased prosperity, people began to be more discriminating about the fish they bought; such luxury fish as lobsters and crabs and, lately, Dublin Bay prawns (miscalled 'scampi') began to fetch high prices. Now there are more cobles than ten years ago, and the few yards that are building them cannot turn them out fast enough to meet the orders.

The cobles at Seahouses (*Emblem, Clan Gillian, Glad Tidings, Boys' Own, Welcome Home* and *Remembrance*) are big fine open boats with diesel engines, capable of going very fast and holding the sea in any weather, some of them with canvas wind-dodgers stretched over their forward parts. They all have power capstans for hauling pots. Their mainstay throughout the year is the lobster pot, and each boat works from three to four hundred of these, generally with three men, or two men and a boy. The pots are nowadays made of Corlene netting stretched over cane frames, and the 'parlour' pot, recently introduced from America, is replacing the older ones. The parlour pot has two compartments: one reached by a funnel from outside, the other by another funnel from the first. The first compartment is baited with fish (generally salt herring), the lobsters get in to the bait, find they are trapped, and try to get out which they can only do by crawling through the funnel into the second compartment or 'parlour'. There they must stay until taken out by the fisherman. The bait lasts much longer in this kind of pot, which can therefore be left down much longer – after a week or a fortnight it will still have lobsters in it.

The pots are fished in fleets of about forty, all joined together by

BAMBURGH: *Above*, the Castle; *left*, Grace Darling's tomb.

SEAHOUSES: *Above*, boatbuilding; *below*, fishing boats in the harbour.

Corlene or nylon line. At either end of each fleet there is an anchor and a buoy. The pots are shot on rocky ground, and most cobles now have an echo sounder to tell where this ground is, although experienced fishermen very seldom have to look at it. They know where they are from shore marks. When a fleet is being hauled one man works the rope around the capstan which is driven from the main engine, another throws the pots as they come up to the third, who whips the lobsters and crabs out through a slit in the netting (with his bare hands), throws 'white' or undersized crabs and undersized lobsters back and rebaits the pot with fish. The second hand takes it, replaces the slit, and piles the pot with the others of the fleet on the starboard side of the boat. When the fleet is all aboard (making a high stack in the little boat) the boat goes full-speed to a fresh ground, the first anchor is dumped over, and the senior fisherman then flings the pots over one by one as their turn comes, taking great care that the rope doesn't get tangled up and that the pots hit the water right way up. The boat is going flat out during this operation and if a man got his foot in a bight of the line he would be dragged overboard at high speed and almost certainly be killed. The operation calls for great skill and considerable stamina, particularly during rough weather when it is hard enough to stand on your feet.

In the latter part of the winter most coblemen lay up for a few months and busy themselves mending old and making new pots, and repairing their boats. Some of them, though, follow the old craft of *long-lining*. Each boat shoots a line with about a thousand baited hooks on it, which lies on the sea bottom for a night or a few hours, and is then pulled aboard again with, hopefully, fish on some of the hooks. The fish thus caught are of the best quality, not having been dragged along the ocean bottom for hours in the cod-end of a trawl net, and should fetch a good price. The factor that prevents most men from long-lining though, is their inability to persuade their wives to bait the hooks. This was traditionally the job of every East Coast fisherman's wife. Now wives refuse to do it, for it keeps them away from the television and the bingo hall, and Seahouses is plentifully supplied with both these amenities.

But the cream of the fishing for Seahouses men, and indeed for most Northumbrian fishermen, was the salmon fishery: it is this that kept them going throughout the year and put, as they often point out, a little butter on the bread. But the salmon fishery in Berwick Bay is now illegal – a mortal blow to the fishermen.

I cannot but urge the visitor to Seahouses to try and ingratiate himself with some of the fishermen enough to get taken for a trip to sea. Very early in the morning, often before light even in summer, a group of men in blue jerseys and seaboots begins to assemble in the lee of the big old lime kiln near the harbour, talking in that monosyllabic taciturn way that fishermen have and if the visitor is a southerner I shall be very surprised if he understands a single word that anybody says. Someone will have a transistor wireless set, and this will be tuned in to a weather forecast. Late comers will turn up – one or two young boys – fresh from school – long hair like the Beatles flopping out from under their woollen caps and walking with a swagger that shows they are proud to have joined the men in what, for Seahouses boys, is the only profession worthy of a man. Finally one of the older men grunts something in the impenetrable Geordie dialect, he and his crew pick up their rolled-up yellow oil-skins and their sandwich boxes and slope off down to their boat. The rest soon follow, and soon the noise of engines waking into life comes from all over the harbour.

For the rest, Seahouses and North Sunderland have several good hotels, some fine pubs (is it the Black Horse that has the name-plate off the *Forfarshire*? There was a law suit about this. A previous land-lord of the present pub found it in his cellar and sold it to another landlord. The brewery that owned the Black Horse thereupon went to law to get it back – saying that it was theirs. They won the case). There are two big caravan sites, one each side of the town, both well-equipped and very pleasant. There is a scruff of 'amusements' down near the waterfront: pin table alleys and bingo halls which fit very ill in this fine fishing port. There is a small but very good boat-building yard which can turn out a first-class coble, and a life-boat station with a very good record of service and an inshore rescue craft.

The harbour looks much better than it is. In fact the north-east basin is quite unusable because of a strong *send*, or turbulence caused by the waves that come in the entrance to the harbour and are re-flected by a reef of rock to the south. A plan has been prepared, however, which, if it receives government approval (it will cost £320,000), will cure this trouble and turn Seahouses into a fine little all weather, all-states-of-the-tide harbour, and ensure its future prosperity as a fishing port. The plan is to extend the North Pier by about fifty feet, thus narrowing the entrance, and then to cut away and remove the reef of sandstone that reflects the waves, so that the latter will just spend themselves on the shelving beach south of the harbour. There will also be dredging and other improvements. It would be very sad if this improvement were not carried out, and if the fishing element in Seahouses was overwhelmed by the holidaymaking, with the little place given over entirely to pin tables and bingo. Nothing is duller than the seaside resort that is nothing else.

CHAPTER 5

The Farne Islands

❧

SEAHOUSES is the port of departure for the Farne Islands, and every day in the summer, in fine weather, passengers are taken out.

All the way along the coast from Holy Island we have been conscious of this group of small islands, sometimes looking sharp and clear as if we could swim to them, at others looking hazy and far-away and quite unattainable.

From the sea they look impressive enough, for in places they rise up in vertical cliffs seventy to eighty feet high and the rock of which they are made has a fluted, or pillared nature which makes them very strange and beautiful. They are in fact part of the Great Whin Sill, which we have met at Holy Island and Bamburgh, and which we will meet again at Dunstanburgh and Craster. This sill is an intrusive sheet of hard dolerite, from about eighty to a hundred feet thick for most of its length but about two hundred and forty feet near the head of Weardale, that starts from High Force in Teesdale, passes through County Durham and Cumberland into Northumberland, through Dunstanburgh, out to sea to Farne Islands, then bends back to England at Bamburgh. It is intruded into the carboniferous rocks in the interval between the Middle Coal Measures and the Upper Brockram of the Permian Period.

The islands themselves vary in number according to the state of the tide: there are perhaps fifteen of them which never become submerged at all. As several of them never become exposed (not islands really of course) the place is very dangerous for shipping. At low tide there are about twenty-eight islands (above the water). They are notable for birds and seals and also for their history as a refuge from the world for saints.

The eider-duck has been called 'St Cuthbert's chicken' because that holy man gave special protection to these birds. They breed in profusion on the island where the saint lived, the Inner Farne, and also on several of the other islands. The best time to see them, and other birds, is in May and June (late May is better than early). The puffin is the most noteworthy bird on the islands. These nest in holes on many of the islands, and it is at evening that they may be seen in their greatest numbers as they come in from the fishing. Then there are razorbills (not many) which nest on the bare rock, and guillemots which suffer from the most ghastly overpopulation problems – the tops of some of the vertically-sided rocks are so packed with them that a lot of eggs get pushed overboard. There are terns, principally Arctic but also common, roseate and sandwich. There are cormorants, notably on the inaccessible Megstone, shags, and a handful of fulmar petrels. Of gulls there is the kittiwake, which is an amiable and harmless bird, and the herring-gull and lesser black-backed. These latter two are harmful if too numerous for they are most piratical birds and surely – you don't have to live on the Farne Islands to be aware of this, nor indeed even within miles of the sea – if there is one thing we have enough of in the British Isles it is sea-gulls. Traditionally, since long before St Cuthbert's time, men have collected gulls' eggs to eat. They are very good food. The collecting of their eggs does not, in fact, have much effect on their numbers because nearly every bird, including gulls, if you remove one egg, will lay another. But the collection of gulls' eggs by fishermen has been beneficial for three reasons: it provided good food, helped to support members of the most worthy and useful community in the country, and did to some extent keep down gull numbers. Now, since bird watching has changed from being a sport to being a religion, watchers are stationed on the Farnes and other places to prevent fishermen from following their age-old pursuit. They follow it just the same, of course, but now they have to do it by stealth. It will be a good day when conservationists realise that fishermen are part of nature too – just as much as kittiwakes are, and equally worthy of encouragement and protection.

Fishermen and conservationists come into conflict again in the matter of seals. Seals and fishermen are competitors, for they are both after the same quarry. Anyone who has been drift-netting for salmon knows how often a seal will bite the salmon in the net in half, and scare the others away. Seals eat salmon, no matter what scientists believe, and the huge number of seals on the Farne Islands do great damage to the fisheries. When we get further south we shall notice that there are no fish at all in the Wash, and the reason for this is undoubtedly the fact that the Wash is chock-a-block with seals. Again it is a matter of recognising that there should be a balance in nature, and that man should play his part in it. From time immemorial seals were a crop in the Farne Islands: they were an immensely valuable source of oil, meat and hide. Thus they were kept within reasonable numbers. Now we obtain these commodities so very easily in other ways they are not hunted – except as a positive policy to contain their numbers, a policy that is only arrived at after great questionings and heart-burnings.

The fact is that seals are intelligent, charming and beautiful animals. To wander about the Brownsman, the Wamses, Staple Island or the Megstone in November and December, when there are hundreds of big-eyed calves about – babies that can be stroked and fondled – and to watch the amiable old cows and bulls, who seem quite unafraid, is to realise that however desirable it might be to limit their numbers it is even more desirable that somebody else should be the executioner. There is another small factor in this seal problem that few outsiders perhaps know about. The fishermen of the Northumbrian coast are very – is superstitious the word? – about seals. It might be hard for the landlubber to credit that such a belief could really exist in the twentieth century – but there are fishermen on the coast who employ all the latest electronic gear imaginable, and understand how it works, but who at the same time believe that dead sailors transmute into seals! I know of one of the most modern-minded men in Seahouses who used to bang away at seals with a rifle when they came near his salmon net; but since he lost his eldest son he will go below and hide his head when somebody else has to perform the same office, and if a seal is hit he doesn't want to know about it.

But throughout the year there are seals about the Farne Islands, and they come out on the rocks to rest at all times. It would be a very sad day if they were all exterminated, for *they* are part of the balance of nature, too.

Now for mankind. There is a story (I have seen it related in Grace Watt's most excellent book on the Farne Islands (*The Farne Islands*, Country Life 1951)) that before St Aidan came the islands were inhabited by little people 'clad in cowls and riding upon goats, black in complexion, short in stature, their countenances most hideous, their heads long'. But by AD 651 we come to a hard rock of certainty on which we can build – the Venerable Bede. He tells us that about this time Bishop Aidan used to retreat to the islands when he wished to be undisturbed, and from this spot saw the flames as Penda tried to burn down the city of Bamburgh; by miraculous intervention he caused the wind to change so that the city was saved. He then tells us how, in AD 687, the most reverend Father Cuthbert died on the Farne Islands, and wished his body to be buried there; only after most earnest entreaty did he consent to having it removed to Lindisfarne, where it became the most valuable stock-in-trade.

As St Cuthbert was perhaps more closely associated with the Farnes than anybody else, it is here, perhaps, that we ought to consider his life. He was born in 637, in the Lammermuir Hills, and is said to have spent his boyhood as a shepherd near Doddington in Northumberland. He was called to become a monk, and entered the priory at Mailros (old Melrose) under Boisil, the famous prior of that place. He was a favourite of Eata, Prior of Ripon, who took him to Ripon with him where he became *hostillar*, then sent him back to Mailros, where Cuthbert became prior when Boisil died. In 664 he was transferred to Lindisfarne as prior. In 676 he retreated to the tiny island of Hobthrush (where his hermitage is still marked with a cross), but found it inadequately remote for his spiritual needs and so took himself off to the Inner Farne Island, where Aidan had been before him, and there built a round wall of stone and turf, which cut off his view of all but Heaven, and in it a tiny oratory and a living-room. There was no fresh water when he arrived but prayer solved this problem. He determined to be self-supporting. He tried to grow wheat, without success. He then tried barley, sowing it far too late, but it miraculously grew to a good crop. Birds infested it – but he asked them to go away, which they did. There are many charming stories about him. One about how a crow, when he scolded it, would come and stand at his feet and hang its head in shame until he forgave it. He ground the barley between stones and made cakes of the flour and dried them in the sun. At first he would give audience to pilgrims, then only through a small window, and afterwards not at all except just to give them a blessing. After nine years of this he was elected Bishop of Hexham, and only accepted the honour after King Egfrid and his nobles had come to the island and begged him on their knees. He exchanged the bishopric of Hexham, though, with Bishop Eata for that of Lindisfarne. In 686 he was convinced his end was near, and retired to the Farnes to die, and there he survived for two months and three weeks. For the last five days his diet was half an onion. At nine o'clock on 20th March 687 he was carried by attendant monks back to his cell and he died at midnight. The monks signalled with torches to their brothers on Lindisfarne, and later the saint's body was buried next to the altar at Lindisfarne and the fragments of his carved wooden coffin can still be seen in the library of Durham Cathedral.

After this there was a succession of hermits on the Inner Farne. There was a notable one, Bartholomew, in 1150. The Vikings raided the island – and St Cuthbert's well immediately dried up. It ran again as soon as these heathens left the island. Various monks farmed the island, and it always grew good barley. In 1370 we read that there was a community of monks there who had three acres of barley, two of other crops, and kept a bull, two cows, a pig, four sheep, six capons, six hens and a cock. In their granary they had twelve quarters of wheat, twelve of malt of oats, twelve and a half of malt of barley, three bushels of salt, half an ox and three sheep down in salt, five codfish in salt, two hundred red herrings and twelve quarters of coal. These monks derived an income by selling surplus barley, and also sea-birds and their eggs, as well as lobsters, fish, seal oil, porpoises and young seals. They also engaged in wreck salvaging. They had a boat and tackle which was worth, when new, 117s.: ten oars, a fifty fathom line and a hundred hooks.

In 1407 the Master, John de Rypon, was sacked for extravagance, it being said that he kept horses and strolled about the country frequenting 'eatings and drinkings'. In 1461 John Kirke was rebuked for 'haunting a womanse house over ofte a for noon'.

And what is there still to see? Surprisingly quite a lot. There is St Cuthbert's chapel, which was rebuilt (if not completely built) in about 1370 by those jolly monks who had all that malt (malt of *oats* too! and my own brewing experience tells me that twenty-four and a half bushels of malt would have made about two hundred and fifty gallons of very strong beer!) and it was restored by the Venerable Charles Thorp, between 1831 and 1862 when that ecclesiastical dignitary took the tenancy of the islands. He filled up most of the windows, put a new one in the east end filled with Flemish glass, and brought seventeenth-century woodwork from Durham Cathedral. The archdeacon lived on the islands for some time, and he intended that the chapel should be a memorial for Grace Darling.

In 1927 the National Trust took over, and repaired the chapel the next year, and, incidentally, built a cottage for bird watchers on the Brownsman with stone from the abandoned lighthouse there.

The big tower was built by Prior Castell of Durham from 1494 to 1500 as a fortification and was a typical pele tower of the period. One Captain Robert Rugge commanded it in 1637 with a gunner, a gunner's mate, and two soldiers. It was then used as a lighthouse. It had four storeys (the top one is damaged) and has a pointed barrel vault on the ground floor, a piscina on the first floor, and St Cuthbert's miraculous well is said to be on the ground floor.

Of other buildings, a light tower or beacon was erected on Staple Island the remains of which are still to be seen, and there was one on the Brownsman. In 1809 a round lighthouse was erected on the Inner Farne, which is now working but unmanned. It used to be

run on acetylene gas and the great white splodge on the cliffs below
it that can be seen so clearly from the mainland, was made by the
spent carbide being chucked over the cliff. In 1810 a lighthouse was
foolishly built on the Brownsman – right in the centre of the group –
and Robert Darling, Grace's grandfather, was keeper of it. Grace
was here until the age of ten, when she moved to the Longstone,
and before they moved the family kept goats and sheep on the
Brownsman.

The Longstone light was built in 1825, when it became obvious
that the Brownsman was a mistake. It is still a fully manned lighthouse.

There is the ruin of a small hut on West Wideopens that belonged
to a seaweed cutter.

The **Kettle** is a good anchorage for landing on the Inner Farne.
It is delightful to explore these islands in your own boat. You should
go there at least once in a northerly gale at half tide to see the water
spurting ninety feet into the air from the Churn, which is on the
north-west end of the Inner Farne. To hire a boat for the Farne
Islands from Seahouses costs about £4. One passenger may have to
pay 37½p for the trip, but during May, June and July he should
have a landing permit, obtainable at most hotels in Seahouses, and
which costs 12½p. You are not supposed to land on the Brownstone
and the Longstone End in the breeding season, and should only
tour the Inner Farne under guidance. The bird population of the
Farnes managed to survive quite well a couple of thousand years
of unchecked human visitations of the islands. By far the best thing
to do is to go in your own boat, and then you need bother nobody.

And to end our discussion of the Farnes, as we should do, with
St Cuthbert, Aelfric, a monk at St Abb's Head, relates the following
story. When the saint was on the Farnes he used sometimes to
immerse himself in the sea up to his neck to say his prayers. Once
a brother monk joined him at this. 'Then did Cuthbert, as his wont
was, sing his prayers, standing in the sea-flood to his neck, and,
after, bowed his knees on the sand, stretching the palms of his hands
to the heavenly sky. Just then came two otters from the bottom of
the sea, and they with their fleeces dried his feet, and with their
breath bathed his limbs, and, after, with beckonings, begged his
blessings, lying at his feet in the yellow sand.'

CHAPTER 6

Seahouses to Warkworth Harbour

✤

SOUTH from Seahouses takes us along a rocky knuckle of shore, backed up by a caravan site and a golf course, past a strange fresh-water lagoon at a point called the Snook, to a delightful sandy bay with sharp rocks off-shore, past Annstead, a fortress of a farmstead crouching behind the sand-dunes, and you soon come to **Beadnell**. If you stick to the coast road here you come to think that the place is entirely given over to the dreariest of holiday villas, most of the year empty, and flibberty gimcrack modern 'racing yachts' until you come suddenly to Beadnell Harbour – where lie, when not at sea, five magnificent cobles, tied out into the middle of the tiny harbour by ropes from the walls. They look simply superb: romantic in the extreme. Their names are: *Research, Golden Gate, Joan Dixon, Eileen and David*, and *Jane Douglas*. Their owners tend to be oldish men, mostly named Douglas, nearly all staunch chapel men and when I asked one of them the way to the pub he said: 'It's next to the church and the graveyard – and the three go well together!'

By the tiny artificial harbour, which one might guess was built somewhere near the beginning of the eighteenth century (there is no mortar between the big dressed stones) is a group of fine lime kilns, the porticoes of which are used by fishermen to store their pots. These kilns are fortunately the property of the National Trust and will not be pulled down to make room for worse things: it is a pity that they are no longer used for their proper purpose. The little harbour itself has been the target of a take-over bid which, thank God, has so far failed. It has been reported in the press at various times that yachting interests would pay £20,000 for the harbour (from which now the fishermen very rightly exclude pleasure boats) but the five boat-owners, who also own the harbour, stead-fastly refuse. The common talk locally is that the little fishing fleet will die out, because no boys are coming into them and their crews are ageing. If this is so it is sad, for never has there been a better living in fishing along this coast, but of course the larger centres, such as Seahouses, which have a small bunch of fish merchants waiting on the quay for the boats to come in to bid for their catches,

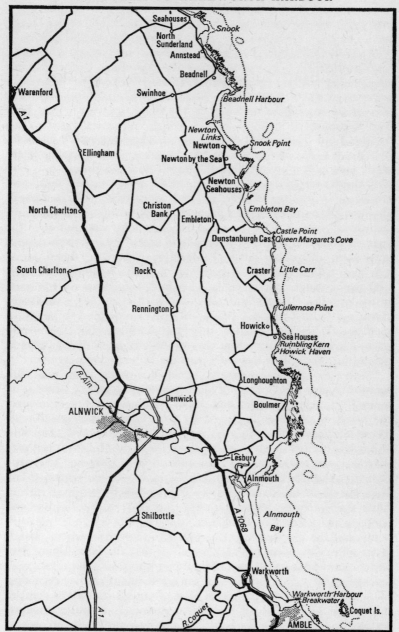

Seahouses
North
Sunderland
Annstead
Beadnell
Snook
Beadnell Harbour
Warenford
Swinhoe
A1
Newton
Links
Newton
Snook Point
Ellingham
Newton by the Sea
Newton
Seahouses
Embleton Bay
North Charlton
Christon
Bank
Embleton
Castle Point
Queen Margaret's Cove
Dunstanburgh Cas.
South Charlton
Rock
Craster
Little Carr
Rennington
Cullernose Point
Howick
Sea Houses
Rumbling Kern
Howick Haven
R. Aln
Longhoughton
Denwick
Boulmer
ALNWICK
Lesbury
Alnmouth
Shilbottle
A 1068
Alnmouth
Bay
A1
Warkworth
Warkworth Harbour
Breakwater
R. Coquet
Coquet Is.
AMBLE

are attracting the boats away from the smaller places. Water skiing, in the bay, is currently doing great harm to the salmon fishing.

Beadnell Harbour has undoubtedly seen busier days. There is a big turretted house by the harbour which is almost hidden behind signs saying NO WAITING, which is where kippering kilns once were, there was a good export trade in burnt lime, the place was famous for smuggling, and in 1538 seventy-one able-bodied men were accounted in the population. It is an old place, too, for on a headland just north of the harbour are the remains of a thirteenth-century chapel dedicated to St Ebba, and it is thought that there was a very early Anglo-Saxon chapel on this same spot.

Beadnell village itself (near which a large 'estate' of modern houses and bungalows is growing up) is north half a mile and inland a hundred yards or so and is very attractive, with an early eighteenth-century church of most wonderful aspect, and a pub called the Craster Arms, built in front of an original pele tower. The tower was built by the Forster family in the fifteenth century. The vaulted basement is now the beer cellar, there is a vestige of a newel staircase and a fireplace on the ground floor. The Craster coat of arms adorns the front of the pub, along with the sign of an insurance company, so that the fire engines of that company should know that they were to put fires out there if nowhere else and conversely fire engines of rival companies should know that they were to stand by and watch the building merrily burn.

South of Beadnell Harbour, near where there are caravans, is a most beautiful sandy bay, backed by the sand-dune country of Newton Links. These sand dunes are excellent for children to play Indians in and are interesting from a botanist's point of view. At one place is what looks like a totem pole: a heavy varnished post planted in the ground with timber steps up each side of it. To divine the purpose of this object (and there are many more the same around our coasts) might tax the ingenuity of the cleverest. In fact it is a mast for the Coast Guards to practise their rocket apparatus on. They rig up their tackle and their breeches buoy and practise taking each other off it over the sand-dunes.

Newton-by-the-Sea is a tiny village not by the sea at all but about half a mile away from it. There's a nice little pub and a walled garden with a tower in which Dorothy Forster is supposed to have been immured. Down by the sea is **Newton Seahouses**, where the Ship Inn stands at the back of a lovely quadrangle open in front to the sea but enclosed on three sides by the most delightful cottages. This little ensemble of buildings is charming: one of the nicest places

to live, one would think, on the whole coast. Unfortunately the
motor-car is invading even such lost fastnesses. The landlord of the
Ship has a fine moustache, and the pub should be visited for this
alone, although it is also a very fine pub with a good atmosphere.

Embleton Bay has good sands, dunes and a golf course. At North
Farm, inland, lives Mr Manners who owned Pravona, Cheep-
Cheep and Garçon d'or, three very fine race horses. He still owns
race horses.

Embleton is a fine example of a Northumberland village with a
pele tower built in 1395 for £40 and now part of a big house, the
central part of which is of about 1720 and the rest about 1820. The
latter part was designed by the Dobson who designed Newcastle
Central Station. The lower part of the church tower is Norman, the
rest of the building predominantly fourteenth century. The chancel
is Victorian, and the vaulted floor of the tower is extremely interesting. We are now in Craster country, and in the church are memorials
to:

William John Craster, Colonel of the Royal Bengal Artillery, seventh
son of Thos. Wood Craster, who served throughout the Indian
Mutiny, was besieged in Delhi, took part in the North West Frontier
campaigns of 1858 and 1860 and the Afghan War of 1879 and died
at Beadnell Hall 1922.

John Charles Pulleine Craster, Captain in the 46th Punjabis, and,
while attached to the 40th Pathans, fell in taking Gyantse in Tibet,
28th June 1904.

Shafto Craster Craster, Captain in the 8th King's Regiment, died of
fever in Kangra, India, 11th April 1856, aged 29.

There are also memorials to the Greys of Fallodon.

The Crasters have had one of the longest unbroken tenures of
an estate in England, for they are said to have lived at Craster
before the Conquest and they live there still. Unfortunately, of the
two surviving male Crasters, Sir John has no heir and his brother
Shafto is unmarried. They are both very fine naturalists, and have
played leading parts in the life of the district in which they live.
Sir John has fought valiantly to further the interests of the fishermen,
not only in his own harbour of Craster but all along the coast.

But before we get to Craster we must walk the mile or two around
that marvellous Embleton Bay to **Dunstanburgh Castle.** Here
we are back at our old friend the Great Whin Sill, that natural
foundation of castles, and this particular castle has a most
romantic aspect. It dominates the coast for miles: we probably saw
it from the Farne Islands if it was a clear day. Unlike the castles

that we have so far seen Dunstanburgh has never been restored; it is now no more than a ruin and we know that everything we are looking at here, except the caretaker's wooden hut, is medieval.

The site is a perfect one for a fortified camp, and certainly the British were here: sherds of Samian pottery have been dug up indicating habitation in Romano-British times. The name itself would suggest that it was a fortified place in Anglian times, but it first comes really into written history when Simon de Montfort got it by swapping other lands for it in 1255. When he was slain at Evesham, Henry III took the castle and gave it to his second son, Edmund of Lancaster. Edmund's son, Thomas, inherited it and built much of the castle starting in 1313. He was executed by Edward II and the castle taken in hand by the king, and thereafter by the various earls and dukes of Lancaster. John of Gaunt had it through his wife who had held the barony of Embleton, and he came himself to Dunstanburgh in 1380 and strengthened the place considerably against the Scots, blocking up the gateway and turning the gate house into a keep and making a new gateway, with portcullis and barbican and mantlet north-west of it. The Scots attacked the place, but it withstood them, and thereafter during the troubled times on the Border in Richard II's reign it was kept well stocked and garrisoned. When John of Gaunt's son Bolingbroke usurped the crown, Dunstanburgh, as part of the Duchy of Lancaster, became a royal castle, and was governed by a constable.

During the Wars of the Roses the castle was steadfastly Lancastrian, until attacked by 10,000 men under the Earl of Warwick, when it was surrendered upon honourable terms by the commander of its garrison, Sir Ralph Percy – the 'Falcon of Dunstanburgh'. The Falcon turned coat and became a Yorkist, turned it back again and became a Lancastrian, and was killed by the Yorkists at Hedgely Moor. On 24th June 1464 Warwick attacked and took the castle again, and this time it was held for the new King who was Edward IV. But after this, castles such as this one were of small avail, for the siege cannon had been developed, and Dunstanburgh was looted and fell into disrepair and in disrepair it still is.

As a fortification it relied more on its natural position, the vertical or nearly vertical walls of the Great Whin Sill and the sea, than on sophisticated artificial defences. Towers are but sparsely placed along its enormously long curtain walls and the very long, and weak, east wall could have been attacked very easily by escalade by seaborne troops. Perhaps though the English, even when Dunstanburgh was built, felt they could rely upon their floating wooden walls to prevent seaborne attack. The north boundary of the castle is unassailable because it is a vertical cliff falling straight into the sea: the west wall is approachable by the enemy only up a very steep bank; only the comparatively short length of the south wall had to be really seriously fortified and here there is a fighting tower every hundred feet or so, and a moat in front, cut out of solid rock.

We enter the castle by the early fourteenth-century gateway, now reopened since John of Gaunt closed it. We can clamber up into the two massive drum towers of the gate house, which later became the keep, and it is exhilarating to do so, particularly on a windy day. Inside the gate we come into the Inner Ward, created by John of Gaunt when he built his new gate and barbican; it has a tower at its corner. Working east now, along the south curtain wall, we come to the Constable's Tower, with the ruins of that important man's house behind it, then a small fighting turret, and then to the interesting Egyncleugh Tower, which was once a gate to the sea and had a draw-bridge and a barbican of which nothing remains. The curtain now follows the edge of the Egyn Cleugh, a little inlet also called Queen Margaret's Cove, and reaches the edge of the sea cliff where it changes in nature to a wall of very poor construction, punctuated by three privies which are still useful. After a couple of hundred yards we come to Castle Point which sticks out into the sea. Here we may see fulmars, kittiwakes, guillemots, and if we are lucky puffins and eiders (as we walked along the sands of Embleton Bay to get here we probably saw terns, Arctic and sandwich, swooping down to take sand eels at the water's edge).

Walking west along the northern boundary of the Outer Ward we may well feel that the defenders were safe enough from this side. The Rumble Churn, alas, rumbleth no more, its rumble having been cut off by a fall of rock. We come to the Lilburn Tower (John Lilburn was constable of the castle around 1325) which was very well built because it is still in good order. We keep on going and get back to John of Gaunt's gateway.

The size of the place (eleven acres) must have been a big embarrassment to the defenders, but it would not have been possible, owing to the lie of the land, to have made it any smaller without sacrificing the natural advantages of the position. It had one enormous asset: a small viable harbour right at its door to the south, now completely silted up and cut off from the sea. This harbour was connected with Embleton Bay, to the north of the castle, by an artificial ditch which must have turned the castle into an island. A huge castle, the garrison of which could be supplied by its own harbour, was obviously a great asset (compare Beaumaris, on Anglesey). But the castle had serious disadvantages. It was far off the beaten track: the road to the North was five miles to the west of it. It was not the centre of a rich district, and therefore never the seat of its lord, and was thus never developed as a lordly residence. It was too far from the Scots border to be an effective advanced base. It has one great advantage today though, and in this it is most unusual. You cannot get to it by motor-car.

South, a mile and a half of lovely rocky shore brings us to the village of **Craster** where, perhaps for a thousand years or more – certainly for seven hundred – the Craster family held out against all comers in their fortified house of Craster Tower. The Tower was mentioned in a list of 1415. The present house has a wing of 1769, the rest more modern. Sir John, however, no longer lives here, but in one of the farmhouses of his old estate..

Forty years ago the Craster estate was a model of the best that the English squirearchy could produce. The little artificial harbour, built by the Crasters just before the First World War as a memorial to one of the family, used to contain a good fleet of fine cobles, and besides this, East Coast sailing barges and small steam coasters used to come in and load stone, which was gravity fed to them from great hoppers on the end of the east pier the foundations of which can still be seen. The stone was taken to the hoppers by cable-way from the Crasters' big quarry in the Whin Sill just behind the village. Big kilns worked away smoking kippers from the herrings that the cobles brought in. The farms surrounding the village on the landward side were well farmed and productive, and the woodlands well tended. Game abounded, for the Crasters were a great sporting family. Even now it's a superb little place, substantially unspoiled although like everywhere else infested with cars in the holiday season. There is a tiny (but I think growing) fleet of fine cobles and kippers are still kippered but on a much smaller scale than formerly and now with herring bought from North Shields and not with local fish. These kippers are probably the best in the world and are supplied to the Queen, among other people. They are only available in the early summer, when Mr Robson, who kippers them, thinks the herring are in the best fettle for the job. They are *not* subsequently deep-frozen, nor are they made from frozen fish and Mr Robson does not approve of people buying his kippers and deep freezing them. They should be eaten in prime condition or not at all.

Kippering is a simple process. The fish are split down the back

Left, Beadnell lime kilns; *below*, Dunstanburgh Castle.

WARKWORTH: *Above*, the fourteenth-century bridge; *below*, the Castle.

(Messrs L. Robson & Son have a German machine which does this job and replaces an army of fisher girls), soaked in brine for twenty minutes, then hung on tenter hooks (hence the expression) which are just bent nails in sticks about five feet long, and the tenter sticks are then hung on the racks inside the kiln. The kilns are very tall, and if a kiln is to be filled men clamber up the racks and then, perched there precariously, pass the loaded tenter sticks up from man to man – the topmost man putting them on the racks. Then a smouldering fire of sawdust and chips (always supposed to be oak, but many curers like a little soft-wood mixed with it) is lit on the floor of the kiln and is kept going for from fourteen to twenty hours. Salmon have five hours in the salt and four days in the smoke.

Opposite the kippering sheds is the Jolly Fisherman Inn and a jolly good inn it is too.

The quarries for which Craster was famous were in the whinstone, and setts of up to six feet in length used to be produced from one of them for kerbs of pavements in London and other cities. This spur of the Whin Sill, which starts at Castle Point in the north, runs to Cullernose Point a couple of miles to the south. On our journey southwards we shall not meet it again. Strangely, the two reefs which give shelter to the tiny Craster Harbour, the Little Carr and Muckle Carr, are made of limestone. The fishermen know that the lobsters grow better and quicker on the limestone than they do on the whinstone.

There are rugged cliffs south of Craster, and a little estate village at **Howick**, and another Rumbling Kern (although I have never seen it rumble yet) and Howick Haven where recently the boiler of a French trawler has been dragged up out of the sea for salvage. She was the steam trawler *Tadorne*. She went ashore on those vicious rocks on 29th March 1913, and five of her crew are buried in Howick churchyard. Twenty-two were rescued, three never found.

If we keep on past where the *Tadorne* was wrecked (there is an old fisherman's hut there) we come to where a little valley runs down to the sea, with a stream, and there is a bridge over the stream and a strange concrete quay the use of which seems to have been forgotten. A footpath here takes us up the valley, or burn, which is delightfully wooded and planted with ornamental trees, and it is obvious that we are in some gentleman's, or nobleman's, park. If we keep going, up this most delightful of glens, we come to an ornamental bridge over the public road, to a little Norman-style church among woods (the *Tadorne*'s men lie to the east of it, down near the fence) and then are perhaps ten acres of superb garden and parkland with a great house in the middle of it. Lord and Lady Howick allow people to walk round the grounds between two and seven in the afternoons from Easter to September, and if you enter by the way I described, you should go to one of the gates and pay your 12½p. One most excellent gardener and a lady assistant look after this enormous pleasure park, helped by Lady Howick herself who is passionate about gardening, and the amount of work they get through is enormous. There are six hundred rhododendrons, magnolias galore, at least one Chinese handkerchief tree and tulips and daffodils in great profusion. Howick Hall, built for Sir Henry Grey in 1782 to a design by William Newton, is the centre of a 17,000-acre estate. Northumberland is nothing if not feudal: cross the Pennines and you are in a country of small farms, most of them owner-occupied. Northumberland is nearly all huge estates with big farms farmed by tenants. Howick Hall was the home, from 1801 to his death in 1845, of the second Earl Grey, the Reform minister.

A lovely rocky shore brings us to **Boulmer**, pronounced 'Boomer' by those who know. This is a stark and spartan little place: a simple row of fishermen's cottages right on the seashore and for each house a big and beautiful coble either lies out at anchor in the little Haven, or is out at sea, or is hauled up just south of the hamlet. The Boulmer men are alleged by other fishermen (e.g. those of Amble) to be the pampered pets of the Duke of Northumberland, their land-lord, who always sees to it that they get salmon licences. If they are, then jolly good luck to them. They have a beautiful lifeboat house, and the first boat was put in it in 1825. Sadly it was decided to withdraw the RNLI boat from Boulmer a year or two ago. The Boulmer men would not take this lying down, and formed an RNLI of their own which they call the Boulmer Voluntary Rescue Service, financed by sympathisers in the locality. They have bought a fibreglass speed boat of foreign origin and large engines. Many people (including some from Boulmer) think that if they had bought their old lifeboat off the RNLI she would have served them a lot better (besides being enormously much cheaper), but there was a difference of opinion about the whole business. Of course as lifeboats get larger and more powerful they tend to get fewer: the boat from Amble, for example, can quickly get to Boulmer (if she can get out of Amble Harbour which she quite often can't). But places like Boulmer badly need a small lifeboat, perhaps of the 'Liverpool' type, to help and escort their own fishing boats when bad weather comes up – to say nothing of rescuing the increasing number of racing yachtsmen who spend as much time upside down as they do right way up.

The glory of Boulmer is the marvellous painting inside the pub. This is by one A. H. Marsh (I have not been able to date it) and is of the women of Boulmer dragging their lifeboat through the sand-dunes – so as to launch her at some other point along the coast – a common practice in sail and oar days. The women dragged the boat in order to conserve the strength of the men who would have the ferocious task of rowing the heavy boat off through the breakers and maybe several miles into the teeth of a gale. Most of the women in the picture can be recognised by old Boulmer people today, and whether we approve of this kind of representational art or no, to most of us this picture must be extremely moving. The pub at Boulmer, the Fishing Boat, is best appreciated during an easterly gale at high spring tides in the winter. It then seems as if the tiny hamlet is about to be overwhelmed, and the safest place seems to be not very far from the bar.

Inland from Boulmer is an airfield and radar station of hideous aspect. Then we come to the inevitable golf course. Then to **Alnmouth**. Like many English rivers and other old natural features, the Aln has a Celtic name, *A* being Old Welsh for water and *lain* for clear or clean.

Alnmouth has become a very popular little resort for people who like quietness, bathing, and golf. There is a small boatyard and some dinghies and racing yachts. The little town itself is pleasant, but it suffers from having no industry except that of being 'residential' or a resort. A hundred and fifty years ago it was an important trading harbour, but in 1806 the sea broke through the sand dunes and the river changed its course and the harbour became silted up and unusable. At one time ships of many nations called here to load corn, and the very road to Alnmouth was called the Corn Road. It is an ancient place, for on the little hill beside the abandoned harbour are the ruins of the Saxon church of St Waleric and the Norman church of St John the Baptist. Alnmouth claims to be 'Twyford on the Alne' where Bede tells us a synod was held in 684 in which Cuthbert was elected bishop. The Schooner Hotel is large and popular: the Red Lion is an ancient inn.

If we can get a lift over the river there are marvellous sands all the way to **Warkworth Harbour**, but there we will have to get somebody to put us over a river again if we want to get to Amble. Otherwise we will have to cut inland to Warkworth and go by road. But the point north of Warkworth Harbour is interesting, if only because the River Coquet used to reach the sea well to the north of it: the present harbour mouth is a recent invention. The old bed of the river has sunken barges in it: one or two of them original Tyne keels (of 'Weel may the keel row' fame). These were once loaded with stone here and towed south to the Tyne by tugs. This exit to the sea was once the port of Warkworth. The point of land itself is called Monkey Island, but is an island no longer. The long north wall of the new Warkworth Harbour takes a tremendous bashing from the sea – it is most impressive to watch a north-easterly gale breaking against it – but don't try to walk out on it on such an occasion or you will probably have to swim.

CHAPTER 7

Warkworth to Amble

჻

THE little town of **Warkworth** doesn't seem to have changed
much since Harry Hotspur, according to Shakespeare, took his less
than cordial farewell from his wife before he set out for the battle of
Shrewsbury. The town is crammed into a horseshoe loop of the
River Coquet, and thank God still not blanketed by straggling
suburbs. The neck of the horseshoe is cut off by that 'worm-eaten
hold of ragged stone' as Shakespeare made his Henry IV call the
castle, and the medieval bridge across the river at the front of the
horseshoe is guarded by a tower. The whole town is a fortress. The
only sad thing about it is that the new motor bridge is beside the
fourteenth-century one – thus spoiling the latter and also channel-
ling the growing volume of through-traffic through the town. Of
course they should have put their new bridge half a mile downstream of the town and by-passed the little place altogether.

The town is most beautiful: it seems to have everything that a
little town should have – including a restaurant down by the church
that serves *cordon-bleu* food. It still has that excellent institution
which makes a town part of its countryside: plots of land outside
the town which belong, by right, to the burgesses. Every townsman
thus has one foot in the country, and the architecture of the town
shows this in that some of the houses have passages through them to
allow the cow to be taken to the back, for milking, after having
come back from grazing. These plots (called *stints*) are some half
acre in extent, and still exist, excepting in such cases as when the
foolish owners sold their rights to the Duke of Northumberland and
now regret that they did so. The crop that replaced cows on these
holdings was caravans, but recently the planning authorities have
banned these and there is a nice tidy caravan site instead between
Warkworth and the sea. It was much more fun before. There are
several hotels – Warkworth House has Adam fireplaces and bronze
stair rails brought from Brandenburg House, in London, by the
Forster family.

The name Warkworth comes from *Werceworde*: the homestead of
a woman named Werce, and a Werce was mentioned by Bede but

it might not be the same one. Ceolwulf became king of Northumbria in 729, and himself founded the church of St Lawrence of Warkworth and thereafter gave it, and the town, to the monastery of Lindisfarne. Osbert, the last king of Northumbria, took it back again and this sacrilege was thought to have been responsible for his death in 867, fighting the Danes at York. But the Danes were overrunning the whole country then and Lindisfarne itself was in eclipse. William the Conqueror parcelled the place out to Mowbray, and thereafter the history of Warkworth was the history of its castle, for the town was merely an appendage of the latter, and the latter was the most important castle in the north of England. A significant share of the history of England was played out in **Warkworth Castle**.

The church is one of the most interesting in the county. It is very much a Norman church: the chancel and its arch are still beautiful Norman work: the twelfth-century vaulting of the chancel is rare and beautiful. The south aisle was stuck on by the Percy family in the fifteenth century. The nave is Norman and very long: the tower and spire later. The east window of the south aisle is worth looking at, for it has the only medieval glass in the church and very beautiful it is. There are fragments of very early Celtic crosses, a tomb effigy of a knight west of the main door – about 1330 – and with fine features, very much an officer and a gentleman. The whole place has great atmosphere. The great bulging north wall may be structurally unsound but it is beautiful.

So up the main street we go to the castle, and the great Percy lion looks down at us from high up on the north wall of the keep. We can walk round the castle either way, along the road to the east of it, or the grassy bank to the west of it: in any case we should walk right round it to look at it from the besieger's point of view before going inside.

This castle had the most varied and exciting career, until seven shots from the cannon of Henry IV told its defenders that the day of the castle as a serious weapon of war was over for ever.

Henry of Scotland, the son of David I, was created earl of Northumberland by the treaty of Durham in 1139, and he started the first serious castle building there, because by the treaty he was denied the much stronger castles of Bamburgh and Newcastle and needed a fortified place from which to govern his country. Henry II of England got the castle back from the Scots (together with Northumberland) and gave it to Roger Fitz Richard for the latter's bravery in the battle of Coleshill, near Flint, in which the marauding army of Henry II was nearly destroyed by a Welsh ambuscade. In 1173 the Scots William the Lion, who had been lord of Northumberland before being ousted by Henry II, attacked the place and overthrew it and went on to attack Newcastle, but there was repelled.

Roger's son, Robert, built much more of the castle, including the great gatehouse, very early in the thirteenth century. He also built the Great Hall and other buildings inside the bailey (the Keep was not in existence then) and the Carrickfergus Tower. Edward I stayed in Warkworth on his way to one of his Scottish forays, and during his and his son's reign the castle was strengthened very much against the Scots. In 1327 the Scots besieged it, were beaten off, but tried again the same year under Robert Bruce but again it withstood them. Indeed without notable siege engines it is hard to see how anybody could have got into it.

The heirs of Roger Fitz Richard got into debt, and the castle passed into the hands of the Percy family after 1332 when John Clavering, the last of the old family, died. It was about then that the Grey Mare's Tail Tower was built, and the inside of the present keep. The castle became then the chief home of the Percy family: the home from which Hotspur rode forth to 'kill me some six or seven dozen of Scots at a breakfast, washes his hands, and says to his wife, "Fie upon this quiet life! I want work." ' It was here that the plans were laid to put Bolingbroke on the throne of England, and afterwards to take him off again, but the latter plan went wrong. The earl of Northumberland took refuge in the castle after his son had been killed at the Battle of Shrewsbury, and it was then that the king attacked him with 37,000 men, fired his seven cannon shots (this was in 1405 when the large siege cannon was a horrible new device) and the garrison surrendered. The Crown took the castle back again, but later restored it to the Percy family, in the person of Henry Percy, the son of Hotspur. He was killed fighting against the Yorkists at the battle of St Albans. It was probably during his tenure that the marvellous keep was planned and started, and also the collegiate church, the foundations of which still lie across the bailey, and the building of which, one could only imagine, would have detracted considerably from the castle's military value. The castle was a Lancastrian stronghold until 1462, when Edward IV gave it to his brother George, Duke of Clarence. Warwick the kingmaker made it his headquarters in 1462 in his successful campaigns against the Lancastrians in Bamburgh, Alnwick and Dunstanburgh. In 1469 Henry Percy did homage to Edward IV, all was forgiven and forgotten, and the Percy family once more regained their old home. It was he who heightened the internal tower at the entrance to the Great Hall (a tower which surely had no military significance?) and put the Percy lion on it, which still remains looking like the embellishment of some Sinhala palace in the jungles of Ceylon, and gives the tower its name of the Lion Tower.

In the reign of Henry VIII though the castle passed from the Percy family to the Crown, and Lord Parr, Lord-Warden of the Marches, lived there and repaired the place, but in 1557 Queen Mary restored Warkworth to the Percy family. The current earl then joined the Rising of the North in 1569 against Queen Elizabeth and paid for it with his head, and the Percys again lost their stronghold. Sir Henry Percy, however, was forgiven, given back Warkworth and created eighth earl of Northumberland, but he died in the Tower charged with high treason. The ninth earl got put into the Tower because he was mixed up with Guy Fawkes (one is tempted to believe that the Percy family just wouldn't take no for an answer) and thereafter it was leased out to the sort of people who merely let it fall down. When James I reached Warkworth on his way to Scotland he remarked that the Percy lion on the keep was holding up the castle, and his courtiers were much moved to see the place 'so spoiled and soe badly kept' with sheep and goats in many of the chambers. The Scots captured it in 1644 and the Roundheads in 1645, and the latter gave it back to the tenth earl. In the last three decades of the seventeenth century it met the fate of most English castles: it fell into the hands of the sort of sharks who delighted in tearing down and selling the work that better men had done. But in the mid-nineteenth century the fourth Duke of Northumberland repaired part of the keep to make it habitable, and did some maintenance to the rest of the fabric to prevent its further decay, and in 1922 the eighth duke placed it in the care of the Ministry of Works. The Duke of Northumberland still has private rooms in the keep, but for a very long time the restored castle of Alnwick has been the seat of the Percys.

Inside the castle there are careful drawings showing the date of every part of it, and the custodian, Mr Haswell Anderson, is a splendid man who knows all about it all (and who, as a matter of purely marginal interest, brews very good beer in his lovely house half a mile up the river). But it is a magnificent castle. It can show architecture of every period from old Mowbray's early Norman (the keep is on the Norman motte and the curtain walls follow the line of the old Norman bailey) to late fifteenth century. Unlike Dun-

stanburgh, this castle was for most of its time the principal seat of its
lord, and therefore great care was lavished on it, and besides being
a bare fortification for soldiers, it was also a home. It is instructive
to imagine the place in use and to see how well designed it was to
fulfil its function at the various stages of its history.

The range of buildings behind the Lion Tower should be considered apart from the keep, because it was in use long before the
keep was built. Here is, or at least was, everything for the simple
comfort and hearty cheer of the lord and his family and a large
body of retainers. No modern architect has come anywhere near the
efficient and beautiful arrangement of buildings of the early medieval
Great Hall, with its kitchen and other offices, its solar for the lord
and his family to withdraw to, its chapel. The great Keep of Warkworth, which duplicated much of this, must be one of the most
advanced of its kind, and is a highly sophisticated piece of building.
This too should be considered as a place for use. Where would be
the best place for, say, the goods hall, or the beer cellar, or the pages'
room, or the great hall? In most cases the answer to such questions
is: right where they are. It is a superbly designed dwelling place for a
large community, besides being a very strong fortress. Most of it
was built late in the fourteenth century and so it came at the very
peak of the medieval castle-builder's art: the cannon were already
speaking the doom of all such castles when it was built. Notice the
clever use of the thickness of the great walls over and over again for
the siting of passages, stairways, cupboards or privies. Observe the
complicated flushing arrangements for the lord's latrine.

There is one other thing we should do before leaving Warkworth
and that is go and look at the **Hermitage**. In the summer Mr
Anderson arranges for parties to go up the river to it by boat, and
this is very much the way to go; but when the river is in spate, and
the boats laid up, you can go by land, taking the first turning left
after crossing the bridge north of Warkworth and proceeding until
you come to a cottage standing all alone on the left, with a farm
gate just beyond it. Go through the gate (on foot only) and follow
the subsequent path and it will bring you to the river. Notice the
strange enclosure of weather-boarding there – it is a salmon pass to
allow salmon to by-pass the weir. Turn left and go downstream and
you will come, after a beautiful walk on the wooded banks, to the
Hermitage. If you have managed to borrow the key so much the
better, for without it you cannot get in.

Nothing much is known about the origin of this hermitage. There
is a corking ballad about it – and 'The Hermit's Tale' by Dr Percy

73

is splendid too, but both stories are completely fanciful. At all events it was a cave hermitage presumed by its decoration to have been excavated in the fourteenth century, and later enlarged and embellished. The latter hermits did themselves proud and we well might envy them. Sir George Lancaster was the last one recorded. He was appointed hermit in 1531 with a yearly stipend of twenty marks, was allowed twelve cows and a bull, with calves sucking, two horses, twenty loads of firewood and every Sunday a draught of 'fysshe'. Who would not be a hermit under such circumstances, and in such a lovely place? Sir George had a hall, a solar and a large kitchen as well as a chapel and a sacristy. The chapel is beautifully decorated by vaulting carved out of the solid sandstone cliff, and a decorated-style window into the sacristy, the tracery of which is also carved from the 'living rock'. Do not miss the lady who is reclining in the arched recess south of the altar. It has been thought that she, with her attendant all but obliterated figures, is Our Lady in the Nativity. Over the inner door were once decipherable the words, in Latin, meaning 'My tears have been my meat day and night', and over the door to the sacristy: 'They gave me gall to eat, and when I was thirsty they gave me vinegar to drink.' It is most important to visit the hermitage, at least once, alone.

And so we move on to **Amble**, which in its day might have thought that it was to be the successor to Warkworth's greatness, but which now, just for the moment at least, appears to have had its day itself. It's a tough little place, though, and may well rise like a phoenix out of the ashes of closed coal mines.

For, in our saunter along the Northumberland coast, we are about to leave the innocence of a truly rural countryside. From here to the Tees we are to know the influence of King Coal, for we are at the most northerly edge of the readily workable Northumbrian coalfield.

Amble has a Bronze Age burial ground on its golf course, and 'Ambell' was granted to Tynemouth Priory by Robert de Mowbray in 1090. The latter was given it by the Conqueror. For a long time it was a place of very little account. Until the great storm of 1799 the mouth of the Coquet was further north, as we have seen, and ships went right up to Warkworth without bothering Amble. But several of the coal seams outcropped nearby, and at one time there were eighty small shafts down to the coal between Amble and Hauxley which is only a mile away! And then in 1837 the Warkworth Harbour Commission was formed and Amble became 'Little Liverpool', and had Danish and Swedish consular offices in it, and the

Duke of Northumberland managed to extract £10,000 from the harbour company claiming that his salmon fishery had been impaired. Amble built up a fine little fleet of brigs and brigantines and schooners – at one time there were twenty-two ships owned in the town, all engaged in the coal trade to Scandinavia, or to London, or timber trade, or fetching slates from Dinorwic in Wales. Mines were opened up to the south and connected to Amble by railway and the place became a flourishing coaling port with a special connection with Denmark and Sweden. Most of Amble was built late nineteenth century or early twentieth. All seemed set fair for permanent prosperity. A new mine at Hauxley a mile south, started sending up coal as late as 1926. Little steel coasters (not locally owned) replaced the old wooden ships, and at one time ships of 2,500 tons' burden were using the port. This fell away recently to ships carrying about 1,500 tons. And then, in 1968 and '69 the staggering blow fell. Mine after mine had closed down (after all – mining is an extractive industry), ships were getting bigger and needed bigger ports (there is seventeen foot six over the bar at Amble but only at spring tides) and the National Coal Board closed its staithes. Amble was finished as a coal port. The railway lines to it were ripped up.

Unfortunately the harbour authority had not developed the harbour as a fishing port, although there is a little local fleet, both of decked boats and cobles, and Scottish boats use the place. They still do not seem to have grasped the necessity of doing this, but if there is a future for the port it is in fishing. Small coasters still sometimes come into the harbour to load stone, and this trade might be developed, but Amble could have a very good future as a fishing port.

There has been some attempt at diversifying industry – ladies' underwear is being produced in an old Baptist chapel for example, but Amble was more than anything else a coaling port and a mining centre and nothing of this is left at all. The wonder of it is that most people seem to have jobs. There is one good industry, which is expanding fast and which is just the sort of industry for a place like Amble, and that is boat building. Messrs Harrison and Sons (now owned and run by the brothers John and Hugh Matthews) have developed from a very small yard building small cobles into a business employing a lot of men and turning out big motor cobles and 'keel boats' as fast as they can make them, and further expansion is being undertaken now. The yard hasn't a hope of keeping pace with the orders it gets, for the demand for cobles is increasing all the time.

They have even started building big motor cobles, with tunnels for the propellers, for the west coast of Scotland, where cobles were never heard of before. The Matthews brothers do more for Amble than build cobles. Hugh is pilot in the harbour – now that the place is in decline a full-time pilot cannot make a living there and Hugh is doing it just to keep the harbour going until better times return. John is secretary of the lifeboat, and both brothers (and their wives) take a keen interest in RNLI affairs. There is a flourishing yacht club in Amble, small now but growing, and when the new spine road gets driven through from the Tyne, no doubt Amble will develop as a yachting port. Blyth is likely to become more and more busy commercially, and less attractive to yachts. Amble is a perfect place to keep a small yacht: the place has great atmosphere, it is at one end of a long stretch of coast (to the north) of special interest and beauty, and it is a fine little harbour. It may seem strange to recommend a late nineteenth-century coaling port as a holiday resort, but certainly I do so recommend Amble. Somehow it still has the smack of an old sailing ship port about it, its coast and river are varied and interesting, it offers fine sea fishing and not far away fine trout and salmon fishing, it is a mile and a half away from Warkworth but half as expensive, it is full of real Northumberland people, about as friendly as people can be, it is full of good pubs (the Schooner and the Ship are great) and the little fishing fleet is of constant interest and adds flavour to the place.

The best time to see the harbour is in a howling north-east gale. If you walk out on the wooden extension of the south breakwater then (if you can do so without being washed away) you not only have the experience of seeing huge waves break around you – but under your feet too. And you see the waves hurling themselves against the North Breakwater and overtopping it and surging down like great waterfalls – the smoke that thunders! Outside, north of Coquet Island, is a hell of breaking water, for there are reefs out there and the great waves are feeling the bottom. It was here, and in such conditions, that in 1969 an RAF rescue launch was overturned, and towed in, upside down, by the Amble lifeboat, and hours later a hole cut through the hull to release a man who was trapped inside. Coxswain Willie Douglas got a bronze medal for it.

Coquet Island is just a place with a lighthouse now, but at one time it had a cell of Tynemouth priory on it, and supported the saintliest of saints. Henry the Hermit, a Dane of noble birth, came here after a vision, to escape marriage. His view of the delights of marriage is indicated that he considered preferable living on this fourteen acre island on a small loaf of bread and a draught of fresh water every day for many years, then only food three times a week, and for the last four years of his life nothing to eat but the barley that he grew himself, crushed between two stones, wetted, and dried in the sun. So much did he afflict himself that the monk in charge of the island gave him harsh words and opprobrious epithets. He developed a loathsome affliction of one knee, but he continued to cultivate his little garden hobbling on a crutch. He had second sight, and knew when his half-brother in Denmark had been killed, and foretold the wreck of a ship for he said that he could see a woman following her. In the winter of 1126/27 the pain in his knee became intense but he would allow no one to administer to him, nor approach his cell. On 16th January 1127 a man heard two choirs of angels singing alternate verses of the *Te Deum*. A monk then heard the hermit's bell ring and he ran to his cell to find him sitting up with his hand on the bell rope, quite dead. A candle burnt beside him which the hermit would have had no means of lighting. When the body was washed it became as white as snow. The Warkworth people tried to retain the body as a relic but, when they were shipping it across, divine interception caused the winds to blow it to Tynemouth Priory where it became a profitable attraction for pilgrims.

A later hermit built, with great ingenuity and out of driftwood probably, a little windmill to grind his barley with but the baron of Warkworth sent men to smash it down as windmills were the baron's prerogative. In 1415 a small fortress was built on the site of the old cell, and this now forms the base of the lighthouse. Leyland wrote that there was 'secoal' digging there in 1528. In 1644 the Scots captured the island. In 1730 it was said to be uninhabited. In 1747 there were huts inhabited by diggers of coal. There are traces of coal diggings and also salt pans on the west of the island. Stone from Coquet Island was used to repair the battlements of Syon House at Brentford.

CHAPTER 8

Amble to Seaton Sluice

❧

SOUTHWARD ho from Amble, along a rough and rocky coast, past the first of many man-made hills the tip of Hauxley mine, to **Hauxley** itself, a tiny fishermen's village built in a piece by a Captain Widdrington about eighty years ago. The Widdringtons had owned Hauxley at least since the middle of the fourteenth century, when Sir Gerard claimed some land nearby from the prior of Tynemouth. The case was to be tried by combat, and the prior appointed one Sir Thomas Colville as his challenger, Evidently Sir Gerard didn't like the look of the fellow, for he backed out.

Just inland from Hauxley is the mining village of Radcliffe, and it was completely razed to the ground and its site excavated for coal, in 1971. Geological *cognoscenti* can discern the Hauxley Fault (which has a throw of a hundred fathoms) on the shore at Hauxley Head. Near this there is a fossil forest on the beach when the tide is very low, and there is a bed of shale in the cliff there very rich in fossils. Just south at Bondicar is boulder clay much studded with boulders left there by the Ice Age,

Just here, in the 1926 strike, miners sunk shafts of their own down to the coal and ran their own little unofficial coal mines.

After Bondicar we embark on the shore of **Druridge Bay**, which goes on for ten or a dozen miles, and which is sand, all sand: there are empty sandy beaches in Northumberland to satisfy every spade-and-bucket wielding toddler in the British Isles, all at once, and still leave room for daddies to recline in deck chairs.

Chevington Drift might be taken as an archetypal mining village on the Northumbrian coalfield: two rows of tiny terraced brick cottages nearly a mile long stuck out on a dreary treeless moor. Its pit is closed but it is not to be pulled down – its inhabitants like it too much.

But before Chevington we come to a new and strange world: the world of the National Coal Board Opencast Executive – an organisation busily engaged in creating if not a new Heaven, at least a new Earth. For this is the Coldrife Opencast, quickly followed to the south by the Radar Opencast, and huge excavators are busy

78

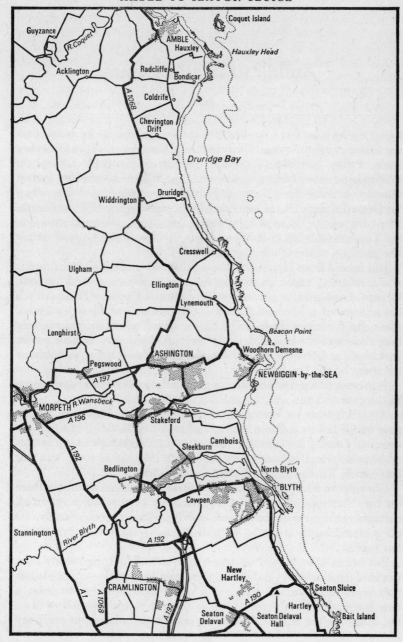

digging out two thousand acres of land, for five miles along Druridge Bay, to get at ten million tons of coal. In places they have to go down to two hundred feet below sea level to do this, and just the 200,000,000 cubic yards of overburden will have been removed – and put back again – before the ten million tons of coal all sees the light of day.

This might seem like terrible desecration of the countryside, but the fact is that the countryside has already been desecrated, and when Derek Crouch (the contractors for the NCB) have finished with it, it will be far pleasanter than it was before. The whole of this flat and treeless boulder clay area has been partially mined out by underground workings, and there is that look about it of desolation that seems common to undermined countryside. Subsidence has occurred leaving swampy 'flashes' or shallow lakes, often with rubbish in them, there are tips and dumps about, natural drainage has been interfered with: the whole area, pre-opencast, has the air of desolation you might expect of a land that has been fought over. When the opencasters have finished with it the topsoil is all replaced, the surface carefully graded to help drainage, hills and hollows placed where needed, trees planted, tile drainage provided, and the land handed over to the Ministry of Agriculture for a year or two for the surface to be rehabilitated for agriculture. There is plenty of land thus treated to be seen at Coldrife and Radar and the contrast with the old land is striking. Agriculturally and aesthetically it is far better land. Druridge Bay is at present a weird hellish world of vast pits, huge machines covered with lights working all night, large areas of dreadful mud, and heaps of earth and rock. But when it is all finished it will be a peaceful land again, and far more productive and fertile than it was before. And as the NCB officials will be quick to point out to you, the value of coal produced is about 140 times that of the value of the crops that could be taken from this land in the time that it is under the diggers. They will also point out that the coal thus produced is far cheaper than deep-mined coal, and also better, because it is not pulverised in the way in which modern underground coal cutters pulverise their coal.

There is much very shallow coal about here, for several seams – the Queen, and the Little Wonder, the Top and the Main and the Bottom and the Chevely – outcropped about this place: at least they outcrop under the overlying blanket of glacial drift, which in places is only a few feet thick. Old underground miners of defunct mines will tell you that they used to mine 'canny nigh the day', meaning very near the surface. Sometimes they could see the sky through cracks in the clay above. Once a sheep fell down into some workings. When the giant diggers now rip out the rock they sometimes break into old workings, into an old private world that might have thought itself safe from prying eyes until eternity.

As for machinery, 'Big Geordie' – a new working dragline – can swipe up a hundred tons in one bucket load, and her engine room is like the engine room of a big ship. She weighs just about 2,857 tons as she crawls over the ground. Great bucketwheel conveyors gnaw at the clay overburden, and conveyors with endless belts take it away. A shovel takes the next bite (clay and shale), and the enormous draglines, either 'Big Geordie' or the Marions, lift out the rest of the overburden, mostly hard shale and sandstone which has been previously drilled and blasted. The coal is taken away to the screening plant in dumper trucks: about six thousand tons of it every day.

There is a plan for creating a two-hundred-acre pleasure park by Druridge Bay, with a forty acre lake on which children could boat, a 'marina' or at least a jetty for yachts, trees and pleasure gardens. The scheme is being hotly opposed by the National Farmers' Union. Although I am a loyal member of the latter I hope the NFU loses its case. Two hundred acres out of two thousand (previously almost useless for agriculture and after the scheme to be highly productive) is not much, and for the working people of the Northumberland coalfield, and the people of Tyneside, such a pleasure park would be wonderful. Here is a chance to *create* any kind of landscape we want – at practically no cost. We no longer have the improving squires of the eighteenth and nineteenth centuries to park and landscape the country for us. The NCB could here take their place. Druridge Bay could be a heaven for families with small children. I would love to see *miles* of the sort of little beach chalets that one sees around the coasts of Denmark – the kind of thing that stirs planners in England to apoplexy. Such chalets give health and happiness to tens of thousands of people and the planning authorities were made for man – not man for the planning authorities.

Cresswell is a little shore village with a church and an old tower, very much overwhelmed at present by the coal workings. In 1750 a huge whale was towed into Cresswell, and in 1763 an angel fish which was $4\frac{1}{2}$ feet long. We know more about the 'spermaceti' whale which got stranded at Lynemouth, wounded, on 8th August 1822, and could not be put out of its misery by the local fishermen until the blacksmith had forged a spear to kill it. It was 61 feet long, 37 feet 4 inches in circumference, breadth of its tail was 14 feet 6 inches, width of head 10 feet 9 inches, and height of it 12 feet, it had ivory teeth in its lower jaw but none in its upper, it yielded 9 tons of meat and 158 gallons of oil. It was claimed by the local squire but the Admiralty came along and claimed it from *him* – saying it was a *droit* of the Crown.

A weird erection a mile south along the road from Cresswell is a new supply shaft for Lynemouth Colliery. **Lynemouth** is a big mining village, and a big mine, being one of the few chosen to be developed, and not closed down, by the N.C.B. It was flooded in 1966 on purpose to douse an enormous fire, but has been reopened, with a new drift (or inclined shaft) which also handles the output of nearby **Ellington** colliery, and two new vertical shafts. The workings go three miles out under the sea, the output is well over two million tons of coal a year and over fifteen hundred men are employed.

Tremendous new developments are taking place south of it. A big new power station has been built, into which the coal from Lynemouth will go by conveyor, and an aluminium factory is being built to the west of the coast road. The bauxite which will be required for the production of the aluminium (over 300,000 tons a year of it) is to be unloaded from ocean-going ships in Blyth and carried to the smelter by a new railway line.

Just along the road from this new industrial development is the remains of an old one: a superb tower windmill, only recently fallen into disrepair. It is in a most prominent position and surely the new aluminium undertaking could spare a few hundreds, out of the millions which it is spending, to put this industrial predecessor in repair? Actually the students of Ashington Technical College are planning to try to repair it themselves, but they could do with some financial help.

Woodhorn Demesne is a little oasis of pre-industrial England in the industrial desert. Coal mine to the right, coal mine to the left of it – coal mines in fact all round it, but it seems to live in an older world, with its windmill that we have already mentioned, its squire's house, a farmstead or two, a few cottages, and, hiding among the trees, a Saxon church. Much of the exterior may have been restored in the mid-nineteenth century, the top of the tower may indeed be horrid, but there is most palpable Saxon 'long and short work' in the base of the tower and a Saxon window in the north aisle and another in the south. The pillars in the nave are Norman, the magnificent chancel arch Early English, as are the two big arches in the nave. There are plenty of pre-Norman fragments about – bits of a Celtic cross (pre-Saxon even!) on top of the

screen, some stone in the porch bearing strapwork decoration
probably Danish, and up on the west side of the tower, outside, is a
beautiful effigy, believed to be that of a Saxon priest. Inside there is
the effigy of Agnes de Valence, the wife of Hugh Balliol the brother
of Edward, king of Scotland. This is a very beautiful thirteenth-
century piece indeed, and an astonishing thing to discover by
chance, as it were, among a lot of coal mines.

And now we come to that splendid place **Newbiggin-by-the-
Sea**. If we arrive at it by following our usual plan of walking south
along the coast we come first – yes of course – to a golf course, but
with a fine point of rock to seaward of it: Beacon Point, just south of
which lie the Fairy Rocks. The Fairy Rocks should be visited on a
warm summer's night in moonlight, when we might well expect to
see fairies on them. We cannot see much of the Northumberland
coast without developing the art of rock-scrambling (although as we
have seen there are uncounted miles of sand) and here we can
indulge this pastime to the full. These rocks are flattish but full of
fissures, and potholes, and fresh water bubbles up out of them somewhere if you can find it (troops once camped there used this for
their supply, although the place is covered by the sea at high water),
and at various states of the tide the sea bashes powerfully up against
ledges and surges into crannies causing blow-holes to spout.

As we walk on south we notice a tall beacon with a light on it, and
this is one of a pair of beacons at the north end of the measured
mile. This measured mile is used by ships from the Tyne and Blythe
for their speed trials. Then, standing out near the end of a pretty
desolate spit, is the most astonishing church. It is astonishing because
it stands there, like a stranded hulk on the foreshore, apparently
deserted by its parish, and with its thirteenth-century tower and
stone spire above it acting for a beacon to seamen far out at sea. It
may astonish us slightly, too, to find, when we get as far as the
outside of its churchyard wall, that we are walking on partly
pulverised human bones. The sea has been breaking in towards it.
(The *Gentleman's Magazine* of 1886 has a story of two lovers sitting
by the sea here, and a skull rolling down the bank between them.)
The church was built in the thirteenth century, but both aisles were
destroyed afterwards although the arcading of the south aisle was
retained. The entirely unsuitable Perpendicular-style north arcade
(how could any architect be so crass?) was plonked on in 1914, and
plonked so badly that it is now falling apart. The chancel is very
early fourteenth century. Cobles and lifeboats are depicted in the
carving of the modern clergy and choir stalls.

Outside, we should walk a little way into the graveyard to the north of the church to pay our respects to the graves of the men lost in the *Anglia* disaster of 9th December 1904. The steam collier *Anglia*, bound from Hamburg to Sunderland, ran aground on Needles Point. Eight men in the coble *Henry Jane* rowed out to her, the coble capsized, one man, John Armstrong, was rescued by the Newbiggin lifeboat, but seven were drowned. As the traveller will see from the names on the tombstones, all of the men who were drowned were either Armstrongs or Dents: two very common names among Newbiggin fishermen. John Dent, one of the lost men, was seventy at the time: a ripe age for an old gentleman to face a raging December gale in an open boat.

But the men of Newbiggin have paid a heavy toll to the sea. In the great gale of 14th January 1801 five boats from here and Blyth and Hartley – all small villages then – never returned and ninety people ashore were said to have been left without bread-winners. Since then many men have been lost (nineteen once when the lifeboat overturned), until as late as 1966, when the coble *Eventide* was over-turned while driving for salmon and three men were drowned. She was salvaged from twenty-one fathoms of water though, and renamed the *Northern Light*, and she still fishes.

Before we leave that strange no-man's land around the church, however (the land to the north where the golf course now is is known as 'the Moor') let us consider the question of the Newbiggin freeholders. These ladies and gentlemen claim that their rights go back to 1235, and they own *stints* on the Moor, rather as the burghers of Warkworth own *stints*. They also claim rights along the foreshore, and claim that they can stop people picking up coal on the beach. Indeed they *do* stop people picking up coal on the beach if they do it in so big a way as to appear commercial about it. Perhaps this is not a bad thing. For we have reached the coal-gathering country now, where we will see people, old and young of both sexes, filling plastic bags with drift-coal, pushing home great loads on cycles, and even loading the boots of motor-cars. But we will deal with this weighty subject when we get to County Durham: the Mecca of coal-gatherers. But not all of the men of Newbiggin own *stints*, and the ones that don't are apt to resent the powers wielded by the ones that do. Once a year, to placate them, the freeholders beat their bounds, in great style, and hand out largesse to the hoi polloi – in the form of *nuts*.

It is hard to believe now, but at one time Newbiggin was a considerable port. In 1319 Edward II gave a charter for a market and fair which was to levy tolls for the upkeep of the harbour. Before this, in 1310, he had ordered the town to furnish ships against the Scots. In 1328 he gave the town power to seize, or lay an embargo on, any ship that might come into its hands, for his service. In 1331 he ordered that all the ships of Newbiggin should muster in the Orwell, in Suffolk, and join the royal fleet there. Grain and grind-stones were shipped from the harbour, and we hear of vessels of sixty tons' burden loading grain. Blyth did not become a port until the early 1800s of course, and I often wonder if the River Lyne did not once flow out at Newbiggin and thus keep the little harbour scoured out, and allow vessels to run up-stream for safety in south-easterly weather.

In 1852 the first lifeboat came to Newbiggin. There is still one there. In 1868 a great event occurred: the landing of the English end of the undersea cable to Denmark, and the sending along it of a message by Queen Victoria. The cable terminus can still be seen: an ugly building right in the middle of the 'prom' and now a Bingo Hall – *sic transit* . . . In 1908 the first sod was cut for the sinking of Newbiggin pit. In 1910 the first coal was drawn (after terrible difficulties sinking a shaft through wet peat and quicksands). It is now closed down. There are lobster wells cut in the rocks off the point, in which men keep their lobsters before sale. The reefs that run south from this point and which shelter the harbour are called the Hully Rocks and the Down-over Rocks. Fossilised hazel-nuts and deer antlers have been found in the peat beds on Newbiggin beach. There is a fine fleet of noble cobles fishing from Newbiggin now, belonging to assorted Armstrongs, Robinsons, Renners, Clarks and Dents. There were twelve of these beautiful boats in 1970, and I cannot resist giving their names, because these seem to show the strong romantic streak in fishermen: *Evening Star, Endeavour, Adventure, Dayspring, Endurance, Mary Robinson, Royal Diadem II, Children's Friend, Our Girls, Crystal Sea, Golden City* and *Fisher Lass*.

A couple of miles inland is **Ashington**, said to be the biggest mining village in England and a huge and sprawling place full of clubs and chapels and co-operative society shops. The River Wansbeck is insalubrious near the sea, having North Seaton Colliery on its banks and various tips and rubbish dumps near by. It has though a collection of old boats owned by colliers and others who go to sea on a shoe-string. **Cambois** is a strange little colliery village strung out right along the beach, now backed by a mighty power station into which coal is poured from surrounding mines but which,

85

incredibly, has been getting coal too from the *Midlands*. At last – coals to Newcastle, our age has achieved it. The point of land which sticks out north of Blyth Harbour, and which is called **North Blyth**, is the strangest place imaginable. There is first a biggish tidal basin, then a ship-breaking yard (Hughes Bolckow Ltd) carries on its mournful business, then massive timber coal-loading staithes – all backed by railway lines of course – then a big area being developed with great haste and great secrecy by the Alcan Aluminium Smelter Ltd to land their bauxite (see Lynemouth), then – wonder of wonders – stuck right out beyond all this mess and uproar – a tiny row of old cottages, some still lived in, and a tiny pub called The Seven Stars. Alas and alack – how I would like to be able to report that The Seven Stars was still operative! It is not. In 1969 the second biggest rock-cutter-dredger in the world (Dutch of course – the cutter-sucker *Beverwuk* 31) was gnawing away at the rock in the harbour to get a deep enough draught for the aluminium ships (32 feet at low water). To walk right out then along the North Pier is a long walk (nearly a mile in fact) but it is one that is worth it if you like harbours. Rocks protect the pier from the full force of the north-easters, including a group known as the Sow and Pigs.

Assuming that by some divine intervention we can get across the harbour mouth we will quickly find ourselves in the South Harbour of **Blyth** itself. There are two pleasant things here to be seen: a considerable fleet of small, decked fishing vessels (many Scotsmen put in here) and the headquarters of the Royal Northumberland Yacht Club. The latter is in an old wooden lightship, there is a fine bar on board, and the most hospitable lot of members imaginable. Many of them have decent cabin cruisers and think nothing of popping across to Norway for a week.

The fishing fleet is increasing in importance: the value of fish landed having gone up from £20,360 in 1965 to £78,063 in 1968. The port of Blyth holds its own very well, in spite of the falling off of coal outgoings (but still 2,868,744 tons in 1968) and the complete disappearance of a major industry: shipbuilding. A yard that could launch vessels of up to 40,000 tons' deadweight has simply sunk without trace. The first aircraft carrier in the world, H.M.S. *Ark Royal*, was built in Blyth shipyard in 1914.

Meanwhile, the town itself is modern, and you either like it or you don't. It has good shops and a very extensive and helpful library for a place of this size, and if you ever get the chance, don't miss seeing the Royal Earsdon Sword Dancers. These are supposed to be the oldest *rapper*, or short sword, dancers in the kingdom and the dance they perform is superb. With amazing and intricate skill, while performing the most terrible leaps and bounds in quick time to the music, these men weave their rappers into strange designs – and end up, incredibly, with one man holding them all aloft – woven together in a knot!

One sad story about a Blyth fishing expedition. On 22nd April 1769 one Richard Twizell went fishing from the port with his two sons and a man named Short. They were fishing at the 'gretlins', which is what Northumberland men call *long lines* – baited lines with about a thousand hooks on them. A gale blew up from the land, they could not make the shore and struggled for several days out at sea. Twizell's eldest son died and John Short shortly followed him. Twizell sensibly wanted to lighten the load but his remaining son pleaded with him not too. The remaining son then died himself. And one cold dawn some fishermen from Hauxley found a boat drifting with three dead men in it and old Twizell, who was still alive.

There is sand, and beach huts and pavilions and other delights, along the gentle bay south of Blyth, and a pub which used to be – and still ought to be – called the Boiling Well for that is its name, and we then come to the astonishing place of **Seaton Sluice**. We see before us a bold headland of rock, bringing to an end the sandy bay, we cross a tidal creek by a road bridge, turn left before a small village and come to an ancient disused harbour, the huge dressed stones of which look unmistakably seventeenth or early eighteenth century. There is a cut, or canal, hewn through the solid rock so as to turn the headland into an island. This too looks old, and at first it is hard to see what it was for. A fine-looking octagonal building stands near by, a good old inn, and the whole place gives the impression of great activity in the past. It would be a fascinating exercise in industrial-archaeological detection to try to unravel what went on here, without asking anybody, and without reading the following pages.

In fact, this tiny place was one of the very birthplaces of the Industrial Revolution, and in time to come it will be ranked near in importance in this respect with Coalbrookdale. The early history of the manor of Hartley (of which Seaton was a part) was fairly typical of other such places. Hartley was Saxon (Harthalaw – not Hartlea), the Normans made it part of the barony of Ellingham and it eventually, probably about 1166, came into the hands of the de la Val family: a family which had come to England with the Conqueror. According to William Tomlinson (*Archaeologia Aeliana*, Vol. XXIV), in 1311 the estate was divided into husbandry holdings which were let for ten shillings a year – a cottage went for 1s 8d, arable land 4d an acre and meadowland 1s 8d an acre. But in 1574 Robert Delaval compulsorily bought *all* the freeholders out and enclosed all the land for himself. No doubt it was this drastic action that allowed the Industrial Revolution to hit Hartley and Seaton.

We know that coal was worked in 1291, so it must have been pretty near the surface. Wherever there was coal near the sea, there were salt pans and there are records of salt being produced in the thirteenth century and by 1550 we hear of salt being shipped to Yarmouth and Hull and in Queen Elizabeth's reign there were eight pans producing two tons of salt a week, all owned directly by the Delaval family. It was 'esteemed by sutche as buye same to be better than any other white salt'. The salt trade went on vigorously until 1820, when the pans were closed down and certainly I have been able to discover no trace of them.

But in 1595 the coal mines were really developing, and Sir Ralph leased them out to Edward Grey and Anthony Felton. In the next century the harbour began to be developed, for neither coal nor salt could be dispatched without shipping. In 1660 the next Sir Ralph Delaval had the pier built at the mouth of the river. At first the huge blocks of stone which he used (and which are still there) were lifted by the sea, so he had his men dovetail them together with heart of oak. In this year too he placed a battery of guns on the pier and on 14th June 1665 the place was attacked by Dutch privateers and the guns drove them off. In 1670 Charles II granted £1,500 to Sir Ralph for the improvement of the harbour for the shipment of salt, grindstones and coal. In 1671 Seaton was trading with Norway, for we read that Sir Ralph had written to his agent instructing him to trade with a Norwegian skipper for his timber and to 'trafick with him if he pleases, either store him with good English horses, fine breeding mares, or salt or cole'. But it was in 1690 that the development was made which gave Seaton Sluice its present name. A sluice gate was constructed across the river at the point where the road bridge now crosses it and this was used as a very ingenious form of dredging engine. The harbour bed, which tended to silt up, would be ploughed by horses at low tide and then the waters of the river, impounded by the sluice, were released to scour the sand away. This was very effective, and Seaton was all set for its Industrial Revolution. The tiny harbour was now working to capacity. By 1704 1,400 chaldrons of coal were shipped to London, and £6,000 duty paid on salt. By 1760 things were really moving:

an engineer, William Brown, constructed a 'fire engine' (i.e. a steam engine) for hoisting coal from the pit. James Watt came and looked at it and advised the addition of a fly wheel.

The harbour was difficult though, and if there was any northerly wind, vessels could not get out for weeks at a time. So in 1761 Sir John Hussey Delaval, the squire at that time, sent for his brother Thomas who had been practising engineering in Germany. Thomas started work immediately, and it was he who directed the making of the great cut, or canal, that we see there today. This may not seem great to us, in this age of pneumatic drills and gelignite, but when we think that all the drilling of this very hard rock had to be done by hand with soft steel bits and that the explosive used was *quick lime* (the lime would be tamped into the drill holes and then wetted, when it would expand), we realise that they were indeed great men who did it. The job cost £10,000, the cut was thirty feet wide and fifty-two feet from the cliff top. When it was opened in 1764 three oxen and a small flock of sheep were roasted, free ale was served all day, and on 22 March of that year the sailing ship *Warkworth* sailed through it with 273 tons of coal towards London.

The Delavals were insatiable industrialists, as avid at making money as they were at spending it. They even opened a shipyard, which went on building ships until it closed in 1810, and they also had a copperas industry. But the big industry was glass. Here were sand, salt and coal, and in 1763 Sir Francis Blake Delaval granted his brother four and a half acres by the harbour for a glass manufactury. Trained men were brought from Hanover, twenty-four glass blowers were employed and ten thousand bottles began to be made a month. The bottles were sent to the harbour by an underground railway – one of the first in the world to have iron rails (on the advice of George Stephenson) – and in 1777 sixty-three men were working in the factory, besides women employed at five shillings a week carrying and loading the bottles. Seven ale houses stood about the harbour to quench the thirsts of all these workers and of sailors waiting for a wind. They had to wait for a long time, sometimes: it was said in 1848 that there were occasions when they could not get out of the harbour for ten weeks. The fact was that ships were getting bigger, and Seaton Sluice Harbour was not. It is instructive for a sailor now to look at this harbour and imagine the skill and daring needed to get ships in and out of it at all, perhaps with an on-shore wind, in the days before tugs or engines, or even fore-and-aft sails.

Ashore work went on underground as fast as men could be made to forsake their little farms and holdings in the countryside and go down below to toil in danger and difficulty and almost certainly lose their health if they didn't indeed lose their lives. On 16th January 1862 the pumping beam of one of the great engines broke in half and the half which broke off, weighing twenty tons, crashed down the shaft. It instantly killed five men and entombed 199 men and boys, all of whom died. Amazingly, the little harbour and its enterprises lingered on into the new world it had helped to pioneer until 29th July 1871, when the bottle works was closed down. The last ship, the *Unity* of Boston, sailed out of the harbour on 20th May of that year with a cargo of bottles for the Channel Islands.

And what remains of all this activity? Strange grown-over heaps and unevennesses in the soil of the land round about the harbour, the Octagon, already mentioned, by the Waterford Arms, once the customs house, a very early Presbyterian chapel near the King's Arms, St Paul's church which was once a brewhouse, and a black ram's head in the building of the Seaton Sluice Volunteer Life Saving Company, which once adorned the office of the Delavals' glass works. New 'estates' creep up and threaten to obliterate the village, and, on the steep path leading down into the little bay south of the place is a sign board which says: 'Any person taking coal from these cliffs will be prosecuted.'

And what was the fruit of all this ingenuity, and labour and toil? Why, **Seaton Delaval Hall**, just a mile up the road.

CHAPTER 9

Seaton Delaval Hall to North Shields

❧

Seaton Delaval Hall owes much of its impact to its surroundings. Here is this fantasy-child by the English Gothic dream out of the Italian Renaissance as imagined by Claude Lorraine, sprawling over the ruined countryside of the Northumberland coalfield – a most extravagant and disdainful aristocrat faced by an encroaching egalitarian sea of council houses. But the creators of the Hall created the council houses, by sparking off the Industrial Revolution in their demesne, and these 'Gay Delavals' lacked prescience or they would never have built where they did. Or maybe it would have been better if other aristocrats and developers of the coal country had built their family seats amid their coal-mines and stayed there, and then the industrial areas of England would not be so uncompromisingly proletarian.

Built by Sir John Vanbrugh for Admiral George Delaval between 1718 and 1728, it was Vanbrugh's masterpiece and probably the furthest point to which this particular limb of the tree of the human imagination could go. It needs to be seen when by some happy chance a tremendous thunderstorm coincides with a splendid rainbow – and then we would long to watch the whole great pile split asunder by a fork of lightning and crash to the ground like the House of Usher. (Actually if this did happen it would be most unjust, because one of the family, Edward Delaval (1729–1814), was the inventor of the lightning conductor.) The house now belongs to the Astley family, of Melton Constable in Norfolk, having passed to it by marriage late in the eighteenth century, and the present owner, Lord Hastings, has at least stopped the place from falling down (there were disastrous fires) and sometimes even lives in one of the wings for short periods. The house is open to the public in the summertime and many thousands of people visit it. The great central block, with its main hall and gallery, is a splendid ruin, having been calcined by fire and slaked by the weather, and subsequently roofed over to save it from going further, but would still be a fine place for some high drama to be enacted. The west wing has a vast kitchen, most suitable for the production of gargantuan feasts, the east wing has what is for me the glory of the place: the stables. These stables are simply beautiful and it is most sad that they no longer ring to the stamp of shod hooves and smell of that most supreme of all perfumes: the sweat and dung of horses. One of the Delavals once invited all his neighbours to a banquet and when they were arrived they were astonished to find that no preparations had been made in the house and thought that they were being made the victims of one of the Gay Delavals' numerous practical jokes. And then they were taken down to the stables – in which the sumptuous feast had been prepared. Some guests, on other occasions, were alarmed to find, after they had gone to their beds in the house (and not unaccompanied) that the walls of the bedrooms suddenly disappeared upwards to reveal the laughing faces of the rest of the household. Yet more had their beds suddenly drop down into baths of water. Sir Francis (1727–1777) was the greatest of the practical jokers. He was noteworthy in other ways too, being called in London the 'Prince of Fashion'. He acquired his wife Isabella, widow of Lord Nassau Paulet (who had just £150,000), by getting a friend to masquerade as a fortune-teller and tell the lady, when she consulted him, that the best thing she could do was to marry Delaval. He quickly managed to get through the £150,000. He practised for a year as a fortune teller in London himself, and is said to have beaten all the match-making dowagers at the making and breaking of marriages. The whole family (there were eight sons and five daughters in this particular generation) acted *Othello* at Drury Lane in March 1751 and parliament was adjourned early so that the members could go and see them.

Sir Francis was by no means only a dilettante though. He joined, for fun, the Royal Navy, served with Prince Edward under Howe, was in the landing at Cherbourg in 1758 which destroyed the French forts and exacted a levy of £3,000 before the British would go away, and the landing at St Cas in Brittany in which a thousand British were killed or wounded. Sir Francis played a gallant part in both these actions, and on getting home was created Knight of the Bath. He got himself elected to parliament at Andover by the interesting process of firing five thousand golden guineas over the heads of the crowd from a cannon. He was a great friend of actors, and one day Samuel Foote bet him a hundred guineas he couldn't build a castle in a day. He could, and did, and the castle is still there in the grounds for all to see and was the dwelling of one of his many lady loves. His excesses made him bankrupt, and thereafter his more careful brother, Sir John, had to give him a pension of four thousand a

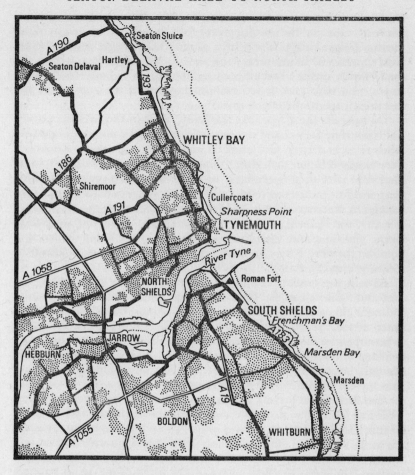

year, which could scarcely have been adequate for his inordinate needs.

Vanbrugh's great dream was not only attacked by occasional bursts of penury, but by a fire in 1752 which destroyed the west wing (thereafter rebuilt) and another in 1822 which was the one that did all that damage to the central block.

The pictures and furnishings in the west wing are interesting as relics of the Delaval family but by no means a great collection. Banquets are held nearly every evening in part of the house by *Historic Productions* who do the thing in medieval style (£3 a head which includes the *mead* – made on Holy Island). The banquets start at eight in the evening and you can book by telephoning Seaton Delaval 2085. If you wish to see the house ghost (the 'White Lady', who will haunt until such time as an heir is born within the hall, which doesn't seem likely to happen as nobody really lives there) you will have to see her peering out of the window of the north-east room of the first floor.

Do not miss the chapel of Our Lady, built in the twelfth century by Hubert de la Val and a pure specimen of Norman architecture. Hubert went on the first crusade, and helped his uncle Robert of Normandy rescue the Holy Sepulchre from the heathen. The beautiful west door is original, as is the sanctuary arch. A modern east window in an east end built in the fourteenth century. Two effigies in sanctuary: one a knight of from 1250 to 1275 – so possibly Sir Eustace Delaval, and the other his wife Constance de Baliol. Some glass of about 1500 in the south side of the choir depicting a kneeling prince; a rare credence shelf over the piscina, a fifteenth-century bishop's throne.

Also in the ground is a mausoleum built in 1776 for John, the last and final heir of the Delaval family, whose unfortunate demise brought this ancient family to an end. Alas – he was kicked in a vital organ, or organs – by an enraged laundry maid in 1775, whereupon he died, and his father died in 1808 at the age of eighty leaving six daughters. The mausoleum was never consecrated though, because it was considered that the fee demanded for doing this service by the Bishop of Durham was exorbitant.

And before we leave this idiosyncratic estate we must mention William Carr, the strongest man in the world. He was born at Hartley Old Engine on 23rd April 1756 and at seventeen weighed eighteen stone and stood six foot three and a quarter inches. He could lift seven hundredweight and throw a sixty pound weight twenty-four feet. By thirty years of age he had got up to twenty-four stone, and was a blacksmith by trade, once working six days and five nights, without dropping asleep once, to repair a steam engine. After this he had a night in bed and then returned to the job and worked another five days and nights. The Delaval of the time painted his portrait in the guise of Vulcan.

Big Ben, the great London prizefighter, journeyed all the way to Seaton Delaval to challenge Carr, but when they met before the battle Carr shook his hand to such effect that the blood oozed from his fingertips and Ben decided not to fight. A press gang overpowered Carr once by knocking him out and actually got him aboard the long boat, but he came to and managed to brace his shoulders against one side of the boat and his feet against the other and he split the boat and sank her, and swam to the shore, to freedom.

He forged a lot of harpoons, for at that time the whale fishery based on the Tyne had reached large dimensions. He made a boxful of harpoons for the whaler *Euretta* and missed the carrier with them. Afraid that this might hold up the sailing of the ship he walked to North Shields carrying the enormous weight on his shoulder, delivered the goods, and walked home again, and on the double journey refreshed himself with no less than eighty-four glasses of gin. Everybody liked him, for he had the most mild and kindly disposition, and he died at the age of sixty-nine on 6th September 1825.

Just south of Hartley is **St Mary's Island**. This is a small rock joined to the mainland by a causeway at low tide. St Mary's Island was once called Bait Island, after a former owner, Thomas Bates, surveyor for the North for Elizabeth I. In medieval times there was a chapel here dedicated to St Helen with an endowment of five shillings a week, but all such coastal chapels displayed lights to aid mariners, which were called 'Our Lady's Lights' or 'St Mary's Lights', hence the present name. There is a graveyard filled with shipwrecked mariners, and when the lighthouse was built in 1897 the remains were dug up and re-buried at Seaton Delaval. The old stone house near the lighthouse was built in 1855 and was an ale house, and from the floor of its predecessor the skeletons of seven Russian sailors who had died of cholera and been buried here, were discovered. The tiny hamlet on the island, clustering round the lighthouse, has great charm.

The place has had its excitements. On 17th April 1810 the usual fleets of fishing cobles put out from Cullercoats and Hartley, and a gale blew up, and the Hartley boats, having the weather gauge, got home while the Cullercoats ones didn't. It was then that the Blyth lifeboat went out with a crew of seventeen, and rescued eleven fishermen and, not being able to get back to Blyth, tried to make the lee of St Mary's Island. Two huge waves swamped the boat and the twenty-eight men were flung into the sea. Two men got ashore but the rest were drowned including one Thomas Brown, the son of the Hartley pilot. The father, being on the island watching the disaster, saw his son floundering in the breakers and rushed in to save him and was drowned too.

Another Hartley man, Thomas Langley, was lowered twice on 28th October 1880 down the cliffs near Hartley to save the lives of two wrecked ships' crews, and for this he got a purse of gold from the Merchantmen of Newcastle, the Royal Humane Society's medal and a medal from the Dutch Board of Trade.

On 26th June 1891 another sort of ship's company was saved from a wreck – the wreck of the iron steamer *Gothenburg City*. She had gone ashore just south of the island and five hundred head of cattle had to be salvaged out of her. The rescuers were greatly hampered by the army of rats, that fought to get into the boats to save themselves from the sea.

And so we come quickly to **Whitley Bay**, which is a large modern holiday resort. Such places are always lauded for being 'very clean'. Whitley Bay is very clean. **Cullercoats** is now part of it. It was once famous for its coble fleet, which was very numerous, and more so for its 'fisher lassies' who used to buy the fish from the fishermen and carry them in baskets to the railway station, take them into Newcastle, and hawk them through the streets. The fisher lassies wore a distinctive costume, and there is a statue of one in the park at Tynemouth known as the 'Dolly' by tradition. Her predecessor once stood down near the North Shields fish quays and was made of wood, but she got entirely eroded away by the habit of fishermen of hacking pieces off her to take on voyages for luck. Her modern successor carries her fish, not on her head, but comfortably fastened on her back. At Cullercoats is a snug little fishermen's reading room complete with snooker table, and the reproduction of a painting by John Charlton of the lifeboat *Lovely Nellie* being dragged for three miles across country by the women of Cullercoats in 1861 – a similar theme to the much greater painting of the Boulmer lifeboat in the Boulmer pub. In the Bay Hotel is a list, on the wall, of the vast number of shipwrecks that have occurred just off the coast here, and on the prom is a nice stone fountain to Lieutenant Huthwaite Adamson, R.N., who sailed from Singapore in H.M.S. *Wasp* on the 10th September 1887 and, like the ship he sailed in, was never heard of again. Just below this, actually built up from the beach which was handy for a constant supply of salt water, is the Dove Marine Laboratory, built in 1908 and no thing of beauty, in which, when I visited it anyway, a dental gentleman was carrying out experiments with barnacles to see if the stuff with which they stuck themselves on to rocks could not be used for filling teeth, and a diving gentleman was making experiments with shrimps to see how it was that they could suffer rapid decompression without getting the bends. This place is a branch of Newcastle University and used to have a public aquarium attached to it but no longer does.

Above, Blyth Sands; *below*, the south front of Seaton Delaval Hall.

Above, St Mary's Lighthouse, near Whitley Bay; *below*, North Shields, from across the River Tyne.

One thing that Cullercoats was famous for, and for which it lingers on in the memories of all old Tynesiders, were the rows of beautiful single-storey fishermen's cottages. All have bowed before the onslaught of mass housing, excepting for one row in Simpson Street, which is still there, and reminds us of Danish fishermen's cottages at such places as Marstal or Aeroskobing. The great fleet of cobles that once made Cullercoats famous is almost entirely gone: there is about one left.

Tynemouth is taken nowadays to include North Shields, but the two places always seem quite separate to me.

After walking about half a mile along a fine sandy beach from Cullercoats we come to the rocky headland of Sharpness Point and, over a little rocky cove, see the noble sight of Tynemouth Priory and castle. The little cove itself is charming, and has boats in it, including a coble or two, and a rowing club. The headland, which Leyland tells us was once called Benebalcrag (*Pen Bal Craig* would make it Welsh for 'Head Summit Rock' which is a good description) stands up steep and impregnable before us: a great lump of magnesium limestone. Leyland goes on to tell us that he read a twelfth-century chronicle which stated that Edwin King of Northumberland, who reigned from 617 to 633, and who founded Edinburgh, built a wooden chapel here in which his daughter Rosella took the veil of chastity. But Bede, writing in Jarrow just over the river in about 730, says that no church was built before the Battle of Heavenfield when the Christian Oswald defeated Cadwalla in 634. Leyland goes on to say that Oswald built a stone chapel to replace the wooden one. The Anglo-Saxon Chronicle, for the year 792, tells us that Osred, last of the Northumbrian kings, was buried at Tynemouth (Bede tells us that he died in 716). And the Danes sacked the place in 800.

But what is quite certain is that Oswin, King of Deira (one of the two Northumbrian kingdoms), was buried here, after being murdered by Oswy, king of the rival Northumbrian kingdom of Bernicia. Oswin, a proper pacifist like that other sainted king, Edmund of East Anglia, refused to fight and disbanded his army, wherefore he got murdered, sainted, and buried at Tynemouth Priory to become its chief attraction for pilgrims. Osred, also martyred, joined him, and until the priory was made untenable by the Danes it was an important place. St Oswin's grave was lost for centuries, but revealed to a hermit a year before the Conquest, and when the Normans arrived, in the shape of Robert de Mowbray to whom most of the North was given, it became a priory again under St Albans and the Benedictine rule.

When de Mowbray rebelled against that shadowy monarch, King Rufus, Rufus twice attacked, and took the fortified headland, and de Mowbray, after his second defeat, had to go away and become a monk himself. In 1127 St Henry, whom we have met at Coquet Island (p. 76) was buried here. But the priory became more and more of a military place, being heavily fortified during the Scottish wars, and a worldly place, acting as a rest house for numerous monarchs and other notables when they came to the North, so much so that the monks became impoverished by the demands of hospitality. Edward III counted Tynemouth to be the strongest fortification of the Marches. Richard II and John of Gaunt gave large sums of money for the fortifications, and in their time the Gate Tower was built, through which we have to go to visit the priory. After the dissolution the place became a royal castle, and the nave of the church was walled off from the transepts and east end and used as a parish church, and it continued to be so used until the seventeenth century. This is why the plan is a little hard to unravel now.

As for what we see today, we approach the gateway along a road which winds round a very steeply banked dry moat, at least half natural, down the grassy sides of which small boys delight to slide, particularly if there has been a fall of snow. We come to the late fourteenth century barbican, well built and solid but much messed about with in 1783 by the military who used it for the purpose for which it was built: a fortification. They added on to it in brick, knocked holes here and there, but a fire in 1936 (when it was still a military building) made it unsafe and the brickwork was pulled down. The Gate Tower behind the barbican is contemporary with it, and contains a great hall and kitchen and other offices. Such is the strength of the natural position of the place that nearly all the defensive work was concentrated on the west side, the narrow neck of the peninsula, as vertical or at least very steep cliffs fall down to the sea for most of the rest of it. Thus on the west side, besides the medieval fortifications, are Elizabethan artillery-age bastions comparable with the much finer ones at Berwick. The place served as a military fortification right up to the Second World War.

Of monastic buildings, there is the massive west front which was added to the Norman church in about 1200: the great deep west doorway is particularly impressive. Just the base of the tracery of the Perpendicular-style west window remains above the door. The nave was predominantly Norman. Beyond the new east wall put up after the dissolution, the foundations of the Norman apsed

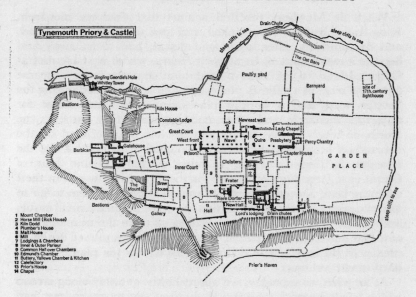

Tynemouth Priory & Castle

1 Mount Chamber
2 Horse Mill (Rick House)
3 Kiln Dodd
4 Plumber's House
5 Malt House
6 Mill
7 Lodgings & Chambers
8 Inner & Outer Parlour
9 Common Hall over Chambers
10 Edmund's Chamber
11 Buttery, Yallowe Chamber & Kitchen
12 Calefactory
13 Prior's House
14 Chapel

presbytery can be seen, but the glory of the place is the towering Early English east end with its narrow lancet windows, its set of recesses for tombs, aumbries and piscina. In the deep recess west of the piscina it is thought that St Henry of Coquet Island lay: is it possible that some of his dust is still there? St Oswin is thought to have been transferred to the lady chapel (at least he is by Mr R. N. Hadcock, the author of the excellent Ministry of Public Works *Guide*) in the middle of the fourteenth century.

But the astonishing surprise of the place is the Percy chantry – a little fifteenth-century stone gem, right in the east end of the old church, still complete, with a marvellous vaulted ceiling which has thirty-three carved bosses, all still sharp and easily decipherable. A key to them is given in the above-mentioned Ministry of Works guide. The rose window in the east end is modern. Over the door is the figure of St Oswin, with the particular Percy who founded the chapel. Sometimes when the door of this little place is open and the sun is shining through the stained glass of one of the south windows on to the altar, the effect, seen from some yards outside the building, is magical.

For the rest, the priory had, at one time, practically every sort of building that a very big and important priory might well have had, from the Lord's Lodging to a prison. Not much of this remains, most of the foundations of the old buildings being covered by a later graveyard and the tombstones of the latter are beautiful and interesting. The Lord's Lodging remains in part, with a most interesting and complicated series of drain chutes jetting over the cliff into the Prior's Haven below. But the probable sites of the various buildings have been worked out from ancient maps, and such scraps of the foundations as have been unearthed, and are shown on the plan on page 99.

Now just at the bottom of the great bluff of the priory lies the little Prior's Haven, in which no doubt the ships bearing wine for the prior and gunpowder for the guns of the castle, used to come, and from here, out to sea for half a mile, stretches the North Pier of Tynemouth Harbour, and on fine days the citizens of Tyneside like to stroll up and down it in a civilised procession that reminds us of a Spanish *paseo*. South of the Prior's Haven is one of the most strange little places: **Tynemouth Village**, a sort of island or oasis of quietness and peace in the hurly-burly of modern Tynemouth. Here are small cottages, a coast guard house, and the headquarters of the Tynemouth Volunteer Life Brigade. By all means see this, and ask to go inside, for in the summer at least it is open to the public. Here are many relics of the vast number of services that the Brigade has performed in its lifetime. On 24th March 1864 there was a tremendous gale in the North Sea, and the Aberdeen passenger steamer *Stanley* and the schooner *Friendship* were driven on to the Black Middens, a group of rocks on the north side of the mouth of the Tyne. The *Stanley* managed to launch a boat with four men and five women, but she was stove in and all but one man drowned. The lifeboat from Tynemouth (the *Constance*) tried to reach the schooner but was driven against the steamer and had all her starboard oars smashed (the effect of this on the oarsmen can be imagined), three of her crew managed to leap aboard the schooner and another was killed in trying to do so. The rest got ashore. The South Shields lifeboat *Providence* managed to get across but most of her oars were smashed and several of her crew injured and knocked out. The Tynemouth coastguard managed to get a rocket line across the *Stanley* and two men got ashore on the breeches buoy but the hawser had been slung too low and a man and a woman were drowned and thereafter it was given up. In the subsequent night the *Friendship* broke in pieces and her crew of five were drowned as also were the lifeboat men who had got aboard her, and at eleven p.m. the *Stanley* broke in two. A rocket apparatus had been brought from Cullercoats and at five a.m. a line was thrown over the remains of the *Stanley* and a few passengers got over with it. But meanwhile twenty passengers and five sailors were washed away and drowned before the eyes of the hundreds of spectators who stood helplessly on shore.

Watching all this as helplessly as everybody else was a young man, a member of the Rifle Volunteers, who afterwards went to a meeting of Quakers, and suggested to some of the Friends that, as they could not, owing to their religious persuasion, go in the Rifle Volunteers, they might do something even more useful, i.e. form a Rescue Brigade. This they did, on 13th January 1865, and the Brigade is still going strong, and – under the command of H.M. Coastguards – has helped at innumerable rescues, for the mouth of the Tyne has always been a most dangerous place for shipping.

The Spanish Battery, with its cannon and its monument to Admiral Lord Collingwood, is a fine place on which to sit and watch the shipping going up and down the Tyne. In 1545 Sir Francis Leek built a battery here with the aid of Spanish mercenaries.

We have to go back, up Pier Road, to get to the centre of **Tynemouth**, and Front Street and its contiguous roads make up a splendid urbane piece of town planning, all of about 1800, with a great feeling of good taste backed by solid wealth. But alas, as we progress up-river along Tynemouth Road things fall away sadly, and we are confronted with all the dreary bleakness of the twentieth century. The Knott Memorial Flats, to make way for which the whole of the Duke of Northumberland's Percy Square of 1758 was knocked down, is perhaps a dubious memorial to Sir James Knott. It is absolutely vast and – unless you like huge brick human ant hills – absolutely horrid. But some of the denizens at least have a good view. You can walk down below it, by the waters of Tyne, until you come to the most interesting waterfront of **North Shields**. Now North Shields, or such as is left of it, is one of the most interesting places on the English coast. Part of its extraordinary atmosphere is due to the fact that it is built up a steep and high bank, so that building stands above building, and roads run steep up or down, and even though most of the buildings would be ugly in isolation they are most evocative in mass: evocative of a roistering age of whalers and fishermen and sailors, swaggering home from the seven seas.

Camden, writing in Elizabeth I's time, gives us a hint as to the origin of the name Shields: 'All over the wastes . . . you would think you see the ancient Nomados; a martial sort of people that from April to August lie in little hutts (which they call sheals and shealings)

here and there among their several flocks.' Again in 1225 it was
recorded that Prior Germanus, of Tynemouth Priory, had begun to
build a town at 'Sheels', and that here he had a great saltery. (One
derivation of the name is from St Hilds.) And in 1267 the corporation
of Newcastle won a case to put down North Shields, and South
Shields as well, alleging that 'the Prior of Tynemouth has raised a
town on the banks of the water of Tyne at Sheles on the one side
of the water and that the Prior of Durham has raised a town on the
other side of the water where no town ought to be, but only huts for
sheltering fishermen'.

But nothing could stop North Shields, just as nothing could stop
South Shields, and North Shields developed into a fine big fishing
port, and that it still is, and for anybody with the remotest interest in
boats, or the sea, or fish, or men, a walk around the modern fish quay
is indispensable. Here the little 'keel boats' come crowding into the
basin, lying so thick that you can sometimes walk right across on their
decks, wriggling their way out of the crowd when they want to put
to sea, slinging their catches up in baskets. Many of them, these days,
are after 'scampi', or Dublin Bay prawns, properly known by the
improbable name of nethrops. These are like gold, and fetch from a
pound to two pounds a stone. The boats trawl for them on muddy
ground (you do not find them on hard ground, which is why they
were not found much before: they were not thought to be saleable
and if men did catch them they threw them overboard again). Up
they come, in the fine-meshed trawls, and up come a lot of other fish,
with them, and as the little boats come speeding in from the rough
sea, followed by screaming gulls, the men carefully go through the
great pile of creatures on deck, flinging seaweed and rubbish overboard, the nethrops into one pound, saleable fish in another, crabs
in a third: about 280,000 hundredweight of 'prawns' are caught a
year. Many of these little ships are Scottish. Some of them are
engaged not in 'prawning' but in seine netting or else trawling for
fish, chiefly haddock. There are about thirty boats in this 'inshore
fleet', all under eighty feet, that actually belong to the port of
North Shields. Besides these are five middle water trawlers, all
about 120 feet long and fishing the North Sea, the Faroes and South
East Iceland, and the Ranger Fishing Company has three distant
water trawlers, all over 170 feet long, with twenty-eight men of a
crew, which catch fish as far afield as the Barents Sea. They stay out
for ninety days at a time, filleting, packing and freezing the fish
aboard. Their names are: *Ranger Aurora*, *Ranger Apollo*, and *Ranger
Ajax*, and four more are a-building and by the end of 1971 North

Shields will have the biggest fleet of these factory ships in the kingdom.

Besides these native vessels we will often see long, old, somehow
very old-fashioned-looking, Polish trawlers come in, and the Polish
government runs a large depot here to provide for them: they need
never make use of local chandlers or ships' stores.

It would take a full day to get even an idea of this splendid place,
North Shields. Early in the morning, when the boats are running
in from their night's fishing, or the big trawlers are unloading their
frozen catches, the place hums with life and activity, hundreds of
strong-armed ladies invade the big fish-packing factories, ice is
shot into holds, fish buyers bid at auctions on the quayside, lorries
come and go, stores are bought at the big ships' stores along the
quayside and transferred on board, boats jostle to get at the fuel oil
pumps, or the ice chutes, or the fish quays for unloading. And later
in the day there is solace for the seafarer. There is a fine little pub
called the *Low Light*, near the small lighthouse of that name. This
lighthouse and the Top Light were built in splendid palladian style
in 1808, and still give a lead to shipping entering the harbour. There
is a vast pub, further up-river, called The Jungle, and many a pub
higher up in the town with many a lady looking for a sailor with a
poke full of money, and perhaps a poker-work sign up in the Golden
Fleece (near The Jungle) sums up perfectly the life of sailor and landlubber alike. Set amid a plethora of pennants brought back by
seafarers from the furthest corners of the Earth the board says,
quite simply: 'BLESSED IS HE WHO EXPECTS NOTHING FOR HE
WILL NOT BE DISAPPOINTED'.

CHAPTER 10

Jarrow to Whitburn

❧

WE can cross the Tyne by the ferry if we like, or else take the new motor tunnel which will dump us on the south bank at Jarrow, but whichever way we cross, to **Jarrow** we must go. For here is the shrine not only of one of the greatest Englishmen, but also, as many people believe, of the first Englishman. Bede was the first writer, at least, to lump the Northumbrians, and Mercians, and Wessex men and the men of Kent into one *gens*, or race, the *Angli*. Further he was a historian and a writer of such a calibre that he has never been surpassed before or since. During his life he wrote some forty books, besides his famous *Ecclesiastical History of the English People*, and probably more than anybody else in the world was responsible for transmitting classical learning and science on through the Dark Ages. He was not only the father of English history but he was one of the fathers of history (as Sir Frank Stenton has said: 'In an age when little was attempted beyond the registration of fact, he had reached the conception of history'). When we consider the tools that he had to work with: a library certainly much smaller than that which could be contained in a mobile library in a bus, writing by hand in unheated chambers in the bitter winter (Cuthbert, Abbot of Jarrow after Bede's death, had to apologise to a correspondent in Germany that he could not send him many copies of Bede's works, in AD 764, because the hard winter had stopped the monks writing) and the state of writing and learning at his time, we must stand amazed at the finish and perfection of his work. Bede was the first historian ever to reveal scrupulously the sources of all his information (he gave strict instructions to scriptoria in which they were to be copied that his footnotes and sources should be included as he was 'not wanting to steal the works of greater men'). He recounted of course innumerable miracles, which we may believe or not as we like, but never a miracle does he tell us of that he saw himself: it is always that he is recounting the stories of other people, and as far as facts, dates, or happenings recounted in his History can be checked, they have always been found to be completely accurate. But further, as with the very best of Roman and Greek

writers, we have a feeling when we read him of complete modernity:
it is hard to believe that here is a man writing 1240 years ago. And
nobody could read the Ecclesiastical History without coming not
only to like but to *love* him. Abroad, his works were sought all over
Christendom, for Jarrow and Northumbria carried the flame of
learning during a time when most of Europe was laid waste by the
barbarian, and even today he is more highly thought of by foreign
scholars than by English ones.

And we can go to his old home today to see exactly how far
English iconoclasm can go. In any other country in the world, here
would be a great goal of pilgrimage, a centre perhaps of learning
and culture, a Bede Memorial of one sort or another attracting the
scholarly, religious or the curious from all over the world. Here is
the actual place where he lived and worked, the actual stones his
habit brushed against, or his sandals trod upon as he walked by,
and what in fact do we find?

Dumped down just outside the uncompromising industrial town
of Jarrow, by the side of a noisome lagoon, with a giant timber
yard on one side of it and a lot of petrol tanks on the other, is a
hideous Victorian church. True, something about the tower attracts
us for that is most certainly *not* Victorian, and there are the unkempt
ruins of monastic buildings to the south. Except for these, the place
looks no different from any other small Victorian church in an
industrial area: it even has posters of extreme vulgarity stuck up on
boards by the gate: one of them, when I last saw it, had a very bad
picture of a leopard with the writing 'The leopard doesn't . . . But
Christianity *does* change human nature!' What would Bede have
thought of *that*?

But this church was founded in 682, by Bishop Biscop, on land
given him by King Ecgfrith, and the dedication stone is still there
for all to see, set in the stonework above the chancel arch. It says
that the church was dedicated on 23rd April 685 in the 15th year of
King Ecgfrith and the 4th year of Abbot Ceolfrith (a month later
the king was killed by the Picts). Bede was entrusted, as he tells us in
his writings, at the age of seven, to Abbot Benedict and then to
Abbot Ceolfrid, was ordained deacon in his nineteenth year and
priest in his thirtieth, and he spent his whole life in the monastery
of Jarrow and Wearmouth, which were one and the same foundation.
He died on the evening of 25th May 735, after First Vespers of the
Feast of the Ascension. His remains were eventually stolen by a monk
of Durham and placed in that cathedral where they were held in
great reverence; after the depredations of Henry VIII's time they

were buried under the Galilee, and his remains were thought to have been revealed in 1831.

The central tower of the church was probably built by Prior Aldwin in 1074, as were the monastic buildings to the south. Some excavation has been done, which uncovered, amongst other things, the biggest area of Anglo-Saxon paving in the country, and although this has been covered up again, some more excavation is planned if money and interest are more forthcoming. Foundations have been discovered by accident to the north of the church, while laying a cable, and there are some fascinating fragments of carved stone in the north porch, some of which were certainly seen and touched a hundred times by Bede, there is an ancient chair in the sanctuary known as 'Bede's Chair' and it might or it might not be (carbon tests place it at about the right date), there are Saxon windows on the south side of the chancel and built-up doorways on the north and south sides. That on the south side, seen from outside, gives us a feeling of being very early Saxon. The church is adequately looked after by a courteous and informative caretaker who lives in the cottage next door, but it all looks very forgotten and deserted. Maybe before we leave it we should read the words written by Abbot Cuthbert, twenty-nine years after Bede died, to Lul, the Bishop of Mainz:

And indeed it seems right to me that the whole race of the English, in all provinces wherever they are found, should give thanks to God, that He has granted to them in their nation so wonderful a man, endowed with divine gifts, and likewise living so good a life; for I, reared at his feet, have learnt by experience that which I relate.

South Shields is a county borough and a big place with a very interesting history, little of which is, however, left to see. But first we should go to the Roman fort because this is where the history of South Shields effectively began.

The foundations of the fort have been well and carefully laid bare, and clearly signposted, and immediately we step over the wall into the area on view we are aware of one peculiarity of the place: it is nearly all granaries. There are at least nine of these. We then realise that the place was in fact a grain storage depot for the Roman army of the north, and that grain was shipped here from the south and stored until wanted. Such troops as there were in the fort were to protect the grain, and never numbered more than a *cohors quingenaria*, or five hundred men. Such a cohort was there (the 5th Gauls) during the campaign of Severus about 209 to 212, and it was at this time that most of the great granaries were built. The design of the granaries, which can still be seen from the foundations, is of great interest to anybody who has had the job of trying to store bulk grain in our English climate. The medieval method of storing grain (and the method indeed employed right up to the invention of the combine harvester) was to store it in the straw, in either ricks or *mows* (small circular ricks left out in the fields), and to thresh it as it was required for grinding and not too long before. The Romans, however, had to store it after it had been threshed, for they could not transport whole ricks by sea, and therefore they had to provide for ventilating and drying it, and so the walls were plentifully pierced with ventilation holes and the floor supported on low stone pillars, and I wouldn't mind betting that there were ventilation holes too in the now-vanished floors. It is interesting that we have got back, now, to the Roman method of storing grain, for the combine harvester means that it cannot be stored in the straw any longer, and elaborate methods of artificial drying have to be resorted to. The headquarters building is still, as to its foundations at least, in good repair, and reminds us very strongly of the headquarters building of a modern British battalion: we can almost imagine offenders being marched in, hatless, by the regimental sergeant-major in front of the C.O. There was a strong room down below for money, and a shrine for the regimental colours above. The strong room was much larger than it would need to have been for storing the pay of the garrison, and it has been surmised that here was kept the treasure to finance Severus's campaign. There are barrack buildings, and many of these were overlaid by the spate of Severine granaries. It is interesting that around the beginning of the fourth century the troops stationed at South Shields (or Arbeia as the Romans called it) were the *Barcarii Tigrisienses*, or Tigris Lightermen. These men had been before on the River Lune at Lancaster, and so had obviously been brought over to help lighter the grain and other cargoes out of the ships.

The most interesting things, though, are in the little museum. There is a beautiful inscription to Alexander Severus, commemorating him for having provided one of the interesting aqueducts to the fort (part of which can still be seen), there is an altar to Brigantia the guardian goddess of the North Country, there is a fine collection of small articles: snaffle bits, scores scratched on tiles for pints of liquor, pottery, lead seals, roof tiles stamped cvg for the Fifth Cohort of Gauls (and one stamped by a dog's footprint); bronze brooches, enamelled clasps, skulls of boars evidently eaten in feasts, damaged skulls of people killed when the fort was overrun by the barbarian (about AD 400) and a superb Roman sword. This is interesting in that it was pattern welded – that is forged together of alternating rods of soft iron and steel so as to produce the intricate pattern that we see nowadays on 'Damascus' shot gun barrels, which were made the same way. It was previously thought that this technique did not come in until the heyday of the Vikings. There was gold-bronze decoration on the blade: on one side an eagle bearing a palm branch between two military standards, and on the other Mars, in full armour, with spear and shield. There are two most moving tombstones both of which tell us something about the relationship between Roman citizens and their slaves, as well as about the extreme cosmopolitanism of the Roman Empire. One was put up by a Syrian merchant from Palmyra – one Barates – to his British wife, who came from the Catuvellauni tribe from the country around St Albans, and who was a freedwoman whose master had married her. Besides a Latin inscription it has one in Palmyrene, the only one in Europe. The other was put up by a trooper of the Asturian Horse to his freed slave Victor the Moor, who had died at the age of twenty. Victor's master records that he 'most affectionately followed his servant to the grave'.

After the Romans left, the English came and somewhere at South Shields there was the nunnery of St Hilds. In a metrical life of St Cuthbert of the mid-fifteenth century we read:

> In takenyng of this thing we rede
> Be the telling of St Bede
> How some tyme was a monastery
> That eftir was a nonry
> Bot a litil fra Tyne Mouth
> That mynster stoode into the South
> Whare Sainte Hilde Chapelle standes nowe
> There it stode some time trewe.

– and it still stands there – only rebuilt by the Victorians. The nuns, however, took refuge in 865 from the rage of Hinguar and Hubba, the Danes, in Tynemouth Priory, but the priory was taken, and the nuns were 'translated by martyrdom into Heaven'. St Hild, incidentally, has been commonly called St Hilda, but there is a strong and sensible movement now to change the name back to its original form. Hild was an Anglian name (meaning 'Battle'), Bede consistently calls the lady Hild as do all other early writers, and it was not until the monks of the Middle Ages, with their craze for latinising everything, got to work that the name was changed to

Hilda. The present incumbent of St Hild in South Shields, Canon Berriman, insists on the original spelling, which I think we should all adopt.

After the Conquest the history of South Shields was one of constant harassment by Newcastle. Newcastle had been granted the charter to trade from the Tyne, and bitterly resented the rise of upstarts such as South Shields. But shipmasters resented going all the way up the river, probably against the wind, to take on smaller loads than they need have done in the deeper water near the mouth. Besides, there was coal at South Shields just as there was at Newcastle. In the mid-fourteenth century shallow seams were being worked on the Deans. Wherever coal and salt water occurred together, salt pans opened up, and South Shields early had a great salt industry: so much so that the huge piles of cinders that grew up beside the pans became a menace. Another menace was a man-made range of mountains that had come out of the holds of ships. Colliers, in sailing days, could not sail empty, but had to carry ballast. This ballast had to be put somewhere before the ships could load coal, and it was piled up in great heaps at South Shields on what are now the Marine Parks, and the skippers didn't see why they should have to unload ballast at Shields (they couldn't get up the shallow river with it) and then move again to load coal at Newcastle.

But Shields battled on, and had to win in the end, and a great fleet of colliers grew up there – and were built in the Tyne – the beginnings of the mighty modern Tyneside shipbuilding industry. A typical collier (called variously a 'snow' or a 'cat') made a voyage in May 1770, and the captain (and owner) paid 2s 6½d a ton for his coal at the staithe, loaded 195 chauldrons (516 tons), sold the load for £219 7s 5d in London (just under 8s 6d per ton). His expenses for the round trip were £196 14s 8½d – and this including 'washing the boy's shirt'! Such a ship would make from eight to ten voyages a year.

In the eighteenth century South Shields went whole-heartedly into the whale fishery. In 1751 the Newcastle Whale Fishery Company was floated and the *Swallow* dispatched from South Shields and she came back with four fish. The *Cove of Cork*, a Sunderland ship, was then fitted out for the fishery, the *Lord Gambia* of 406 tons, the *Grenville Bay* of 306 tons (built in 1783) and the *Lady Jane*, built as a privateer in 1771, all took to the fishery. In the late autumn of 1835 ten whaling ships from the Tyne and Humber got trapped in the ice in the Davis Straits and their crews suffered great privations. The *Grenville Bay* managed to break out of the ice (under Captain

Taylor) and reached the Tyne on the 6th January 1836 with three fish and seventy tons of oil. The *Lady Jane* had been in sight of the *Grenville Bay* at the latter's release but was herself driven further into the ice. A gale of 19th February drove her into open water (in 51° 25′ lat. 52° west long.) and when she reached Stromness in the Orkneys only eight out of her original sixty-five hands could *crawl*. Twenty-seven men had died of scurvy. Soon after this the fishery died away, although the *True Love*, built as a privateer in Philadelphia in 1774 and captured by the British, continued whaling until 1866, making altogether seventy voyages to Greenland. She then served in the Tyne coal trade, and was run down in London River in 1897 – at 123 years old!

It would be interesting to enquire why the British whale fleet never took to sperm whaling when the Arctic seas became exhausted as the American fleet did.

The 'foymen' of South Shields have long been, and still are, a race apart. They work small boats taking lines from ships, carrying kedges for them, and similar tasks. When a steam tug was put on the river about 1820 they got angry and wrecked the Northumberland Hotel. The 'hostmen' of Newcastle were also a race apart. They were established in conjunction with the Merchant Adventurers in the reign of Henry IV, and had a charter given to them by Queen Elizabeth I on condition that they paid her a shilling for every chauldron of coal they shipped. They were coal brokers, and ruled the river. In their pay were the 'keelmen', said by some to be descended from the Tigrean lightermen of the Romans! The Tyne keel was a distinctive sailing boat, much sharper-ended than the Humber keel, setting a square sail like the latter, and propelled in default of a fair wind by a long punting pole called on the Tyne a *puy*. (The same tool is called a *set* on the Wear, a *spreet* in the Fens and a *quant* on the Broads). The keelmen carried coal down the Tyne to load into the ships, called their mates 'bully' and their cabins *huddocks*, wore a distinctive dress of blue jackets and flannel breeches and stockings, and mostly lived at Sandgate in Newcastle, giving rise to the famous song.

While on the subject of the Tyne generally, Henry VIII gave the Newcastle Trinity Brethren a charter, but they were in existence long before his time. They were responsible for all coastal marks and pilotage between Whitby and Holy Island, and have exemption from having to bear arms, serve on juries, or be pressed. Their house in Newcastle is the most beautiful thing in the city incidentally, although not officially open to the public. (But sometimes the truly interested can gain admittance.) There is a superb collection of paintings, another of ship models, the building reminds one of an ancient scholastic foundation with a medieval chapel and other rooms, magnificent furniture, and records of the greatest historical interest. To join it you have to have two qualifications. You have to be a master mariner and a Freeman of the Tyne.

As to things to be seen in South Shields today – if you are puzzled as to why a pub should be called The Alkali it is because it served the workers from a factory making 'alkali', or soda, by mixing salt with vitriol. This stuff was needed in the glass industry, and also for soap boiling, and a crystalline mass of it weighing two tons was sent up to London to be exhibited in the Great Exhibition! At one time fifty tons of Epsom salts a week were produced. The place had to be closed down in the end because of the horrible stink. If you are puzzled why another pub should be called the Balancing Eel, I cannot enlighten you.

At the bottom of Ocean Road is a monument to William Would-have, the inventor of the self-righting lifeboat, an example of which is on display behind him. A prize (of two pounds) had been offered for a design for such a vessel by a South Shields club known as 'The Gentlemen of Lawe House'. Wouldhave saw a woman with a tub of water on her head, and in the tub was a wooden dipper shaped like a segment of melon skin. He noticed that however he threw the dipper in the water, it came upright. He designed his boat on this principle, and, after a sordid wrangle by two of the adjudicators who believed they could improve on the design, Wouldhave only got a pound. But his boat, the *Original*, was launched in 1790 and served for forty years, and Wouldhave is generally agreed to be the inventor of the lifeboat. He himself was born in 1748 and apprenticed as a house painter. He was noted for 'eccentricity of manner, versatility, and a peculiarly inventive genius'. He also got the idea of stepping the sides of a graving dock. He died, neglected and impoverished 28th September 1821 and is buried at St Hilds.

> Heaven genius scientifick gave
> Surpassing vulgar boast, yet he, from soil
> So rich, no golden harvest reap'd, no wreath
> Of laurel gleaned, none but the sailor's heart,
> Nor that ingrate, a Palm unfading this,
> Till shipwrecks cease, or Life Boats cease to save.

Certainly the South Shields lifeboat and the Volunteer Life Brigade there too, has had plenty of exercise. The position of the

Tyne makes it the only refuge for many miles of coast, and it is a dangerous one. In one week in December 1876 eleven ships were lost in the mouth of the river, and in two days – the 12th and 13th of November 1901 – seven ships were lost and there have been many more. Thanks to the rescue services many of the crews were saved.

The Tyne is second to the Clyde as the biggest shipbuilding river in Britain, and recently, in early 1970, Britain's biggest ship was launched into it. This was the *Esso Northumbria*, 126,542 tons' gross. She was built by Swan Hunter, of Wallsend. The river was improved enormously as a navigation when the Tyne Improvement Commission got to work in 1852. This built the North Pier, 2,950 feet long, and the South Pier, 5,150 feet. In the heyday, the river was exporting 21½ million tons of coal a year. This has fallen to about four million tons – the same as it was a hundred years ago. Tyne Dock in South Shields imports vast quantities of sawn wood and pit props from Scandinavia, and also has the most up-to-date iron ore discharging plant in Britain. Albert Edward Dock at North Shields has a roll-on-roll-off car ferry to Scandinavia.

South of the South Pier we come to a great expanse of clean sand, the delight of mums with small children, and there are lavish 'amusements'. No one need go long without bingo in South Shields. At Gypsies Green a huge amusement centre is being set up. It is to be hoped that the gypsies, who used to camp there and for whom the place was named, have been offered other comparable accommodation: they have a right to live too. South of Trow Point we come to fifty-foot cliffs and these could very well be called 'killers'. Above them is a fine stretch of green sward along which people exercise their ponies, and the edge of the cliffs is fenced off at places and notices warn you away from the edge. The warnings are necessary, for the edge is continually crumbling away. And here we may as well consider the geology of this part of the Durham coast.

In the Permian period (starting 270 million years ago) this area was part of the Zechstein Sea, which was very salty and which deposited the magnesium limestone of which the killer cliffs of South Shields were made. This limestone rises as it goes northward, thus as far south as Hartlepool the cliffs are of the upper limestone, but at South Shields the middle and lower are what we see, and we see this particularly well at Frenchman's Bay. In places the limestone has been covered with glacial drift and Scandinavian boulders have been found. The limestone disappears north of Trow Point, but reappears again, briefly, at the great rock on which Tynemouth

Above, Tynemouth Priory; *left*, the Venerable Bede's Chair in Jarrow Church.

WHITBY: *Above*, the harbour, with the Abbey on the clifftop; *below*, the Abbey.

Priory is built. Underlying the magnesium limestone is a vast depth of carboniferous rock (starting with sandstone on top), in which lie from twenty-five to thirty seams of coal, embedded in sandstone and slate-clay and with millstone grit underneath it all. It is when the sandstone is eroded by the sea that the limestone above it becomes dangerous.

The cliffs south of South Shields are most interesting. They are fiercely eroded, and have carved away in great chunks. Dangerous it may be to go near the edge of them, but few of us can resist it. We can get down to the beach at places: at Frenchman's Bay there once lived an old man named Willie the Rover. He slept on sacks by a drift-wood fire in a rude hut, in which the window and chimney were combined. He used to mend people's boots and shoes, but one day he announced that he had been left a great fortune in London, and he walked off and was never seen again.

Manhaven is the next little inlet down into which we can get, and here was a cave once that really *was* a 'smuggler's cave'. The schooner *Rob Roy* was captured off it by the revenue men, with 8,000 lb of tobacco aboard (worth £4,000) and another 600 lb were found ashore in the cave.

In **Marsden Bay** we can get down again to the beach, and should do so, for the cliffs here, seen from below, are very beautiful. Great vertical-sided stacks have been isolated from the cliff face, with inaccessible plateaux on their tops: one of them is called 'Lot's Wife'. We come to the famous **Grotto**, which is an inn and is connected to the top of the cliff by a lift shaft and also stairs. The huge rock that stands up to seaward of it was, in the mid-eighteenth century, part of the main cliff. Now it is a challenge to rock climbers. In 1782 a man named Jack the Blaster got a job in the Marsden quarry above, and he and his wife took up residence in a cave in the limestone at the foot of the cliff, and he built the stairs up the cliff which are still known as 'Jack the Blaster's Stairs'. Then a man named Peter Allen, who was son of Sir Hedworth Williamson's gamekeeper, took the cave over, enlarged it and built a front to it and went into the catering trade. He must have been an astonishing man. He kept a menagerie, pegged a series of ladders to the top of the island rock for visitors to climb (so much a head of course), and drove a vertical shaft to the cliff top down which to lower provisions. He even had a ballroom in the cave. Such was the rapacity of the local squire that he was required to pay rent – for something that had been nothing before he had made it – and after litigation he was forced to pay half that asked for.

When Peter Allen died the place was taken over as a sort of club by a group of left wing writers, artists and politicians. This was in the 1850s. After this it became a pub, pure and simple, and that it still is, and a very large one, and a big restaurant too, and it caters for large parties. You can get to it from the beach, or else down the lift from the cliff top above. The cave has been added on to in front by buildings, and it is hard to see where the cave ends and the buildings begin.

On 2nd June 1836 Peter Allen was digging near his grotto and found, three foot down, the skeleton of a big man with a flattened lead pistol bullet in his ribs and a bit of broken knife blade in the vertebrae of his neck. He dug around and found three other skeletons. On the cliff-top above, thirteen more skeletons were found, but these were prehistoric.

According to a paper by a man named Tate in the *Transactions of the Natural History Society of Northumberland, Durham and Newcastle*, that rare and curious seaweed *Sphacelaria plumosa* is found at Marsden, also Sea Spleenwort (*Asplenium marinum*), Upright Sea Lime-grass (*Elymus grenarius*), and Procumbent Meadow Grass (*Glyceria procumbens*). This is as it may be.

And so we come to **Marsden** itself, which is all being pulled down, and Lizard Point, where there is a lighthouse, and a defunct coal-mine on the site of which has been built an enormous office building locally called the Crystal Palace, which houses a moiety of the vast clerical and administrative staff of the National Coal Board (their head office for the Area is on the Team Valley Estate, near Gateshead, and that is about as big as the House of Commons), and hot water gushes out from the flattened slag heap and dribbles over the cliffs into the sea, telling of fire down below.

And thus we come to **Whitburn**, which is what is known as a 'residential village', and is an ancient place, with an Early English church drastically restored in 1865 alas, and a great Hall. The Hall is beautiful, the two-storyed part of it probably sixteenth century, the rest Victorian. The garden is lovely, with graceful Edwardian balustrading and statuary, and is at present open to the public. Unfortunately it has been bought by a speculator who is trying very hard to get permission to pull it down. May he not succeed.

CHAPTER 11

Sunderland to the Tees

᠙

A mile from Whitburn we come to **Sunderland**, at a point where a stately pleasure dome has been decreed, with accompanying scenic railways and roundabouts, this being the grand **Roker** amusement park. We come to a coastguard station and then a big cross put up in 1904, and carved by Milburn of York out of three stones weighing together 3½ tons. This is in honour of Bede (so even if Jarrow can't be bothered to honour him Sunderland can), and then to the North Pier of the harbour (started in 1787) – and *why* are people not allowed to walk along it? How delightful for the inhabitants of the Roker if they could stroll out over the sea as their counterparts do at Tynemouth. How short-sighted of the River Wear Commissioners not to let them. Further south we come to a small fishing basin, with many big cobles moored in it, and into this we would sail with a yacht if we were sailing. There was a beautiful little country cottage here a few years back, most aptly called Rose Cottage, inhabited by a gentleman called Mr Sloane and his wife, who would help the seafarer find moorings and even do repairs to his boat. Alas, Rose Cottage has been pulled down to make room for yet more petrol tanks, and thus progress marches on.

Inland we have to cut, and we come to the other half of the monastery of which Bede was the greatest ornament – for here is **Monkwearmouth**, with St Peter's church standing in a large open stretch of ground. Ships are being fitted out in the river just below it. As a building, St Peter's is one of the most interesting in England, for it is not only Saxon, which is rare enough, but is very early Saxon, for it is remarkable in having been built of stone at a time when practically every other building in the land was timber, or wattle and daub. It was founded by a most remarkable man.

Benedict Biscop was a noble retainer of King Oswy, came under the influence of Aidan, the Celtic missionary from Iona as other Northumbrians did, became converted at the age of twenty-five, and started out on the almost unique journey, at that time, from Northumbria to Rome. He arrived there in 653, two years after St Aidan died. He went to Rome a second time and thereafter, on the Island of Lérins, he took the vows of a monk, presumably then taking on his name of Benedict. He came back again but made a third and fourth trip to Rome (he went once with Bishop Wilfrid, who found him too austere so they parted) and brought back manuscripts and many treasures. It was then that he went to King Ecgfrith (Oswy having died) and persuaded him to give him a large stretch of land to the north of the Wear to form a monastery. But he had seen too much of the metropolitan world to be contented with wattle and daub, and he went to Gaul to get skilled masons and he sent again for glaziers to make and fit glass for the church, the cloisters and the refectory. Glass was an unheard of luxury in early Anglo-Saxon England: can it be that its existence at both Monkwearmouth and Jarrow enabled Bede to get on with his great history? Certainly to carry on prolonged studies and writing without glazed windows in northern England is an intermittent job, to say the least. The manuscripts that Biscop brought back from abroad, too, formed the library that Bede could use, and Biscop gave strict instructions that this library was not to be damaged or dispersed. Alas, the Danes dispersed it, or at least set it on fire, with the rest of the monastery in 870. But Biscop established Monkwearmouth and then established Jarrow, and he made several more visits to Rome. When he was quite an old man, Bede, as a seven-year-old boy, was entrusted to him and he, and his successor Ceolfrith, brought Bede up. Ceolfrith (who also went to Rome) was a man after Biscop's heart, and doubled the size of the library. It was in his scriptorium that the *Codex Amiatinus*, the most important copy of the Vulgate (St Jerome's Latin translation of the Bible) was found. It still exists, in Florence, and eleven leaves of other copies of the same Bible are in the British Museum. He enriched English Christendom in other ways too: he even persuaded John, the Arch-Cantor of St Peter's in Rome, to come to Wearmouth and teach the monks to sing.

After the destruction by the Danes the monastery fell into disuse, although excavations have shown that people were still buried there, but shortly after the Conquest and the terrible harrying of the North, one of the plunderers – the Norman knight Reinfrid – was so shocked at it all that he became a monk and set about restoring the Northern monasteries. He took over the desolated site at Jarrow and rebuilt it, then went to Whitby, and then he and a monk named Aldwin set about restoring Wearmouth. They found the place covered with brambles and bushes and even forest trees: and in 1958 Miss Marjory Crump dug up the hole into which they had thrown the

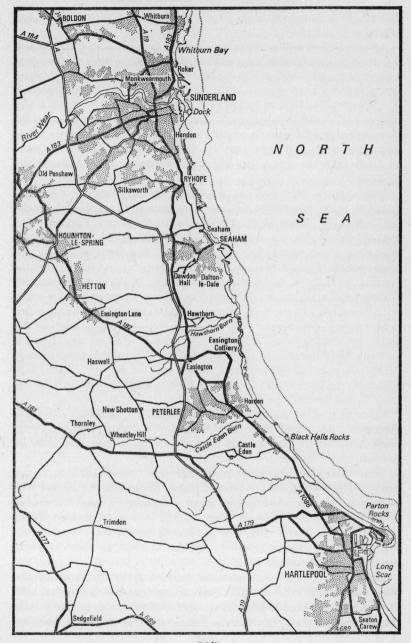

debris! Wearmouth became a cell of Durham, which it remained until the Dissolution.

After the Dissolution it was very nearly buried. The site was used for the tipping of ballast, for the ships that sailed into the Wear to load coal carried ballast just as the ones that sailed into the Tyne did, and this was the place where it was unloaded. But the Victorians in 1866 dug the ballast away, and revealed the base of the tower which had stood there, almost exactly the same as it is now, for thirteen hundred years. The upper stages of the tower were no doubt built later, and at different periods. The top of the tower is supposed to have been done just pre-Conquest (that of Jarrow just post-Conquest).

Much of the west wall is of seventh century and of a kind of masonry found in seventh-century churches in Gaul. Inside, in the north transept, is a collection of carved stones of great interest and beauty, which give a good idea of the workmanship of the Gaulish craftsmen whom Biscop brought with him. Besides two magnificent lions which formed bench supports there is an early eighth-century tombstone, to Herbert, the Priest; there are also carved baluster shafts, a Roman altar used by Biscop's men as a door jamb, a carved scene of two men fighting, some post-Conquest and medieval carving and several other things. Some time should be set aside for looking at all this, for it is very interesting and there is nothing like it anywhere else in England. If the church appears to be locked, go to the vestry door, which may be open, or if that fails climb up to the new vicarage up on the road to the east of the church and borrow the key.

Outside there is nothing to see of monastic buildings, but Miss Rosemary Cramp of Durham University has been doing excavations here, as at Jarrow, and is to do more, so one day a lot of answers may be found.

West of the church there is an *enormous* new clubhouse, of the Boiler Makers' and Shipwrights' Union. It has many palatial bars and lavish entertainments, and huge quantities of beer are drunk, and if you are lucky enough to get invited into it it is an experience worth having. One wonders what Biscop would have made of it. Near by is my favourite railway station, of 1848, by John Dobson, and the purest neo-Greek.

We now come to the successor to that glory of Sunderland – Wearmouth Bridge. This (the original bridge) has been so spread about the world on Sunderland pottery that there can be few people who have not seen a picture of it. The bridge was originally designed by Thomas Paine for Philadelphia, and castings were actually made which were intended to be shipped there by Walkers of Rotham, under Thomas Wilson, Clerk of Works. But the castings got diverted to Wearmouth, because Rowland Burdon, the famous M.P. for the place, sponsored the bridging of the Wear and personally supplied most of the money. The job was started in 1793, Burdon laying the foundation stone 'according to ancient usages of freemasons'. It was an enormous job for its time. The span was 236 feet, 100 feet above low-water mark and with a spring of the arch of 33 feet: it was thrown across in ten days and was the biggest in England. Estimates of the weight of cast iron used in it vary between 214 and 236 tons and there was also 46 tons of wrought iron. On 18th June 1796 a hundred good men and true of the Royal Fencibles marched over it to test it. But the bank of which Burdon was a director failed and he went bankrupt. So a lottery was held to raise the money and the bridge was built, and for a long time, against Burdon's wishes, carried tolls. It was officially opened 9th August 1796 watched by 80,000 spectators! In 1858 Robert Stephenson made a major re-construction to it. The bridge served well until 1929, when the present bridge was opened by the Duke of York. The present bridge was built in the place of the old one in such a way that traffic was not interrupted.

But the potters of Sunderland, of which there were many, seized upon the mighty bridge as their main theme, and myriad are the mugs, and jugs, and bowls, which depict it. Fortunately there is a great collection of Sunderland pottery in the museum here, and this should be missed on no account. Most of this collection was originally accumulated by the same Rowland Burdon who caused the bridge to be built. There is a vigour and a liveliness, and a fine unabashed use of bright colour and gold lustre, about Sunderland pottery that is unbeatable, and a simple folk naivety about the scenes depicted (nearly all nautical), and the verses printed by the transfers make it irresistible. It was by no means all the work of one firm: there were some sixteen potteries in Sunderland and district, and the study of Sunderland pottery could be a lifetime's work. The industry itself seems to have died out without trace, like the dinosaur.

For the rest, Sunderland is the biggest ship-building town in the world – in 1969 the Wear built twenty-two vessels totalling 291,484 tons, beating both the Tyne and the Tees and running the Clyde pretty close. It claims to have been a port for ten centuries. In 1847 work started on the great new dock with a south outlet straight into the sea, now the Hudson and Hendon Docks, and there is a total dock area of 125 acres. A good place to go to meet shipwrights and others is a pub called the Regale, down near Hendon Dock. Many of its customers work at Bartram's yard, which is the only yard which launches ships straight into the sea – through the South Outlet. Bartram's have made a little corner in a standard design ship of some 14,000 tons, to replace the American 'Liberty ships' of the Second World War and they are turning them out as fast as they can. It is instructive to walk to the South Outlet and have a look at them: it is the most accessible of the yards and perhaps the most interesting. Colonel Bartram's grandfather was building small wooden ships higher up the Wear, and so the tradition goes on. It is well worth wandering about Sunderland Docks anyway (it is easy enough to get in, although no doubt illegal, but scores of anglers congregate on the New South Pier – and *they* get in), for here are fine mid-nineteenth-century warehouses built of hefty sandstone blocks, and many things of interest to see.

In the park behind the public library by the way is a spirited monument to Jack Crawford, who nailed the flag of Admiral Duncan to the main-top-gallant mast of H.M.S. *Venerable*, at Camperdown, in 1797. He was a local boy, and is depicted on countless Sunderland mugs.

And so we work on south, along a ruined shore, past **Hendon** which has little to detain us, to the weirdest never-never land where the cliffs seem to be half slag from coal mines, and break dangerously away, and on their tops squatters have built ranges of pigsties and chicken sheds out of drift wood and rubbish. A railway cuts this desolation off from the rest of England, and here we have a glimpse of what the country might be like after the atom bomb. There is little, indeed, to delight the eye until we come to **Seaham**. The first thing that we probably see as we approach this place is the Vane Tempest Mine, or 'Northerner' as the Durham miners call it, one of the oldest of the coastal mines and still going strong. But just before the pit is a *dene*, as the little streams that cut such steep valleys in the country here are called, and on the banks of this a hall and a church, a newer mansion and a few cottages. The new mansion, which is not all that new, is an approved home for young ladies, and we are unlikely to gain admittance. The bigger house, now a hospital, was the house in which Lord Byron got married. The hall was built in 1777, by the Millbankes, and Sir Ralph's daughter, Anne Isabella (born 1792), married Byron on 2nd January 1815 in a room in the Hall. The room is still to be seen, kept much as

Byron saw it. Byron wrote 'Hebrew Melodies' here, and 'The Destruction of Sennacherib' in which the Heathen came down like a wolf on the fold with, according to generations of schoolboys, his *corsets* gleaming in purple and gold, and the couple parted after twelve months. In 1821 the third Marquess of Londonderry bought the estate, and married Frances Anne Vane Tempest and built Seaham Harbour.

Just over the lane from the Hall is the church, and at the risk of being accused of sending the reader into every wayside fane of fruitless prayer, I must urge him to go into this one. Here we are right back in Anglo-Saxon days again. It had always been thought that this church was Early English, but in 1912 a builder uncovered some blocked-up windows which dated the place pre-Conquest. Elements of the church have been tentatively dated as eighth century. The dimensions of the nave and chancel compare exactly with Monkwearmouth, Corbridge, Escombe and Jarrow. But there is herringbone masonry in the north wall, generally supposed to be post-conquest, but with Saxon windows over it – Anglo-Norman overlap. The chancel now is transitional of 1180. The porch, which is currently falling to pieces, is sixteenth century and neo-classical, pulpit of 1579, there is a priest's hand raised in blessing at the back of the aumbry (very unusual), in the gable of the porch a sundial of 1773, 700-year-old font, seventeenth-century cover. The vicar of St John's church, in Seaham Harbour, has the key, and can also be prevailed upon to show Byron's signature in the registry book.

On the grave of William Richardson, killed in Seaham Colliery explosion of 8 September 1880, is:

He is gone O how hard not a friend to be near
To hear his last sigh or see his last tear,
No parting, no farewell, no kind word of love
To cheer his last moments, or point him Above.

The place where the town of **Seaham Harbour** now is was a tiny place before the third Marquess of Londonderry got to work on it. But that nobleman opened coal-mines all about, and laid railway lines to Seaham, and built a large and complex artificial harbour. The little town still has a great atmosphere about it, but the harbour is extremely interesting.

The layout of the harbour was by the Newcastle man, John Dobson, who designed the delectable Greek railway station at Monkwearmouth. It was opened by Charles, the third Marquess, in 1831, and all the earlier parts of it have that look of good craftsmanship and good taste that characterise engineering works built in that era.

In front of the harbour office we have John Tweed's bronze statue of Charles Stewart Vane-Tempest Stewart, 6th Marquess of Londonderry, in the robes of the Garter. He was Postmaster General and Viceroy of England. The harbour itself is an amazing place. The landward side of it has been hewn out of high sandstone cliffs – the North Dock gives the impression of being a flooded quarry rather than a harbour extended to seaward, and two big tunnels provide connection between various parts of the harbour through high, vertically-sided natural ramparts. The inner parts of the harbour particularly repay careful study. The whole place could well form an open-air museum of harbour works. The masonry itself is superb and grand, and all such fittings as bits and bollards, old capstans for hauling ships about or opening or closing lock gates, speak of another age. There are some railway trucks also from another age: it is amazing that they have not been snapped up by a museum. When I sailed into Seaham eight years ago there were still two paddle-wheel tugs *working*. These were just quietly scrapped, and an American, who had a little more sense than the Dock Company, bought them up and shipped them across the Atlantic. Had they been kept, and were the early Victorian coal trucks renovated and looked after, and was one of the abandoned sheds turned into a museum, Seaham Harbour could easily become the harbour equivalent of the York Railway Museum, or the Stoke Bruerne Canal Museum, and this without in any way detracting from its value as a modern port. In fifty years' time those paddle tugs will be worth very nearly their weight in gold, and even now they are extremely valuable.

It would be an interesting exercise for somebody versed in industrial archaeology to examine the harbour carefully, and try to date every part of it. We know that the first dock was started in 1828 and extended in 1845, and that by an Act of Parliament of 1898 the Seaham Harbour Dock Company was formed and work began on the big South Dock which was opened by the Prime Minister, Mr Balfour, on 11th November 1905. Meanwhile on 26th August 1898 the 7th Marquess of Londonderry had laid the foundation stone for the big North Pier.

The first cargo of coal went out on 1st July 1831 in the brig *Britannia*. The peak year was 1930 when 2,314,530 tons of coal were shipped. By 1968 this had fallen to 553,522 tons. Little 'puffers' sometimes come in to load coal for the Orkneys and Shetlands and such outlandish places. A little timber comes in and a little stone goes out. There is a fine healthy fleet of big old cobles, some owned by full-timers but some by part: colliers and others who like 'a bit of sport' with some money attached to it too. They keep their lobster pots and other gear in caves hewn out of the sandstone, or high up on ancient ledges. Their numbers were sadly depleted, though, on 17th November 1962, when their lifeboat was over-turned with the loss of the whole crew.

South of Seaham Harbour is **Dawdon Mine** – sunk 1900, now 1,661 feet deep, where 2,400 men dig out over a million tons of coal a year mostly from under the sea from the High Main, Main Coal and Low Main seams. Like all the other coastal pits the Dawdon dumps its waste rock into the sea. Just south of it, at **Hawthorn**, is a vast limestone quarry, where limestone is mined for the steelworks at Middlesbrough, and also, nowadays, for concrete, which is mixed on the spot. Hawthorn Tower has been pulled down, but there is a folly tower, eighteenth-century 'medieval', on Kinley Hill which hardly anybody in the world knows about.

Hawthorn Burn is crossed, right down near the sea, by a soaring brick viaduct that carries the railway. Underneath are old lime kilns and the ruined cottages of the lime burners. It is a romantic spot. From here on south (and I recommend that you go down to the beach here – further north is too difficult) is a most splendid and dramatic coast. The great vertical cliffs are of magnesium limestone or of dolomite, there are caves and standing stacks and arches. The beach itself is like any other beach, except that it is largely made of coal, and this gives the place a kind of stygian grandeur. All along the beach stoop the coal gatherers. These are miners out of work, or men 'on the sick', or men who do the job full-time for a living, and they walk along the mark of the last high tide and quickly throw pieces of coal into sacks. These sacks they sometimes hump on their shoulders to the top of the high cliffs, where their ancient bicycles await them. A man who knows the job can stow in a bicycle frame a quarter of a ton! Other men pile the sacks into heaps and keen operators come down with four-wheel-drive ex-army trucks and carry the stuff away. Fortunes have been built up like this, and although plenty of authorities have tried by one means or another to stop these operators, so far nobody has succeeded.

As we walk along this dramatic beach we come to one of the reasons for all this coal: the dumping gantry of Easington Mine. An overhead cable brings buckets of waste rock, which are tipped over the sea in a never-ending succession, by night and by day. This waste inevitably has some coal in it, and the coal floats and is washed up, while the rock is washed away. Besides the army of coal-gatherers is often another small army – of beach fishermen. And sometimes they fling their baited hooks right out into the blackened water near the mine tip, and seem to catch as many codling or haddocks there as anywhere else. The sea fishing along this piece of coast is extremely good, and during strikes and depressions many a miner kept his family going, and well, by picking up and selling coal and by catching fish with a rod and line. There are home-made huts, at one point, and cobles drawn up on the beach.

Easington Colliery is perhaps the quintessential colliery village. The old village of Easington, up on the A19, is a typical old English village, with a church with a Norman tower. The new village, around the colliery, is a sea of council or NCB houses. The mine is a huge one. It is now 1,581 feet deep and the workings extend far out under the sea. While the visitor is in this area he should by all means try to get the NCB to let him go down a pit, for it is a great experience for the non-miner.

Fitted out with a battery-operated electric lamp on his helmet and a hand-held safety lamp as well, to test for gas, and a 'survival outfit' which has an anti-gas mask, and two identity discs with numbers on them, you find yourself following your guide up a dreary brick tunnel and through an air-lock door to the top of the shaft. Here you have to give up one of your identity discs to an official. If you don't come up that shift and claim it back again he will wonder why. The cage comes up – surprisingly small and of several decks – and in you crowd with perhaps forty other miners. Down you go, a thousand feet or more down the black shaft, and get out into a tunnel. Here are the 'man-riders', in the case of Easington, a brand-new very fast battery-driven train. You clamber in, and squat down inside, and for what seems hours shake and judder along the track, all the miners with their lights out so that it is quite dark, the younger men shouting broad 'Geordie' to each other, about their girl friends, the dance that night, the chances of Sunderland football team, and how they hate that shift and wish they were on another.

After several miles of this travelling (during which somebody is bound to remind you that you are several miles out to sea) the train stops and you get out, turn right or left at a fork-way, go through an air-lock door, walk perhaps half a mile down a tunnel, and come to a place where much heavy electrical and hydraulic machinery is slung up from a railway line overhead at the tunnel roof. Here are transformers for breaking down the high voltage current and electric motors for driving hydraulic machinery. From here on the ground is a serpentine mass of pipes and cables. Your companions take off most of their clothes, leaving shorts and singlets, but they all wear thick knee guards and helmets, and with them you clamber forward past all the machinery to the coal face.

The tunnel you are in is extended in a heading – being added to by a gang of miners with drills and explosive. The coal-face runs off at right angles to this. It consists of a low tunnel – you have to crawl along it – entirely filled with machines called hydraulic chocks. These are placed side-by-side, touching, and as each is composed of two pillars and a floor and a roof, they form a metal tunnel, through which you can crawl. And through which you do crawl. In front of the line of chocks, towards Norway, is the coal-face – perhaps three foot high. Behind – towards England – is the mined-out seam which has begun to collapse. Then along the coal-face comes the coal-cutter. This is a heavy squat monster, spouting water at high pressure to keep down dust, with a wheel with teeth on which spins round at high speed and chews out the coal. It comes crawling along in front of you – trailing high pressure water and air pipes and electric cables – a man crawling beside it working various levers, and another following it trying to prevent the dragging cables from catching on things. Everything is done on the hands and knees, and the feeling of claustrophobia is intense. You know you would have perhaps a couple of hundred yards of three-foot high tunnel to crawl through to get to where you could stand up – and then four miles of travelling to get to the bottom of the shaft.

The chewed-out coal falls on to an endless conveyer belt below the cutter and is whisked away, and ultimately raised up and shot down into trucks to be taken to the coal shaft. Now when the cutter has made a couple of passes, it is necessary to hoist the whole complex of machinery forward a foot or two, and this is done by a man crawling along and causing the hydraulic chocks to hoist themselves forward one by one. It is known, very expressively, as *snaking*. Each chock is made to loosen its forward pillar, tighten its back one – force its forward pillar forwards towards Norway, tighten it, loosen its back pillar, and draw its back part forward towards its front. Exactly like a caterpillar. And in doing so it 'snakes' the conveyor belt forward too.

In moving forward, the line of chocks leaves the roof behind it unsupported, and the visitor is likely to feel alarmed at first by the creak and crash of breaking rock, as the roof behind him collapses.

But, crouched uncomfortably inside the tunnel of chocks, he is quite safe.

Relatively safe, that is. No miner underground is ever safe. If, when you get back to the surface, you go to the graveyard at Easington you will find the little Garden of Remembrance to the eighty-three men and two rescuers who died down this pit in the explosion of 29th May 1951, a thousand feet down and a mile and a half from the bottom of the shaft. The rescue teams worked night and day for ten days, individuals snatching an hour or two's sleep when they simply had to, and they had practically to rebuild the shattered workings as they went. There are men at Easington, and in the mines round about, who have never recovered physically from this experience. There is many a miner who will tell you: 'I don't want my son to go down pit!', but the one thing that depresses a miner more than anything else is the threat that he will one day himself have to work on the surface.

Easington, like every other big mine, has a big mine club, and this you ought to try to get invited into. There are lush and lavish bars (the present club is not so lush as its predecessor which was burnt down a year or two back but it is sumptuous enough), and on many evenings highly paid entertainers come in and sing, play the guitar, or make jokes. There is a small floating population of professionals, mostly living in trailer caravans (you can often meet them in the caravan site behind Whitburn) who travel the North. The beer is good and cheap, and is consumed in quite frightening quantities.

Horden is the next big mine. These coastal mines are being developed by the National Coal Board as the old mines further inland, that worked the shallower coal, are being closed down. The coal seams dip to the east, and therefore the workings get deeper as they go further out to sea. Early in the 1960s a drilling rig was working out to sea, proving the ground. If coal is still required these workings will get further and further out to sea, and it is not beyond the imagination of man to visualise, one day, shafts being sunk twenty miles out to meet up with them. This would solve the worsening ventilation problem, and enable coal to be discharged straight into ships, moored against artificial islands.

Behind Horden is **Peterlee**, where grows a big new town. Much of the new housing is well and imaginatively designed and reminds us of Chandigar, the brand new capital of the Punjab designed by le Corbusier and his assistants. The consultant architect here was

B. Lubetkin. There is a distinguished manor house north of Horden, of about 1600 at a guess, with a fine front porch on Tuscan columns. The pleasure of living in it must be somewhat mitigated by the enormous potato crisp factory just over the road.

The shore deteriorates south of Horden, the cliffs becoming ugly and the foreshore messy. At Blackhalls Rocks there is an excellent example of a reef talus fan (the detritus from an advancing coral reef). All these cliffs are pretty fossiliferous. The cliffs give way to a low shore of blown sand and we come to **Hartlepool**.

First we have the Steetley Magnesite Company, with its huge factory which extracts magnesium out of the sea. Sand then gives way to the Parton Rocks, which are hard limestone and stretch out to sea making interesting rock scrambling and rock pool gazing ground. And then we turn into Hartlepool itself and, alas, what a horrible sight greets our eyes. Up until twenty years ago the old town of Hartlepool was one of the most beautiful and atmospheric places in England. Crowded on its narrow peninsula, about its marvellous great church, was this Georgian and early Victorian seaport. It only lacked the top gallant masts of tall ships in the background and, such was the atmosphere of the place, these the imagination could easily supply. The houses were old, of course, but like most old houses had been well built, and they were the sort that, had they been at Greenwich or Blackheath, would have been snapped up for large sums to be converted into modern residences by rich people. True some were small and could have done with two being knocked into one. The County Borough of Hartlepool however had quite another solution. They simply pulled practically the whole place down (they are currently mopping up the few streets that are left) and turned the town into one big council house estate, and it is a council house estate of such banality that it has to be seen to be believed. This marvellous medieval walled town with an eighteenth- and early nineteenth-century seaport built within it, has been turned into just another dismal council estate, with row after row of identical blocks of four attached houses, in squares, all looking exactly alike except that some have stupid little bits of pebble dash *upstairs* – and some *down*, to give variety like. The whole thing is an unredeemed – and unredeemable tragedy. Something ancient and beautiful has been ruined for ever, to the end of time it cannot be recaptured. And even the people whom it was supposed to benefit – the people who now live in the council houses – do not like it. Everyone that you speak to bemoans the atmosphere that has gone, and the friendliness of the old organically sited streets. 'The place seems to have lost all its old charm!' they say. By God it certainly hasn't got any new charm.

St Hild's church stands up amid all this like a great stranded whale. Even the council house enthusiasts haven't dared to bring their horrible little boxes to within many yards of its thirteenth-century walls. To the west of the church, running down the hill, what used to be a lively and colourful produce market is now a dismal 'municipal garden', as banal as the housing estate, its most prominent feature a 'gents'. St Hild's looks like a church in a bombed site, but it took worse than enemy bombing, or shelling from warships, to achieve *this*.

But we must suffer it, in order to get to the church, which is one of the finest Early English buildings in the country. Here the austere grandeur of this superb style of building can be seen at its perfection, pure and untouched, and to go into this church, particularly when the sunlight is streaming through the clerestory windows, is a great experience. There is a most excellent church guide, inside, for 5p, and I will leave further description to this. But do not miss the Brus tomb behind the altar (the chancel is new work by Caröe), for this was the Brus or Bruce family that provided the victor of Bannockburn. Also the effigy of a lady having her gown bitten by a dog, and the idiosyncratic memorial to William Romaine in the north wall are of interest. But there are a hundred other details which you should not miss. The purity of the style is due to the fact that, after the building was started in 1185, it was completed in thirty years.

Hartlepool, then Hereteu, was one of the string of early religious houses along the Northumbrian coast that followed St Aidan's mission. Aidan himself founded the monastery, and set an Irish princess, St Hieu, in charge. St Hild, another princess, although this time a native Northumbrian coming from South Shields, succeeded her (both princesses and saints were thicker on the ground than they are now). She moved on to Whitby, where we can find her again. In 800 the monastery was destroyed by the Danes and in 1066 Robert de Brus was given a great estate around here by the Conqueror. In 1200 King John gave (for a consideration no doubt) a charter to the 'men of Hartinpoole'. In 1306 Robert the Bruce the Eighth was declared a traitor to the English crown and his estates confiscated. In 1315 the Scots plundered Hartlepool as a reprisal, but in 1330 a great wall was built around the town, with ten towers to it: there are still some six hundred yards of this wall left, on the seaward side. By 1614 Hartlepool was the most important port in Durham and in the Civil War the place was attacked and overcome by the Scots, who were later dislodged by the Parliamentarians. It was captured again by the rebel earls in the Rising of the North. In 1831 the giant was born which was to swallow up old Hartlepool. The railway and a dock came to what is now West Hartlepool, and from that time on West Hartlepool grew and grew, and became uglier and uglier, and it is now a great sprawling city of a hundred thousand people. The old walled town could surely have been kept, as something from an earlier and in many ways a finer age.

On 15th December 1914 the citizens of Hartlepool were made aware that there was a war on. Four German battle cruisers, one heavy cruiser, four light cruisers and two flotillas of destroyers steamed across the German Ocean; half of them went to Scarborough and half to Hartlepool. After a terrific bombardment with heavy guns they withdrew. The bombardment did surprisingly little damage, considering its intensity, but killed a number of people. On the 27th November 1916 more excitement – a 485½ foot long zeppelin came across and dropped some bombs, which did great damage, before being shot down into the sea.

As for what is left of the old town of Hartlepool, there are still some fine roistering pubs down by the fish dock (there is a fine fish quay with a lively auction). In the Golden Anchor, out near the front, there is a magnificent set of photographs of old Hartlepool. But the place that I like best of all, I think, is way down in dockland, near the West Harbour. This is the old Prince of Wales' Inn, now a club – the Headquarters of the *Small Craft Association*. There are fine fellows in there talking of their exploits in cobles and other small fishing boats (none of your sailing-round-the-buoy stuff) and the steward's daughter, who serves behind the bar, should be the toast of the town. She is my toast anyway. The Tees Sailing Club has its being the other side of the basin, which is sadly silting up.

Out in Hartlepool Bay there are said to be submerged forests, and the Long Scar and Little Scar rocks are outcrops of Bunter sandstone, everywhere else covered by glacial deposits. We say goodbye to the cliffs of magnesium limestone here: they end at the great strike fault that tends from Hartlepool Bay to Darlington. The Cleveland hills are before us now, over the Tees, made up of a variety of Jurassic deposits. The last gift we come to of the salty old Zechstein Sea are the pipes that cross the ground, apparently aimlessly, south of Seaton Carew. These carry brine from the salt measures, 900 to 1,200 feet down: the remains of a salt sea that dried up. There is anhydrite too, to be pumped up, and gypsum down there, and it has all the makings of a great chemical industry that centres round the Tees, and which rivals the chemical industry over the salt measures of Cheshire.

Seaton Carew is by way of being a seaside resort, much over-shadowed by a huge steel works and an even bigger timber yard, with several big hotels, a pleasure park, and very good sands. There is always hope of finding on them silver and gold doubloons of Carolus III and IV, from 1720 to 1804, because a ship named the *Little Duck* was wrecked there. She had been captured from the French in the Napoleonic wars, and was given this ridiculous name. Although it was known that she had been a slaver, it was only dis-covered that she had all this gold and silver in her belly when she was wrecked in 1867. Several honest working men got very rich from her.

CHAPTER 12

Tees to Skinningrove

❧

I CANNOT imagine anybody going to **Middlesbrough** unless they really had to. The place is the result of the single-minded devotion of a small number of early Victorian industrialists to the search for money. As part of the new Teesside conurbation it is due to change very rapidly, and from now on should be an exciting and interesting place to live. But at the moment it seems to have no centre, no shape, no history and no soul. Not a stone had been laid in it until 1830: it was just two farm houses and a ruined hermit's cell on the bank of a muddy and shallow river with a draught at the mouth of three and a half feet at low water.

One of its single-minded founders was Henry Bolckow, born at Sulten, in the Grand Duchy of Mecklenburg on the 6th December 1808. He made a great fortune (£50,000) speculating in corn, came to England and was persuaded to go in for the iron trade. Iron was at that time being mined in moderate quantities under the Cleveland Hills, and Bolckow managed to get a large concession for mining it, and he and his partner, Vaughan, built up what was then probably the greatest iron and steel producing complex in the world. Cleveland became the successor to the dying iron trade of the Midlands, and by 1881 Sir H. G. Reid was able to write the following lyrical passage:

'The iron of Eston' (one of the mines near Middlesburgh) 'has diffused itself all over the world. It furnishes railways to Europe; it runs by Neapolitan and Papal dungeons; it startles the bandit in his haunt in Cicilia; it crosses over the plains of Africa; it streaks the prairies of America; it stretches over the plains of India; it surprises the Belochees; it pursues the peggunus of the Gangtori. It has crept out of the Cleveland Hills, where it has slept since the Roman days, and now like a strong and invincible serpent, coils itself round the world.'

Three hundred and fifty million tons of Cleveland ore was smelted on Teesside before the mines finally closed down. As for Bolckow, he just didn't seem to be able to go wrong. Even when he searched for such a run-of-the-mill commodity as water (sinking, in 1863, some boreholes to a depth of 1,200 feet) he struck instead rock salt and anhydrite, thus opening the great chemical industry of Tees-side today.

Another family which helped develop the iron industry was the Quaker Pease family. Joseph Pease was famous for helping to promote the Stockton and Darlington Railway which was, of course, the first, and he was very largely the creator of Middlesbrough. In about 1875 Dorman Long came on the scene: Arthur Dorman, who was a Kentish man, and his partner Albert de Lande Long, rented

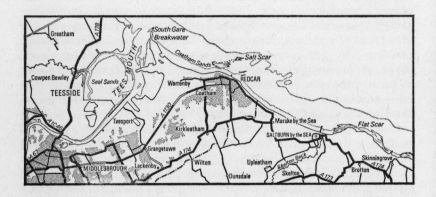

a small iron works on the Tees and went on to become the biggest steel company in the country. Teesside has supplied the steel for Sidney Bridge, Runcorn–Widnes, Birchenough in Rhodesia, most of the steel for the new Forth Bridge and the new Severn Bridge, and probably half the steel bridges in the world outside those of the U.S.A. Dorman Long merged with Bolckow Vaughan in 1929, and more or less swallowed it up. Currently the group is spending astronomical sums (£140 million has been spent since the war) on its Teesside steel plants.

As for the river along the banks of which all this activity goes on, it wasn't much of a ditch until the Tees Conservancy Board was set up in 1852, and by 1861 had dumped no less than 4,500,000 tons of slag south of the river mouth to form a breakwater. This made it possible to dredge a channel which now has a minimum depth for five and a quarter miles upstream of 35 feet 6 inches. Thousands of acres of land have been reclaimed, too, from the sandy expanses of tidal flats, for industrial development, and the process still goes on and more and more acres of the Seal Sands are being raised above the tide by slag-dumping for yet bigger and bigger steel works and chemical factories. The Tees estuary has all the charm of the biggest rubbish dump in the world. The Tees is a considerable ship-building river (172,127 tons in 1968, 75,102 tons in 1969 – the smaller second figure being due to a major reorganisation of the Furness Yard). Teesside is very much a 'growth area', and is expanding at the expense of Tyneside and Wearside and every other East Coast industrial area. It is rather interesting that the village of **Yarm**, up-stream from Middlesbrough, was once the major port on the Tees. It is now a rural village, with a lively annual gypsy horse fair.

If we cross the Tees by the Transporter Bridge (built 1911 by the Cleveland Bridge and Engineering Company), we will have some miles of heavy industry to negotiate before reaching the sea again. We will pass the gargantuan new Dorman Long works at **Lackenby**, with its output of four million tons of steel a year, and then tread the dreary marshes to **Warrenby**, with another great steel works at Tod Point, and the Redcar Jetty, which sticks out into the river a mile and a half, and is currently being improved at just fifteen million pounds' cost to accommodate 200,000 ton ore ships and handle about ten million tons of foreign ore a year.

It may be wondered why foreign ore has to be imported in such impressive quantities when there is still a big reserve of native iron ore under the Cleveland Hills (about 200 square miles of it). The answer is that firstly the Cleveland ore is fairly low grade (from 25 to 30 per cent) and therefore requires much more coke, or other source of heat, to make a ton of steel, and secondly Cleveland ore is highly phosphoric. This increases the cost, and the difficulty, of making steel. In fact, even after Bessemer's great break-through of 1856, it was still impossible to make steel of Cleveland ore, and up until 1872 no steel at all was made on Teesside: only iron. In 1875 Bolckow Vaughan installed a Bessemer steel plant, but made steel from low-phosphorus haematite ore from Spain. It was not until 4th April 1879 that Gilchrist Thomas and his cousin Percy Gilchrist demonstrated a process for making steel from high phosphorus ores, thus starting a world-wide steel-making revolution. In 1911 Bolckow Vaughan went over from Bessemer to the basic open hearth process, and thus started making very high-class steel (and incidentally producing the basic slag which was, and still is, such a boon to agriculture: the most benign of 'artificials').

Now if we like we can slog down to the **South Gare Breakwater**, near which is the Teesmouth Lifeboat Station, and walk back by the Coatham Sands, where is supposed to be a petrified forest, and we come to **Coatham**. This is now just a part of Redcar. Once it had a pier of its own, but so many ships were driven through it in so many gales that it was abandoned and now nothing of it is left.

Redcar is a flourishing seaside resort, a home for commuters from Teesside, and has such delights as a race course, 'gaming clubs', a 'fabulous Roller Ghoster' – and bingo galore. The pleasantest part of it is the coble landing, where perhaps half a dozen motor cobles and no less than fifty pretty double-ended motor boats of a very distinctive type, which I hereby name *Sandsend Beach Boats* since they do not seem to have a name, are drawn up on the pavement above the beach. Only three of the craft, all big cobles, are owned by full-time fishermen. The rest belong to part-timers: men who work in steel works or other places when they simply have to, but who go fishing, commercially, in their spare time. More and more of such men are coming on to the coasts, and many full-time commercial fishermen resent them. Fortunately the sea is free to anybody and nobody can stop them, and what better way can there be for a man working shifts in some unhealthy and gloomy steel works, or down a mine, to spend his time than getting out on the sea in a small boat? And if he catches and sells enough lobsters and crabs and other fish to pay for his boat, and a pint or two of beer to quench the thirst that labour on the sea has engendered, what a very good thing. But part-timers should be careful not to undercut the full-timers when they sell their fish. It might seem generous to give fish away because 'they were only caught for sport', or sell them for less than they are worth, but it is very ungenerous to men trying to make their living at the fishing. As for the boats used by most of the part-timers, the majority of them were built at Sandsend, and a description of them will be found on the pages devoted to that place (p. 160).

A most fascinating thing to see in Redcar is the Zetland Museum. Because of its position, in a bay on the great coal route between the North and London, Tees Bay was a terrible place for wrecks in sailing ship days. Ships creeping along the coast would become embayed by a north-east gale, and often couldn't get out. The only place they could run down-wind to was Teesmouth, and with a depth of only three and a half feet at low water there, to take this course was often fatal. In three bad gales in the years 1821, '24 and '29 *seventy-three* ships were lost in Tees Bay. In the '24 gale alone, a hundred and forty ships were lost along the east coast of England, and thirty-seven came ashore at Coatham and Redcar. For this reason Redcar early became a lifeboat station, and in 1802 the lifeboat *Zetland* was brought from Spurn Head where she had been serving until then. The *Zetland* was built at South Shields by Henry Greathead, the first builder of real lifeboats, in 1800, and she still exists, for all to see, in the fascinating little museum which has been established in the old Lifeboat House at Redcar. She is thirty foot long and ten foot beam, is lined with air cases to keep her afloat and the water could run in and out of her so that the crew sat with its feet in the water. She could not sink and saved five hundred sailors in her time. When the RNLI decided that she was too old and tried to replace her by another boat, she was dragged out on to the promenade for the purpose of breaking her up, but an angry crowd assembled and forcibly rescued the vessel. The fishermen refused to use the new boat and contributed a hundred pounds of their own money to have the *Zetland* repaired at South Shields. This was in 1864, when the boat was already sixty-four years old. She continued in service until 1887. On 29th October 1880 she rescued seven men from the brig *Luna* which had bashed through Redcar Pier in a severe gale. There was another lifeboat in service then at Redcar, the *Emma*, which had been paid for by an organisation called the Free Gardeners. The two boats rescued the crews of five ships that day. Probably the most severe bashing she had was when the brig *Caroline* of Aalborg went ashore on Coatham Sands loaded with coal. The *Caroline* launched two boats which were instantly capsized and all the men aboard them lost. The *Zetland* had by then been launched and one of her crew, William Guy, was in the act of throwing a lifeline to a drowning mariner when he was swept overboard by a wave and himself drowned. The *Zetland* was so smothered by the sea that she was invisible from the shore until she was washed up on the Coatham Sands several hundred yards away from where she had last been seen with most of her oars smashed. The tradition of the lifeboat service being such that the boat is always launched, no matter how apparently impossible the conditions might be, attempt after attempt was made to launch her again, but without success, and the rest of the crew of the *Caroline* were drowned. But to offset this sort of failure there was often success such as when the brig *Jane Erskine* came ashore on 15th November 1854 and the *Zetland* saved thirty-five men, which included twenty-six local fishermen who had gone out in cobles to try to refloat the brig.

The name Zetland, incidentally, came from the squire. Sir Thomas Dundas, an Ulster baronet, was created Baron of Aske in

1794, and his nephew, Lawrence Dundas, became Earl of Zetland in 1838. The family's funereal coats of arms make a noble display in the church of Marske, the next village we shall come to, although there is a testy comment by a student of heraldry beside one of them saying that the supporters are themselves supported on gas brackets.

In the little museum there is much of interest, besides the oldest lifeboat in the world. There is a good collection of ship models, fishing gear, a diorama of some rather thin fishermen in their shed, a poem written by a lord about the old lifeboat, two others written by commoners about the wreck of the barque *Berger* of Raumo in 1898. There is also the drum that was beaten about the sandy streets of the little village to summon the lifeboat crew.

Two scars of rock run out into the sea from Redcar, the most northerly of the two called the Salt Scar, and filled with fossils of the Middle Lias rocks, especially *Protocardia truncata*. In about 1830 an ambitious scheme was promoted to build a harbour of refuge here, to be named Port William. If this had come about many hundreds of ships lost in Tees Bay would have been saved. Unfortunately it did not. There are several paintings, showing how the port would have looked, in the Zetland Museum.

Redcar itself was a small fishing village among the sand dunes until the middle of the last century, when it began its inevitable career as the holiday resort for Teesside. A letter to Sir Thomas Challoner written early in the seventeenth century said this of the fishermen of Redcar:

'Truly, it may be said of these poor men, that they are lavish of their lives, who will hazard twenty or forty miles into the seas in a small trough, so thin that the glimpse of the sea may be seen through it; yet at ten or eleven o'clock in the morning when they come from sea, they sell their whole boat's lading for four shillings, or if they do get a crown they do think they have chafered well.'

On St Peter's Day the fishermen changed their crew mates for luck, dressed their boats, painted their masts bright colours, and sprinkled the bows of the boats with 'good liquor'. A writer in 1863 says there were eight cobles at Redcar each with seven long lines with four hundred hooks on each line, the hooks placed four feet apart. They put to sea at midnight and went fifteen or twenty miles out, catching cod, conger, haddock, ling, plaice, skate, soles, turbot and whiting. They also set crab pots and called this 'trunking'.

Two miles along the shore is **Marske-by-the-Sea**, which is surrounded these days by large housing estates. Indeed we feel that the day is not far off when the whole of this esturial plain will be under either factories or brick boxes. The nicest thing about Marske is the Marske Fishermen's Choir, which sings to raise money for the widows left by lifeboat disasters and for other good causes, and sings very well. The fishermen, nearly all of whom are part-timers, haunt the Ship Hotel. The tower and steeple of Marske's old church, of St Germaine, stands forlornly in the middle of its graveyard, the body of the church having been *blown up* in 1821! The graveyard brings a memory of a deserted wild gale-ridden coast village into the middle of a banal modern housing estate. James Cook's father, who was 'a common labourer', is buried opposite the tower door. He taught himself to read as an old man in order to be able to follow the accounts of his son's voyages. The new church is interesting, although not beautiful. It has a fine collection of funerary coats of arms of the Zetlands brought from the old church, and an ancient font (used as a cattle trough – then a vicar's flower-pot – before being brought here. It had a locked top to prevent the theft of holy water for improper purposes), and other relics including a fine floriated cross. Next to it is Marske Hall, Jacobean and very striking, built by the Pennymans who were royalists in the Civil War and lost Hull, then belonging to the Zetland family and now a Cheshire Home. People are encouraged to visit it in the afternoons.

Sand and gradually rising sandy cliffs bring us to **Saltburn-by-the-Sea**, which is quite a distinguished little place. Henry Pease, one of the Quaker ironmasters, started it all, and the railway arrived in 1861, and the Zetland Hotel, designed by William Peachey of Darlington, was built very soon after. It is still there, complete with commodious stables and coach houses out the back for the horses and carriages of people of quality. A great part of the little town has the feel of this particular era, when labour was so cheap that it was almost free and the ironmasters of Middlesbrough had so much money they simply didn't know what to do with it. The owner of the Skelton Estate (Mrs M. W. Ringrose-Wharton) spent seven hundred pounds on a splendid bridge across the Skelton Beck, and it is still there, and is still supposed to cost a halfpenny to cross on foot, a penny on a horse, donkey, or mule, and progressively more for vehicles pulled by increasing numbers of horses – you wouldn't get a bridge like that nowadays for seven thousand pounds, never mind seven hundred. Below it the Beck valley has been laid out with pleasant plantations, a miniature railway, a boating pond, and Italian gardens, established in the 1860s and still much unchanged.

On the other side of the town, which occupies a piece of high ground, is another valley called Hazel Grove, where grow hartstongue ferns, and next to which is a very pleasant caravan site. There is a pier, which provides excellent cod fishing in the winter and was built in 1869 and is connected with the town above by a hydraulic tramway of curious design. There are a number of big hotels as well as the Zetland: the Alexander Hotel is a distinguished building and is in a row of distinguished buildings – high up on the bluff looking north-east across the sea.

Down a steep hill we cross the Beck and come to **Old Saltburn**, which was originally a bunch of whitewashed fishermen's cottages under the hill called Cat Nab. It is an old settlement indeed, for on what was once erroneously thought to be a raised beach because it had sea shells on it, was in fact the kitchen midden of early *strandloopers*, or beach combers, who had deposited the shells of their dinners there several thousand years ago. They not only dined on shellfish: the bones of the now-extinct Great Auk were also found there.

After the Great Auk eaters came hermits, for in 1215 we read that Roger de Argentum gave land for a hermitage to Whitby Abbey. And in the early part of the nineteenth century the place was the home of a great smuggler and a famous man indeed. This was John Andrew, who combined the office of king of the local smugglers with the landlordship of the Ship Inn and the Mastership of the local fox hounds. He owned a fast cutter the *Morgan Rattler*, and had a partner at Kirkleatham five miles inland, who was a brewer, and very ready to take any rum or brandy that Andrew liked to land. He practised the profession of smuggling with enormous success for a great many years, and only came unstuck twice: once when he was running a cargo at Black Hall, near Hartlepool, and was caught and heavily fined, and the second time in 1827, when he was apprehended again (this time at Hornsea, in South Yorkshire) by the Preventives, and imprisoned for two years. We read that another M.F.H. had to be found in the emergency to hunt the hounds. Besides the Ship Inn he owned the nearby White House, and when Sir Alfred Pease bought this after John Andrew had died he found, in the last stall of the old stables on the sea side, a false floor and cellars under it. He was told that Andrew had been used to stabling a particularly vicious mare in that stall. The Ship Inn is still there, much hung about with brass objects. There are some cobles and double-enders, and a winch to pull 'em up the beach, and, under Cat Nab, a most lugubrious little morgue.

The Ship Inn is just above sea level, and the cliffs now rise rapidly to the south of us. We have a choice before us of either keeping to the shore, if it is low tide, or climbing to the top of **Hunt Cliff** and admiring the splendid views from the top. If we choose the former we will have to pick our way between fallen blocks of the Middle Lias rocks from above, which are rich in fossils. In fact some of the rocks seem to be made up entirely of masses of fossil shells. If we go up the top way we may discover the remains of the Roman Signal Station there, which are scant indeed, and are situated well below the top of the 500 foot hill (the cliff itself is 350 feet of sheer drop and an excellent place for suicides). If there is not much to see at the Roman station, there is plenty to imagine. Actually a scrap of the south wall of the little fort survives. There was a square tower with walls 44 inches thick, surrounded by a wall and outside that a ditch 28 feet wide and 6 feet deep. The tower was probably three storeys high, and had semi-circular bastions at the corners. This was the pattern of all these lookouts of the Saxon Shore. The Hunt Cliff one was excavated in 1911 and 1912. A well was found which contained the skulls of fourteen or fifteen people, as well as a piece of cloth seven inches by five inches in size, and wool and bast fibre.

We have embarked now on a stretch of shore which has been called the Nursery of the Science of Geology, because it was along here that much of the earliest work on this science was accomplished. The great stretch of cliff, much of it vertical and all of it offering the clearest exposure of the Jurassic rocks in England, starts near Saltburn in the north and continues south until it butts with the cretaceous chalk near Filey. Stratum overlies stratum here, clearly visible, each one plentifully marked with the fossils which date it. We can stand on the shore practically anywhere along this stretch of coast, and look up at the cliffs and try to imagine how each horizontal band of rock was laid down under the sea, and, by the fossils, watch the evolution of life, as aeon followed aeon. In places there are faults, and unconformities, and we can unravel what has happened as easily as reading in a book. A short cut to understanding this great exposure is to go to Whitby Museum, where some curator of long ago painted a mighty panorama of the whole set of cliffs, and here, also, is as complete a set of fossils of the exposure as we can find, short of spending many years collecting ourselves.

Broadly, the cliffs at Saltburn are Lower Jurassic, those starting south of Whitby, Middle, and south of Scarborough, Upper. The formidable Hunt Cliff is formed of dark unstable liassic shale and sandstone (the Lias, which forms so much of this coastline, is a blue clayey limestone, but it doesn't look like a limestone: much more like a clay). Sandwiched between the Upper Lias and Lower Lias shales is the ironstone series: the ore is an oolite of carbonate of lime.

There are broadly four seams of Cleveland ironstone: the Main, which is about eleven feet thick, the Pecten, up to six feet, below this the Two-foot, and then the Avicula, which varies in thickness. By the time we get as far south as Staithes the seams have thinned and the Middle Lias shales intrude. At places along the cliffs (particularly just north of Staithes – there very near the bottom) we see a narrow seam of *dogger*. This is a strange formation of ironstone around nuclei of some organic substance – some long-dead plant or animal – and the whole consists of a layer of spherical shapes from the size of eggs upwards, a rusty red, and very hard. It was a rich ironstone, but hard to smelt, and the miners were fined for including it with the other ore. As for fossils, this coast is the richest fossil-finding ground in England.

If we are working our way south along the top of the cliff, we will become much incommoded after a mile or two by the Macadam works. Here large machines are busy quarrying out the old slag heaps to turn what was flung away as useless into something useful: macadam to put on the roads. Then we come, abruptly, to one of the strangest phenomena of the coast: **Skinningrove.** It is a pity really to approach Skinningrove from the west: it should be seen first from the great hill to the east of it (from the map it will be seen that what we have come to regard as the north-to-south-going coast of England has now practically become a west-to-east-going coast here, but if from force of habit I still write of walking *south* the reader will know what I mean). When you approach Skinningrove from the east you suddenly see the great iron works perched high up on a steep cliff like a castle of the Rhine, chimneys fuming, and down below it, hung on the almost vertical slope, that invariable adjunct to Yorkshire industry, the pigeon houses and allotments of the workers. Further down still, right in the sharp cleft of the wyke or valley, is the village of Skinningrove: a few jumbled rows of brick terraced houses which no doubt sager men than I have condemned but which I think, in some strange way, are beautiful. Strangely enough the people who live in them do too, a fact which will be discussed later.

If you came along the beach, however, treading among the fossils, you will arrive first at the massive seawall of Skinningrove Harbour. This has a system of great pipes coming down to it, and running along it, and some strange rusty machines which may well puzzle the non-industrial. They are, in fact, heat exchangers. Hot water from the power station in the iron works is run down the steep slope to the harbour, and cooled by sea water which is pumped from the end of the breakwater. The cooled water then goes up again, to circulate once more through the power station, while the warmed sea water is pumped back into the sea. This harbour, disused now except for small fishing boats, was once very busy and thousands of tons of pig iron went out of it. After a period of chartering ships for this trade the Skinningrove Iron Company, in the 1890s, had built four ships, named the *Skinningrove*, *Hummersea*, *Cattersty* and *Northgate*; the *Skinningrove*, renamed *Mechelin*, still sails under other owners. Her first master, Captain Fryatt, was a famous man in his time. He would often sail with his hatches open, saying that his cargo of pig iron was still so hot from the furnaces that he dare not close them.

The reason for the existence of a large iron and steel works in such an improbable place was the outcrop there of the Main Seam of the Cleveland ironstone and the handiness of a steep cliff over which to dump slag. There is a romantic story of how John Vaughan, Bolckow's partner, stumbled on the Main Seam while out shooting on the moors for partridges. Much the same story (only true) is told about the discovery of the Copperbelt in Zambia: a prospector, having abandoned hope of finding anything useful, shot a roan antelope for meat, and when he was cutting it up noticed a stone which was copper ore and thus discovered the greatest copper deposit in the world. The mine that was opened at the spot is still called Roan Antelope. But in Vaughan's case the legend is not true, for we can read in his own words how he had been advised by a geologist that the main seam should outcrop along a certain line, and he walked along this line examining such signs as the dirt excavated out of fox and rabbit holes, and on 8th June 1850 he discovered the outcrop. This was over at Eston, but the year before, a miner named John Rosebury had already discovered the main seam in Skinningrove Valley, and the indefatigable Bolckow and Vaughan immediately started to mine it. Mine after mine was sunk in the surrounding country, and if we wander around there today we can still see the old waste dumps on every hand. There were sixty mines hereabouts, and by 1883 seven million tons of ore had already come out of them. They are all closed now: Skinningrove Mine ceased operating on 26th September 1958. If you walk up the vale you can still see where it was, with a bricked-up adit into the steep cliffs of the valley and the mine buildings taken over for other purposes.

The ore was formerly taken up to the steel works on the opposite cliff by aerial ropeway, and before that, straight up a vertical shaft that was sunk down to the main seam actually inside the steel works, with a hoisting engine over it which went on working for nearly a hundred years before it was scrapped.

Many of the men living in Skinningrove were iron miners and will tell you what the job was like. The ore bodies were approached by adits, or drifts, not vertical shafts. You walked down them. At the end of Skinningrove's life the miners were walking about four miles into the bowels of the hills. There they worked in pairs, contract mining – in other words being paid for what they mined only, and mining on what is called the stall and pillar method. The ore body was about eight feet thick, and nearly horizontal. They drove drives and crosscuts (what the layman might call tunnels) the height of the orebody in a criss-cross pattern, leaving pillars of untouched ore to support the roof each about twenty-two yards square. They continued in this manner until the surveyors told them that they had reached the limit of their firm's concession, and they then used to retreat, robbing the pillars as they went, leaving the roof to be supported by the timber they had already put in while they stripped the pillars. When the pillars were gone they would try to salvage the timber by hauling it out with ropes before the roof, as it inevitably did, collapsed. They could never get all the timber out. They mined the soft rock by drilling it with rotary drills turned by hand – and then blasting with a slow powder. They loaded the tubs or trucks, by hand, put their tallies on them, and sent them to the main haulage by horse-power, horse boys coming to fetch them. The tubs that they had filled were counted on the surface, and they were paid accordingly.

At first iron was only mined near Skinningrove, but in 1864 the Lofthouse Iron Company was set up to build blast furnaces at Skinningrove and produce pig iron and wrought-iron goods. The company went bust in 1877 and the furnaces were damped down, but in 1880 the Skinningrove Iron Company was formed, directed by the redoubtable T. C. Hutchinson, and took over the iron works and some of the mines for £50,000. Hutchinson, universally called T.C., is still talked of with awe, although he died in 1918. He used to drive about in a horse trap until he got one of the earliest motor cars in the North of England, and then, as his beard used to blow into his face as he drove along (which he used to do furiously) he would have it parted into two parts and tied in a knot behind his neck. He was a hard driver of men as well as motor cars, but a great encourager of new ideas and young talent, and when he wasn't driving his car or his workmen during the week, he was preaching to them on Sunday in the Methodist chapel.

When Hutchinson took over the works it had two blast furnaces, and he built three more. Pease and Partners came into partnership in the firm in 1884 and the place was much modernised. In 1910 machinery was installed for rolling ships' plates. At the present time there is only one blast furnace working, but it is a big one with the capacity of several smaller ones. It is, alas, to be damped down. Under the 'rationalisation' policy of the National Steel Corporation, Skinningrove is no longer to be a producer of iron or steel. But £1,700,000 is to be spent on expanding its present production as a rolling mill, and Skinningrove will produce more and more special-ised steel profiles, using steel from elsewhere to make high-grade steel components such as bulldozer blades, track-lugs and many other things. All this is causing heart-burnings among the blast furnace men and other steel workers, who see their livelihood disappearing before their eyes. In fact they will probably have to go to Lackenby every day, or elsewhere, a thought which doesn't please them at all, for they are among the most closely-knit of clans, and Skinningrove has long been a little world of its own.

It is a world which is threatened seriously at the moment. Loftus Council, which is responsible for this area, has built a large and uninteresting housing estate up at Loftus, and, working on the theory that the world will not be bearable until every inhabitant of it lives in a council house identical with the council house of every other single inhabitant, wishes to pull the village of Skinningrove down, lock stock and barrel, and transfer the inhabitants up aloft where they will be planted out like cabbages. The inhabitants do not *want* this. They *like* Skinningrove, even if the officials of Loftus Council call it a slum. A slum it may be, but it is a happy slum, where families have lived for generations, everyone knows everybody else; there are a couple of dozen good 'part-timer' boats that go fishing in a serious way, a fine big pub called for no reason that anybody can think of Timm's Coffee House, and a good club. Authority does not carry much mandate down there, people can have their allotments and their pigeon houses and do much as they like – and they don't want to move. At least I have so far been unable to find one who does, and I know where I would want to live if I had to choose between Skinningrove and some blasted council estate.

At Skinningrove (as at Orford in Suffolk) a merman was once

captured by the fishermen. He 'showed himself courteous to such as flocked farre and neare to visit him; faire maides were welcome guests to his harbour, whom he would beholde with a very earnest counteynance, as if his phlegmatic breast had been touched with a sparke of love.' In 1779 the Welsh-American privateer, Paul Jones, cannonaded the place from the sea, but didn't do as much damage to it as Loftus Council have succeeded in doing already. At **Brotton**, inland, we can hear very good Yorkshire singing in the Ship Inn on a Saturday night. At **Skelton**, further inland, lived the de Brus family, then the Fauconbergs, the Nevilles, Conyerses, Trotters and subsequently Miss Margaret Wharton, or 'Peg Pennyworth'. Possessed of immense wealth (she once gave a nephew a hundred thousand pounds), she would go to the market and buy a pennyworth of live eels which she would carry home in her pocket, and used to send her pies and other bits of cookery to the bakehouse to have them baked there so as to save fuel. There is a story that she once told her footman to do this, and he refused, saying that it was beneath his office. She then told her coachman with the same result, so she ordered out her coach, made the coachman drive it, the footman stand behind it, and she herself was driven to the bakehouse holding the pie on her lap. John Hall Stevenson lived here, and used to entertain Lawrence Sterne, who derived from him Eugenius in 'Sentimental Journey'. Stevenson wrote 'Crazy Tales' and 'Macaroni Fables'. He would never get out of his bed if the east wind were blowing. Sterne once sent a boy up to sabotage the weathercock, so as to get his friend out of bed.

At **Loftus** was a worm, or dragon, slain by Sir John Conyers, who was a great Worm-slayer. He also accounted for one of these animals at Sockburn, but I have never been able to find where this is.

CHAPTER 13

Skinningrove to Sandsend

❧

ON the next stage of our journey, to Boulby, we are faced with a dilemma which we shall come across again and again along the ensuing coast. Whether to walk along the foreshore or the top of the cliffs. Here I can only suggest that we must make two excursions, because it would be unthinkable to miss either.

If we start by going along the foreshore we pass the boat landing of Skinningrove, where the boat owners have built rough tarred huts in which to keep their gear, and where they can sit and make their lobster pots, and get away, one suspects, from their wives. We turn the corner on to the rocky foreshore, where great flat slabs of rock form rock pools and support boulders and mushroom-shaped rocks which have fallen from the cliffs above in the slow process of their erosion, and we may find an old man or two looking for nice big winkles (there are plenty of little ones but the big ones are harder to find. The white-shelled ones are called 'dog winkles' and are not supposed to be edible), or younger man knocking limpets off the rocks for use as long-line bait (commonly a mussel is put on the hook first, and the tougher limpet put on the end of the hook to keep the softer mussel on. The limpets are called 'flidders'; hermit crabs are 'lelpies' in the North of England), and if a man sees a piece of jet washed up by the tide he picks it up, for a pound of jet is worth 37½p. But of jet later. Here, also, on the infrequent sandy patches, you may see men scraping up the 'sea coal'. The coal washed up along this beach is in the form of fine dust – you seldom see big pieces – and this is the furthest limit south of the coal-gathering industry, which we saw at its peak along the County Durham coast. The coal used to come ashore in fair quantity as far south as Staithes. It does so no longer, and what the reason for this is I do not know.

But before you embark along this shore I must utter a solemn warning here – and this warning must go for the rest of the coast, with a few breaks, right down nearly to Scarborough. Do not attempt the coast walk unless the tide is on the ebb. Once the tide begins to rise it comes very quickly over the nearly-level foreshore, and the unwary will find himself forced by the breakers against un-

scalable cliffs, and unless somebody comes for him with a helicopter
– quickly – he will drown. The safest thing is to follow the tide down
– in other words start walking as soon as you can after high water.
You know you are then safe for several hours. About a mile east of
Skinningrove you will see some concrete slabs up under the cliff,
and also some old brickwork and masonry. The concrete is easily
explained away: it is the remains of a fortification of the First World
War. The other structures are a long story. Look down on the flat
rocks of Hummersea Scar below these works and you will see a sort
of channel with straight sides, slanting out towards the sea. The
rock has been deepened here, loose stones removed, and a rough
breakwater built along one side of the channel. Perhaps you would
hardly notice the place if you didn't know it was there. This was,
incredibly, a harbour, and it is a measure of the extreme difficulty of
land transport in days of old that any ships should try to get into
such a desperate place.

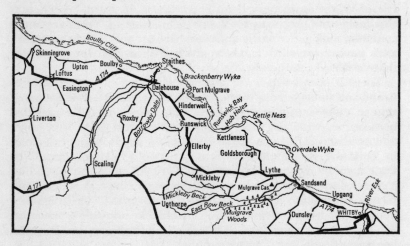

But we are viewing some of the workings of what was once the
greatest industry along this coast: the alum industry. As we go
southwards, nearly to Whitby, we will find that in very many places
the whole sky-line of the countryside has been altered by vast
diggings, dumpings and quarryings, and there are quarries on the
cliff-tops big enough to bury a village in. We may well wonder at
the enormous labour of shifting all this rock and dirt with nothing
but picks and shovels and wheelbarrows.

The history of the industry is this. Alum was known to the

ancients, and was used as a mordant for red dyes. In fact it seems that a really good rich red could not be obtained without it. It was also used for curing skins (still is) and for medicinal purposes. It is a double sulphate of alumina and potash, or else of alumina and ammonia. After the fall of the classical world the secret of its production was kept alive by Arab alchemists, and during the Middle Ages in Europe it was obtained at enormous expense from the East, or else dyed fabrics were obtained, and were known as 'Turkey red'. In 1459, though, it was found to exist in the rocks at Civita Vecchia, near Rome, and its discovery here was hailed as a great victory of the Cross over the Crescent, and a jealously-guarded Papal monopoly was immediately established in it. After Luther, however, the Germans started to make it, having broken with the Pope, and Queen Elizabeth tried to introduce its production into this country. She granted a licence to make it in Devon, but the attempt failed, and another to work the Lower Eocene rocks at Alum Bay on the Isle of Wight again proved no good. Then, in 1595, Sir Thomas Challoner of Guisborough, 'riding a'hunting in Yorkshire on a common, took notice of the soyle and herbage and tasted the water', and, having travelled in Germany and seen the alum workings there, realised that here was alum.

There is now a wonderful story about how Sir Thomas went to Rome and smuggled one of the papal alum workers out of the papal state in a wine barrel, the man being only too willing to be smuggled because he, with the other alum workers, had been kept there almost *incommunicado* as a serf or slave. Sir Thomas brought the man to Yorkshire, and found out from him how to extract alum. The Pope thereupon excommunicated Sir Thomas and placed upon him a curse of enormous length, enormous complexity, and almost complete comprehensiveness, so that almost no part of the knight remained uncursed. In spite of this formidable injunction, however, Sir Thomas prospered, and so did the alum industry, and England became independent of papal supplies.

R. B. Turton (whom one suspects, probably wrongly, of being a Catholic) debunks this whole story, with enormous scholarship, in a book called *The Alum Farm* (published by Horne, of Whitby 1938). He suggests that the curse (a copy of which is in Whitby Museum) was in fact invented by Lawrence Sterne, who used just such a curse in *Tristram Shandy*, and who used to go and stay at Skelton Castle, in the alum country. It seems to me just as likely that Sterne got *his* curse from the papal one; I think the wine-barrel story is a good one, and hope it's true.

Now the 'alum maker's secret', extracted by whatever means from the Papal State, was the secret of floating an egg. Briefly what happened was this. The alum shale was broken up into small pieces and piled on top of an enormous layer of brushwood. More brushwood was put on top, more alum, until a heap was formed perhaps a hundred foot high and two hundred feet square. It was then set on fire. The shale itself was bituminous, and would burn, and the heap would stay alight for up to a year. In the memory of middle-aged men now at Skinningrove, the shale was still smouldering away in the old workings at Boulby. The iron pyrites in the shale – FeS_2 – would lose half of its sulphur as SO_2 (sulphur dioxide) and become a black sulphide of iron (FeS). This would absorb water from the air and become sulphate of iron, or 'green vitriol' ($FeSO_4$ $7H_2O$). At high temperature this would oxidise even more and transfer its sulphuric acid (H_2SO_4) to the clay, the alumina of which would then be converted to sulphate of ammonia. The calcined shale was then steeped in water, and the liquor formed evaporated, and this left sulphate of iron and alumina. These were then separated by an alkaline lees – originally carbonate of potash and *piss*. The latter used to be brought from cities by ship, in barrels, and the former obtained by burning seaweed. (After 1801 chloride of potash was used instead of burnt kelp.) The solution was then evaporated, and the alum crystallised at a less concentration than that needed for the iron salts, and this exact and critical point was determined by floating an egg in the solution! As soon as the egg floated the liquor was run off and the crystals of alum obtained. Of course the empirical chemists of Elizabethan days didn't know all these chemical formulae, they merely knew that if you burnt the shale, and then subjected it to all these extraordinary processes, you got alum, which you could sell for ten shillings a ton. But in 1860 a simpler way of obtaining alum from the shales of the coal measures in the West Riding was discovered, and the death knell was struck to the Cleveland alum industry. This was just as well, for the countryside had already been denuded of trees and bushes, in the effort to find enough brushwood to fire the shale.

But to get back to the foreshore near Skinningrove, there was a pack-horse track down the cliff-face above the old workings by which we stand (we can still see a trace of it, although not climb it), and down this the alum was brought, to be shipped from small ships or keels that came into the little 'harbour'. Up until fifty years ago there was a house down here called 'Alum House', and in it lived a pair of old recluses known to everybody as Ticker and John.

If we keep on towards Staithes (and keep on we must, unless we turn back, for after Alum House there is no way of getting up the cliff) we will see the Jurassic cliffs very clearly displayed. Before Staithes there is a thin band of dogger (the red balls of iron stone) right at the foot of the cliff – and bits of it still adhere to the flat shale where the sea has eaten the cliff away. The bottom of the cliff above this is Lower Lias, above this Middle Lias, Upper above this, then a band of dogger, then lake estuarine deposits, put there when this part of the world was not under the sea but under a fresh-water estuary, and recent boulder clay right on top. The cliffs are vertical, and seagulls screech and cry above us, flying out from their crannies, and their wild cries sound somehow very ancient, as though they are not far removed in evolution from the winged reptiles over whose fossilised bones they fly. Down below, the limpets and barnacles cling to the very bodies of their ancestors who died in these muds a hundred and fifty million years ago.

Another way to make this journey from Skinningrove to Staithes is to walk along the under-cliff – half way up the cliffs in other words, for here the cliffs are double – a vertical one down below, then a level piece, then more vertical. Along this route one sees the enormous scale of the alum workings, for the alum shale, at the top, has been extensively quarried.

The third route is along the top of the cliffs, and this takes us six hundred and fifty feet above sea level, for this is one of the highest cliffs in Britain. It is a most exhilarating walk, and not to be missed on any account. At one point we can strike inland for half a mile along first a footpath and then a farm lane, to see the garden gate of **Upton** farm, and we should do so, for this is a most spirited exercise of the imagination. The gate is entirely constructed of horse furniture: huge horse-shoes off shires or Clydesdales of long ago, hames from cart or plough collars, bits, all welded together by some cunning blacksmith to make a most beautiful and fitting gate. The little lozenges that hang down in the middle are from a mouthing bit – a bit used for the first training of a horse, to make the mouth salivate and give him a 'soft mouth'. The tractor shed, beside the farm, is an old Primitive Methodist chapel. On the kindly light Lias soil, with its good natural drainage, we see sheep hurdled on turnips, and in the summer good fields of corn. In places though, the soil is boulder clay, and has to be drained artificially.

We come down Bank Brow, to the little hamlet of **Boulby**, and here we see not only the equipment of the alum workers, but of iron miners too. There are several fine late eighteenth and early nineteenth-century buildings. One of them was the stables for the horses that hauled ironstone out of Boulby Hill.

Whichever of these three routes we take, we eventually come to **Staithes**, the most beautiful village along the Yorkshire coast. It may not have quite the scenic attraction of Robin Hood's Bay, but it is better because it is inhabited. Robin Hood's Bay is more than half empty in the winter time, and the people who do live there are mostly retired people, or people with adequate private incomes who don't have to work. Staithes is still very much a working village, and long may it remain so.

If you come to Staithes, not the ways I have advised, but in a horseless carriage along the tarred road, I would exhort you to leave your carriage firmly behind in the commodious car park at the top of the hill opposite the Captain Cook Hotel (known to all and sundry as 'The Station'), and *walk* down the hill into Staithes. People do a great disservice to this little town (it is more than a village) by driving down into it. There is only one motorable road down there, and it is very narrow and steep, and motor cars are a beastly nuisance. At the top of the hill, soon after the car park and on the same side (the right of the road), is a footpath which says: 'To the Beach'. I have never been able to discover a beach along it, but it is well worth following, for it brings you to the upper rows – or *jumbles* would be a better word – of houses – and this gives you a perception of what an extraordinary place Staithes is, one you can never get from down below. The houses climb right up the steep hillside, the upper – and sometimes even the lower – windows of each looking over the red tiled roofs of the one below, and winding narrow paths and steep steps connect each house with the rest of the world. Certainly once pack donkeys carried stuff to these houses – now everything that goes up or down goes on the backs, or in the hands, of two-legged animals. The whole place is madly picturesque. Of course now when any house becomes vacant it is liable to be bought at a high price by rich people from the city, who have nothing to do with Staithes. This process has been going on since Dame Laura Knight lived here, and queened it over the 'Staithes Group' of artists (see her *Oil Paint and Grease Paint*). But the process has not gone anything like so far as it has in Robin Hood's Bay and Runswick. The reason for this is the existence of the iron industry. The fishermen of Staithes, when fishing no longer gave them a fair living, were able to turn into iron miners, which they did, and fifty years ago the place was largely a mining village. Now 'buses and cars go off every morning (the first 'bus at half past five) to Skinningrove, and **Warrenby**, and the various chemical works. It is possible for a young working man in Staithes to go on living there, and if he likes it well enough even to bid for his house and buy it, and thus help to stop Staithes becoming the summer holiday – and winter ghost – village it might well become. And a new phenomenon is being seen in the land. More and more young 'working class' people are beginning to see the attraction of living in beautiful places instead of council houses, as the upper and middle class people have seen for generations. In any one of the four lively pubs in Staithes (and also the very good workingmen's club 'oop t' bank') you will find a lively local company winter and summer, the inhabitants far outnumbering the visitors. Staithes has what is very much a living working community.

Four big motor cobles fish full-time (although they are inclined to take a longish break in the winter) which is four more than fished there eight years ago. Besides this there is a big fleet of 'part-timers'. Of course this is a shadow of the former fleet. The early primacy of Staithes as a fishing port along this coast is a little hard to understand, for you could scarcely find a place more cut off from the rest of the world. We read of fish merchants travelling with horse carts from Staithes across the Moors – well they would have had a terrible long way to travel to come to *anywhere*. And yet in the early nineteenth century there were 1,400 people in Staithes, nearly every one of them owing his or her livelihood to the fishery. As late as 1900 there were still fifty cobles working from Staithes, but before that the village not only owned, but built, big decked yawls, each carrying ten men and boys, and two or three cobles on deck to launch out on the Dogger Bank to handline for cod. So cut off was the place that one can find out very little about it. It didn't even have a church: the people had to lug their dead up to Hinderwell to bury them. That is until the whole place went Wesley-mad in the nineteenth century (Wesley actually preached there) and, in 1865, built the existing big Wesleyan-Methodist church. In that year Staithes had 400 men and boys at sea and 500 boat-building. There were also sailmakers, coopers, fish curers and merchants. The place must have had a better harbour than it has now, to support the big fleet that was there, and also the ship-building industry (some people say whaling ships were built there). The present harbour dries right out, and boats have to come in when there is a fair amount of tide and be hauled right up. The whole of this part of the coast is marvellously productive of fish: the Lias rocks seem to encourage lobsters and crabs, long-line or hand-line fishing for cod and haddock is superb (even the invention of the trawl didn't entirely kill this, because you cannot, mercifully, trawl over rocks), and no Staithes girl was supposed to be fit to be married unless she could cook a ling pie. *Besides*, of course, collect enough mussels and 'flidders', or limpets, to bait a thousand hooks – and bait them – and get the line ready to shoot the next morning. The people were, and still are, very clannish. Verrills and Theakers formed many of the families, and they inter-married closely – it was of no use a fisherman marrying a girl 'off the land' – for she would never stand up to the gruelling hard work of being a fisherman's wife. The women used to have to wade into the water up to their waists to help haul the cobles in, or to launch them to sea, sometimes in big breakers. Whereas horses once hauled them up the beach – now at Staithes a winch is used.

Staithes developed another industry besides fishing before the iron mining came along, and that was stay-making, from the whale-bone which was brought in large quantities into nearby Whitby. Staithes is proud of the fact that James Cook was apprenticed here to Mr Saunderson, grocer and haberdasher. The shop in which he worked no longer exists, having been washed away by a gale in 1812.

The Cod and Lobster, right down on the front, has been damaged by the sea three times. The last time, in the tidal surge of 1953, the front of it was practically washed away and barrels and cases of beer were floating about in the harbour for days. There is a tale, which I doubt but which is firmly believed by the present landlord of the pub, that the salt actually worked its way into the bottles of beer so that the beer could not be drunk. This sounds to me like a story put about by the former landlord for obvious reasons. There are two fine little family pubs just up the road, and another good and unspoiled pub, which very few strangers ever discover, is the Fox and Hounds at **Dalehouse**, a village just down the hill over the main Whitby Road. There was an old watermill at Dalehouse; it is all very picturesque, and just up the back there was an iron-mine, which we shall discuss in connection with Port Mulgrave. On the way down into Staithes, on the left, a very steep lane takes us down to a caravan site near a house called Warp Mill. This was a textile mill, driven by water, producing sail cloth, and the owner likes to think that Captain Cook's sails were probably made there. The great viaduct that carried the railway over the valley was built in 1885, and only recently pulled down when the coastal railway was abandoned, striking a great blow to the whole economy of the region.

Another industry has recently been started, the results of which can be seen from "oop t'bank' in Staithes, in the form of two quickly growing towers by day, or a scintillating cluster of electric lights at night. This is the new potash mine at Boulby. Sylvinite, the potash ore, was discovered under the Cleveland Hills when drilling for oil in 1938–39 and a scheme was considered, and attempted, of brining it, or dissolving it in water pumped down boreholes and then pumping it up again. Fortunately this didn't work, or the whole countryside would have been covered with pipes leading the stuff to the evaporating house. So now shafts are being sunk, and the rock will be mined in its natural state. The difficulties of shaft-sinking are considerable. There is a thousand feet of Bunter sandstone to penetrate, which is permeable and full of water and brine, and a protective lining to the shafts will be necessary. The total depth is formidable, in terms of European mining. This mine started production in 1972, and the aim is $1\frac{1}{2}$ million tons a year. The potash is in association with the Lower Evaporite Group of Permian rocks at 3,400 feet to 4,400 feet. About three hundred and fifty million tons of rock at from 20 to 40 per cent potassium chloride have been proved, stretching for about twenty-four square miles around Whitby. The beds thin out to north, west and south, but their extent to seaward is not known. If the mining is successful there will be enough potash here to keep Britain supplied completely, and also a lot to export to other countries.

And we cannot leave Staithes without considering the Great North Sea Coble Race. A group of young coal-miners from far-away Blyth in Northumberland considered that they were the strongest coble rowers on the East Coast. They were challenged by the fishermen of Staithes, and Whitby and a Blyth businessman put up a silver cup and two hundred pounds to be rowed for by the two crews. On 11th September 1866 the *Temperance Star* of Blyth, and the *Jane* of Whitby (the latter crewed by Thomas Coll, Simon Robinson, Thomas Crooks and Burton Verrill) raced, with oars only, along the ten-mile course between Staithes and Whitby bridge, and the *Jane* won easily, completing the course in one hour twenty-five minutes and thirty seconds. The race was followed by a large fleet, including several steam boats, and a contemporary account says the people running along the tops of the cliffs trying to keep pace with the contestants looked like a myriad of seagulls. After the race tremendous celebrations occurred in Whitby, the crew of the *Temperance Star* apparently belying the name of their vessel and being given a large lump sum from the prize money by the lucky, and generous, winners. There is a spirited account of the whole affair written by a contemporary journalist hung up on the wall of the Cod and Lobster.

Samuel Gordon tells us, writing in 1869, that if the fishing was bad Staithes fishermen used to get a sheep's heart, stick it full of pins, and put it on a fire and dance round it. They were keen gamesters and had a cockpit. This had magical properties, and no net laid out for drying must be allowed to touch it: if it did it was not used for the rest of the season.

Choosing again a falling tide, we pick our way along the fascinatingly interesting foreshore to the east of Staithes, among the Middle and Lower Lias fossils, around Old Nab and into Brackenberry Wyke (in the cliff of which old mine adits strike into the ironstone) and we suddenly come to one of the strangest little places of the coast: **Port Mulgrave**. Here, apparently lost at the bottom of a mass of foundered cliffs, is a little artificial harbour, very dilapidated, and inhabited now by a dozen or so part-timers' fishing boats, mostly of the double-ended variety although there are a few cobles, and there is a collection of wife-refuge sheds clustered at the base of the harbour. The walls of the harbour are built of massive sandstone blocks, and it is obvious that it was a good little harbour in days gone by. It is connected with the rest of the world by a steep and muddy path up the sundered cliffs, and at first the traveller may wonder how on earth anything was ever got down to the harbour for shipment, or up from it after landing.

The answer lies in a tunnel, the end of which we see a few yards up in the cliff. This looks bricked-up from below, but if we climb up to it we find a doorway, and it can be entered provided one has a torch. The first few yards of the tunnel might not be considered safe by a careful mine deputy, because the timber supporting the roof has collapsed, but once past this length, the tunnel divides into two parallel branches, both of which are well brick vaulted. The righthand tunnel is fairly dry, and leads eventually to Borrowby Dale, very near the Fox and Hounds Inn which we noticed at Dalehouse, and here was the Grinkle Iron Mining Company's mine. This was opened mid-nineteenth century by Palmers, of Jarrow, to mine ore for their furnaces there. The ore was shipped by small coasters from the harbour that they built – and called Port Mulgrave. The harbour cost them £30,000. There is a painting in the Ship Inn, up on the cliff above and along the lane, showing what the harbour looked like in its heyday, with a raised track coming from the mouth of the tunnel, trains of ore tubs being pulled along it by a steam engine, and the ore being shot into the holds of steamers. Up-cliff there is the village that they built, all the older houses very well designed and built of sandstone: the Harbour Master's house a dwelling suitable for such an august personage, and a long L-shaped row of houses, much larger and better built than most 'workers' dwellings' of the period, sensibly sheltering a large block of allotments from the north and east winds. In the allotments in winter you will see some of the very fine brussels-sprouts this part of the country is able to grow. The whole place is very well planned, and the houses still serviceable.

On the shore from Port Mulgrave to Runswick Bay one can find many pieces of fallen rock from the Upper Lias. Ammonites are abundant here (mostly *Ammonites annulatis*) and *Belemnites cylindricus*, also *Pactylioceras annulatum*, *Harpoceras serpentinum* and *Inoceramus dubius*.

Runswick Bay is a kind of lesser Robin Hood's Bay, situated in very much the same sort of site, with a little village much resembling the other place but smaller, all jumbled higgledy-piggledy down the terraces of a steep slope. Like the 'Bay Town' of Robin Hood's Bay the whole place looks as if it is slipping down into the sea. According to Ord it did – in 1682 to 1684 – with the exception of one house. When the final disaster occurred the whole population would have been lost but for the fact that the fishermen were waking a corpse and were therefore awake and alert and got the population out in time. The place was once entirely occupied by fishermen – although now not one full-timer is left – but Runswick still manages to support a lifeboat station. It is a charming place (although practically a ghost town out of the holiday season), with a fine bay of good sands on which horses can gallop or children play happily. We are told by old writers that the people used to sacrifice live cats on the safe return of the cobles from gales at sea, and when they were still out during storms the women used to light fires around which the children were made to dance. In a cave along the bay at a place still called Hob Holes lived Hob, the goblin, who used to be able to cure children of whooping cough. The present writer has seen none of these phenomena. Beyond Hob Holes, incidentally, the Jet Rock can be clearly seen in the cliffs a little above high water mark, above the Ironstone Series, with the grey *Annulatus* shale above, then two dark bands of Middle Lias ironstone. In the Jet Rock are found (besides jet which we will discuss when we get to Whitby) very fine ammonites, as well as fossils of saurians and fish of the genus *Lepidotus*.

Perhaps it is best to clamber up to the top of the cliffs in Runswick Bay, since the shore is pretty hard going, and here we will find the bed of the disused railway, which makes a good track now for walking, or for riding horses. At **Kettleness** the railway station has been taken over as the *Seonee Lair* of the East Cleveland Wolf Cubs, and these formidable infants are often to be seen inhabiting it. On Kettleness was a Roman signal station (nearer to **Goldsborough** actually) which was excavated in 1919, and a human, and canine tragedy revealed. In the south-east corner were three human skulls and oxen and dog bones, also bones of goats, pigs, deer, hares, rabbits, and the shells of crabs, whelks and winkles and coins of the years from AD 392 to 423 (Eugenius and Honorius) and jet ornaments. The tragedy was revealed in that the skeleton of a man was found on top of that of a dog with the dog's teeth at the man's throat. It was obvious that the dog was trying to defend its Romano-British master from attack when it was struck down and killed, and fell on its dead enemy.

The disused railway dives into a tunnel soon after leaving Kettleness. It is boring to walk through it, so it is better to keep up along the cliff edge. The ground suddenly falls away in front of us, in an almost vertical but very overgrown slope into **Overdale Wyke**. These wykes are common all along this coast: they are where small becks, or streams, have cut down through the soft Lias rock (sometimes aided by a fault or other line of weakness). They are generally thickly grown with stunted trees near the coast, and bigger ones further up where the weather isn't quite so inclement. Here at Overdale Wyke, if the traveller seeks, carefully sticking to the sign-posted coastal path (this is all part of the *Cleveland Way*), he will find some steps cut into the side of the steep wyke, and can here descend to the emergence of the railway tunnel. He will then come to a strange never-never land of old alum diggings, and dumpings, where he will again be amazed at the scale of these ancient workings, and staggered that so much rock could have been hacked out with pick axes and carted away by shovels and wheelbarrows. These workings were opened in 1615 and were still in use until 1867 – the last of the alum workings to close. It is strange that, a hundred years after the huge spoil heaps were last disturbed, they are practically without vegetation. Only here and there a little acid-loving grass and a scattering of heather has managed to take root. Mining went on here on a limited scale after the closing of the alum works: drifts were driven into the cliff for the extraction of cement stones – nodules of carbonate of lime which were used for making cement before Portland cement was invented. In other parts of the world, notably near Harwich in Essex, such stones were dredged out of the sea.

After this rather moon-like landscape you come down into the coastal village of Sandsend. And here you might first turn right up the steep hill to have a look at **Lythe**: a pleasant little stone village, with a pretty little church. This was completely rebuilt in 1910–11, but attractively, and inside is a most beautiful wheel-less plough. There is a nice prayer on a card beside it:

> God speed the Plough,
> The Plough and the Ploughman,
> The Farm and the Farmer,
> Machine and Beast and Man.
>
> God speed the Plough,
> In fair weather and foul,
> In success and disappointment,
> In rain and wind and frost and sunshine,
> God speed the Plough.

There are two ophicleides hung up on the wall, late of the church orchestra. Why have we no ophicleides players now? Why no concerto for ophicleides and flute?

Sandsend is at the end of a long stretch of sandy beach stretching all the way to Whitby. Here something peculiar has happened to the great Jurassic cliffs because they disappear, and don't come back until we get to Whitby. Sandsend itself stretches not only along the shore, but up two wooded wykes, or vales, one the Mickleby Beck and the southernmost the East Row beck. Up one or the other one I solemnly exhort the traveller to go, if the day be a Monday, Wednesday or Saturday, for it is only on these three days every week that the Mulgrave Estate is open to the public. The **Mulgrave Woods** are beautiful, botanically and arboriculturally very interesting, and an example of really first-class forestry and estate management. Lost inside the woods is Mulgrave Old Castle, and it is desirable to come across it unexpectedly and alone. Thus encountered it is one of the most romantic ruins in the country. Heavily overgrown with great trees, sadly split and falling down, bereft of all such hideous objects as rubbish bins (or indeed rubbish), or notices telling us to do this or not to do that, it is just as a ruin ought to be. As for the dating of it, the bulk of the south curtain wall is thirteenth century, that of the north along with the keep circa 1300. The great hall has a fifteenth-century window at one end and a fine fireplace at the other: what the Welsh call a *simnnai fawr*, and there is a beautiful little fighting tower – almost an exquisite miniature – at the east end of the ruined curtain which is fourteenth century.

According to legend there was a castle at Mulgrave before the Normans. Leland mentioned it, and reported that the common people believed it had once been owned by a giant. Chaucer mentions the giant, whose name was Wade, or Wada, in his *Merchant's Tale*. The legend was that Wade and his wife, Bell, built both Mulgrave and Pickering castles, and that when one was working at one and one at the other, they used to fling each other their stone hammer. There is also a Wade's Causeway attributed to this lusty couple. It has heaps of rocks along it. These are supposed to have derived from the fact that Bell used to carry rocks in her apron, and sometimes she spilt an apron-full and there they are still. Camden, in his *Britannia*, says that Wade was a Saxon Duke who, after he was defeated in a battle in Lincolnshire, fell into a distemper which killed him, and was buried between two rocks twelve feet apart which occasioned an opinion that he was a giant. Another story is that Wade was one of the murderers of King Ethelred of Northumbria, and that after the murder he was forced to take refuge in his castle at Mulgrave. I cannot find who King Ethelred of Northumbria was: there was of course an Ethelred of Mercia.

The Fossards got this estate from the Conqueror, and it passed in King John's reign to the de Mauley family by marriage. Peter de Mauley was a commander in King John's army. He was active against the Scots and took a de Brus prisoner and held him in Mulgrave Castle. Peter de Mauley III, in fact, built most of the castle that we see today. The de Mauleys were a boisterous lot. Peter I annoyed his patron King John by being very active in making him sign Magna Carta. Peter IV raided Watton Priory, near Lockington, turned a wagon-load of nuns out of their wagon so that he could pinch the vehicle, and went home having purloined no less than a hundred and forty oxen and forty horses. This Peter was the robber baron *par excellence*. Twice he was had up for adultery: the second time, he was sentenced by the Archbishop of York to fast on bread and small beer every Friday during Lent, also Ember Days, and Advent, for seven years, make pilgrimages to York, Beverley, Ripon, Southwell and Hereford, and to be fustigated (beaten with a cudgel) seven times, in his shirt, before a procession in York Minster. Peter V was pretty boisterous too. On 23rd March

1334, at Blakey Moor in the Forest of Pickering, he killed no less than forty-three harts and hinds, with gaze hounds and bows and arrows, and set the heads of the animals up on staffs for all to see. This took place when Edward III was in his castle of Pickering, hunting his royal deer. Edward must have forgiven him, though, because shortly after this he made him an officer of the law. Peter V was a great Scots-fighter, and it was he who built the pretty little tower on the east end of the castle, which, alas, will fall down if somebody doesn't grout it a little with some cement.

The family that followed the de Mauleys, the Bigods, were a boisterous lot too: not only here but formerly in the family seat of Framlingham in Suffolk. The castle passed to John Bigod in 1418. Sir Ralph had ten sons and five daughters by his one wife. But Sir Francis it was who overreached himself. He started off by carrying on a great litigation against the Abbot of Whitby, and ended up by leading the second, and fatal, Pilgrimage of Grace. He was rather ignored by the organisers of the first, who didn't trust him, and so, when they were defeated but forgiven, he decided to organise his own. He went around telling everybody that the whole of the North had arisen, raised a band and attacked Scarborough Castle, and lit a signal fire on Eston Nab to rouse the country. He did all this much under the influence of his fiery mistress 'Mad Madge', or Margaret Cheyne, who was described as being 'a very fayre creature and a bewtyfull', but 'a perfect firebrand of religious bigotry'. Anyway, Madge ended up by being burned at Smithfield, while Sir Francis had his head cut off. Margaret was the bastard daughter of Edward Stafford, Duke of Buckinghamshire.

The Radcliffes then got the estate by marriage, but only as tenants under the Crown, to which the estate had come on the demise of Sir Francis Bigod. Queen Elizabeth finally handed the estate to the Sheffields. Edmund Sheffield was created Earl of Mulgrave on 5th February 1626. He had served with distinction under Leicester in the Netherlands and commanded the good ship *White Bear* against the Armada, for which he was knighted at sea by Lord Howard and thereafter granted his earldom and Mulgrave Castle. In the Civil War the Sheffields were Roundhead, and Mulgrave Castle was attacked, and taken, by the Royalists under Captain Zachary Steward. These dispossessed the owners and put a stop to their profitable alum works. Parliament, however, compensated the Sheffield of the day by granting him £50 a week! After Marston Moor, Colonel Francis Boyton drew up before the castle and came to terms with the garrison, allowing them to come out with their arms. The castle was then dismantled by orders of Parliament.

John Sheffield, the 3rd Earl, was created Marquis of Normanby on 10th May 1694, and Duke of Buckingham and Normanby on 23rd March 1703. He was a great soldier and sailor, but he annoyed Charles II by flirting with his sister and was banished from court. James II took him back again and Queen Anne, his old girl-friend's daughter, made him Lord Privy Seal. Commodore John Phipps, Earl of Mulgrave, in 1773 was given command of the bomb ketch *Racehorse* and, in company with a ship improbably named the *Carcase*, unsuccessfully tried to discover the North Pole. He was more successful though when he led the van under Lord Howe in H.M.S. *Courageous* at the Battle of Ushant.

A Marquis of Normanby still lives at Mulgrave, in a new and more commodious castle that was built mid-eighteenth century. It is by his courtesy that we are allowed to wander around practically the whole of this beautiful estate at will, un-admonished by rows of notices, unchallenged by game-keepers, and trusted, in fact, to behave in a civilised way. Charles Dickens was so taken by the place that he 'danced on the green of the velvety lawn'.

Sandsend itself has a hotel and a nice pub, a figurehead of Admiral Collingwood outside Miss Dora Walker's door (she is curator of Whitby Museum and a most knowledgeable lady), and two excellent institutions. One is a really effective Boatman's Association, which has achieved that apparently impossible feat of running one tractor on the beach to pull up everybody's boat. Generally, where cobles are beached, we see the absurd and wasteful sight of nearly every boat owner having his own rusty tractor – where one would do the whole job perfectly. The other institution is the boatyard of the brothers Goodall. These are both first-class boatbuilders and turn out about one boat a month – either cobles or the double-enders that we have seen in such numbers all along the coast from Redcar. The Goodalls have themselves evolved this form of boat. She is obviously evolved from the coble, but lacks the flat-bottomed stern and two side keels. She comes to the beach bow-on, but in fact, the bow section differs very little from the stern. The amidships section is pretty flat-floored and there is generally a raised washboard around the stern and quarters to defy the breakers when the boat comes to land. These boats are clinker built and have many coble features and a coble smack about them, but the strakes are narrower (and therefore probably stronger) and the frames lighter and closer together. For anybody who wants a motorboat that will beach, under twenty feet in length, I cannot think of a better craft than the Sandsend beach boat. For anything bigger than twenty feet I would prefer a coble, and the Goodalls are very good at building those too.

And so we walk along the clean sands to **Upgang**, where once the River Esk debouched until the last Ice Age blocked it up and forced it to escape where Whitby now stands. In about 1817 there was a big run of Hollands gin here, and it was discovered by the unfortunate circumstance of the lynch pin coming out of one of the carts that was carrying the stuff inland. The Preventive men thereupon made a search and discovered 500 kegs hidden in a retaining wall at Upgang. But the next night 700 kegs, which they had not discovered, were loaded aboard a big fishing boat, and she was sailed round into Whitby Harbour and beached on Bell Island, ostensibly for repairs. While she was being 'repaired', the stuff was quietly got away. The last bit of the old Mulgrave Castle Inn here, that was much used by smugglers, fell into the sea in 1945.

CHAPTER 14

Whitby I. The Abbey

❧

WHITBY has practically everything that a small town should have, and practically nothing that it should not.

Amongst the things that it should have is a long and interesting history, which has left many memorials, perhaps the first of which we see if we come along the shore at low tide: the Belemnites in the *Ammonites communis* zone of the Upper Lias, which we can find so plentifully at dead low water on the scar outside the harbour. *Nuculana (Leda) ovum* is abundant here but rare elsewhere. About a hundred and eighty million years after these little animals died, the Ice Age started Whitby as a viable harbour by busting the mouth of the River Esk here, through a line of weakness caused by either a fault or an anti-clinal roll. This causes the west side of the harbour to be down-thrown in relation to the east.

Human history starts, perhaps, with a handful of late Roman coins and some pottery sherds dug up near the site of the present abbey, which indicates that here, perhaps, was a Roman signal station. English history starts spectacularly in the year 655, when King Oswy of Northumberland swore an oath before the Battle of the Winwaed that if he beat King Penda of Mercia, that most reprehensible of pagans, he would found no less than twelve new monasteries. He won the battle and so he persuaded Hild, then Abbess of Hartlepool, to found a new abbey at Streonaeshalch as one of the twelve. Bede tells us that this unpronounceable name meant 'the harbour of the watch tower', which would have accorded with the presence of a Roman signal station there (it would have been vacated for a couple of hundred years or more when Hild came to it, but a tradition would have lingered on). Modern writers say it simply meant the harbour of somebody named Streon. The *halch* part has also been derived from *hough*, meaning a bluff with flat land on top, and certainly this description fits the place.

King Oswy, for good measure, had chucked his daughter in with the twelve monasteries, and she, at scarcely a year old, was dedicated to chastity and handed over to Abbess Hild at Hartlepool. Two years later Hild moved to Whitby and took the little princess with her.

162

When the princess, whose name was Aelfled according to Bede but Elfled according to the Ministry of Works, grew up she took the Abbess-ship over from Hild and reigned for thirty-three years. Hild ruled presumably until she died in 680, and was a most influential Abbess. The foundation she ruled over comprised both men and women (not bound to celibacy) and undoubtedly it would have been run on Celtic lines rather than Roman, with the simplicity, austerity and democracy that this meant. St Hild, whom we have met before on our coastal walk or cruise, at Monkwearmouth and at Hartlepool, was of noble blood, born 614, the daughter of Hereric,

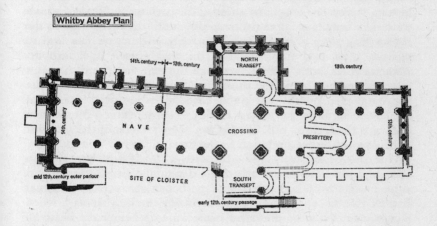

a prince of Northumbria. Just as Monkwearmouth, with its sister abbey of Jarrow, had become a great centre of learning – renowned all over Christendom – so did Streonaeshalch. It produced many great scholars. Alcuin, the foremost philosopher of his age, who founded the University of Paris, persuaded King Charles the Great to send young French nobles to Whitby to 'transplant the flowers of Britain that their fragrance might be no longer confined to Northumbria, but might also perfume the palaces of Tours'. Thus Whitby in some measure can be said to be an ancestor of the universities of Oxford and Cambridge, because the University of Paris derived learning and inspiration from Whitby, and in 1229 many students were expelled from Paris and came to Oxford, and some to Cambridge, and this is said to have been one of the factors that started universities in those places. Whitby was certainly a nursery of bishops. Bede mentions five who were educated here: Bosa of York,

Wilfrid II of York, Aetla of Dorchester, John of Hexham, and
Oftfor of Worcester. So it may be said that the influence of Hild,
and through her, the influence of those early Celtic missionaries
who came from Iona to Holy Island, not knowing a word of the
language of the people amongst whom they were to live, was spread
far and wide.

But alas an event occurred in St Hild's lifetime at Whitby which
had the severest repercussions to Christianity in Britain, and this
was the famous Synod of Whitby. It might not be fanciful to see the
seeds of the iconoclasm that threw down the towers of Whitby
Abbey and caused the downfall of monasticism all over Britain,
in this defeat of Celtic Christianity by Roman in Streonaeshalch
in 664. Everything that we can discover of Celtic Christianity
shows it to have been a purer, less materialistic and less worldly
religion than that of Rome, and, more importantly, it did not
organise itself in a rigidly hierarchical system. Perhaps if we could
have retained it, monasticism in England would not have reached
that stage of temporal power and corruption that gave its enemies
the excuse to destroy it in the reign of Henry VIII. Perhaps, who
knows, if the Celts had prevailed the Scots and Welsh and English
would have become united, the Danes would have been defeated,
and the Battle of Hastings would have had a different outcome. As
it was, when King Oswy made his decision, English Christianity
came under the domination of Rome, and it was over fourteen
hundred years before this domination could be thrown off.

The main issue of the Synod is always said to have been the
question of the date of Easter, and – surely even less urgent – the
question of how monks should shave their heads. In fact it was a
conflict between two entirely different cultures, and attitudes to
religion and life. The Venerable Bede (writing sixty years afterwards) was unreservedly on the side of Rome, although he was
charitable to the losing side (he said of Aidan, the greatest of the
Celtic saints in Northumbria, 'he had *a zeal in God, but not according
to knowledge*'). When the Celts, under their Bishop Colman, main-
tained that Anatolius had decreed that Easter should be on their
chosen date, Wilfrid, the leader of the Romanisers, said that St
Peter had held the opposite. Finally King Oswy sided with the
Romanisers, saying that Peter held the keys of Heaven, and that he,
Oswy, would obey his commands in everything, 'otherwise, when
I come to the gates of heaven, there may be no one to open them,
because he who holds the keys has turned away.'

It is interesting that Colman and most of the Celtic Christians with him, both Scots (meaning Irish) and English, retired to Iona, leaving the field to Rome. The English members of Colman's party then split off and went to Mayo, in Ireland, and formed a monastery there, which was going strong in Bede's time, and Mayo was called *Magheo na Saxan* – Mayo of the English – until the Middle Ages.

The little that has come down to us from this golden age of Northumbria is so good that we can only suppose there was indeed a great upsurge of the human spirit along that northern coast. Consider Caedmon, whose majestic Paraphrase of part of the Scriptures in the Northumbrian dialect most certainly inspired Milton's *Paradise Lost*. The two works have such striking similarities that it is impossible not to believe one was influenced by the other, and after all, Caedmon did come first.

Bede tells us that Caedmon followed a secular occupation (he says nothing about him being a farm labourer – that story is an embellishment of the imagination of our own age), and that until he was well advanced in years he knew nothing about poetry. Indeed, when the harp was going round at a feast and he saw it coming his way, he would get up and go home.

On one such occasion he went out to the stable, for on this night it was his duty to look after his beasts. He went to sleep and in a dream saw a man standing beside him who said: 'Caedmon – sing me a song.'

'I don't know how to sing,' said Caedmon. 'It is because I cannot sing that I left the feast and came here.'
'But you shall sing to me.'
'What shall I sing about?'
'Sing about the creation of all things.'

Caedmon thereupon sung:

Praise we the Fashioner now of Heaven's fabric,
The majesty of His might and His mind's wisdom,
Work of the world-warden, worker of all wonders,
How he the Lord of Glory everlasting,
Wrought first for the race of men Heaven as a rooftree,
Then made he Middle Earth to be their mansion.

The above is Bede's translation into Latin, and Leo Sherley-Price's translation into modern English. And as Bede said: 'verses however masterly, cannot be translated literally from one language to another without losing much of their beauty and dignity.'

In the morning he remembered the whole song and sang it to Hild. She was so impressed that she admitted him into the community as a holy brother, and caused him to be instructed in the events of sacred history. Bede says that he 'stored up in his memory all that he learned, and like one of the clean animals chewing the cud, turned it into such melodious verse that his delightful renderings turned his instructors into auditors'.

Only a little fraction of his work has come down to us (the manuscript of part of his *Paraphrase* is in the Bodleian, bequeathed by Francis Junius, who was a friend of Milton incidentally). But Bede has a great list of works, none of which we have. Caedmon awaits a worthy translator. As a former translator (Robert Tate Gaskin) said of him: 'he may not be the best among English poets – but at least he is the first'.

A runic cross has been found in Dumfriesshire bearing the inscription: 'Caedmon made me', and an Anglo-Saxon poem called the *Vision of the Holy Rood* which is thought to be by Caedmon:

> Now was I upreared, the Rood of Life's Monarch;
> bend me I dared not; dark nails they drove
> through me; the deep scars are on me and the
> wounds of rude hammers. Yet dared I not
> kill them; they mocked us and smote us: with the
> Blood I was dabbled, with the blood that
> gushed forth when He gave up His spirit.

There is a modern monument to Caedmon near St Mary's church.

As for St Hild, little remains of physical evidence of her, for the Danes destroyed her monastery in 867, it lay in ruins for two hundred years, and her bones were later removed to Glastonbury. The great medieval monastery was built over the foundations of her monastery and when it was excavated in this century very little was found. There were, however, several separate cells, fifteen to twenty feet long and ten to twelve feet wide, and the remains of a longer building variously supposed to have been the sisters' dormitory, refectory or school, and part of a *vallum*, or defensive bank around the whole place. To see a living equivalent we have to go to Ethiopia where there are still monasteries just like this, with a cell for each monk; the only difference being that in Ethiopia all buildings are round. Carved stones were found, including one thought to commemorate the Princess Aelfled, daughter of King Oswy, and Abbess until she died in 713 or 714. Small metal, bone and glass objects were found, including three plaques from book covers of gilt-bronze or copper with elaborate decoration: all that is left of the once great library accumulated no doubt by the Abbess Hild and her successors in this power-house of learning and scholarship. They are in the British Museum. When the Norman monastery was founded an 'aged countryman' informed the founders that he could remember the ruins of forty cells or oratories which had survived the Danes.

When St Hild came to Streonaeshalch, we are told, it was teeming with snakes. She charmed them to swarm down over the cliff and there curl up and be turned to stone. Thus ammonites, which abound there, are called 'Saint Hilda's snakes'. We are also told that, in summer, at ten or eleven o'clock in the morning, the sun falls on the north part of the choir of the abbey ruins, and that if you stand somewhere on the west side of Whitby, you will see in a high window of the ruins a woman standing in a shroud.

Meanwhile the Normans came, and William de Percy was given the country around Whitby (it had come to be called Whitby then – presumably the Danes had named it). A man named Reinfrid, who had come over with William the Conqueror as one of his knights, made a pilgrimage throughout the holy places of the North with two companions, a monk named Aldwin from the Benedictine Abbey of Winchcombe in Gloucestershire, and Elfwy, a monk of the Abbey of Evesham. Aldwin, as we have seen (p. 106), stayed at Jarrow. Reinfrid, one story goes, was so horrified at the destruction wrought by the Conqueror's men in the harrying of the North that he determined to stay there and try to build the place up again. So he settled, as a monk, at Whitby, and was given a grant of land by William de Percy. By the time de Percy set out on the Crusades, the new abbey had 'a stout roof and a score of monks'. William de Percy's brother (or some chroniclers say his younger son) Serlo became Prior, and was followed by William de Percy the Second, who had whiskers and was called *Asgernuns*, which apparently means whiskers in some language or other, and from this comes the unlikely name Algernon. Serlo might be installed as the patron saint of *squares*, for he objected to long hair and crusaded in court to have it abolished. After one devastating sermon on the subject all the nobles suffered their locks to be shorn. In the twelfth century the King of Norway ransacked the place, but spilled no blood. The power of the Abbots increased with time. They owned a twenty-mile strip of land, from five to seven miles wide. The Abbot was an absolute prince of his domains, and even as late as 1660 the Lord of the Manor, as the Abbots' successor, ordered the hanging of two poor men.

Various documents have come down to us. One very interesting one is a 'Rolls of Disbursements for 1394 and 5', kept by the Bursar of the Abbey. We read that he paid £6 for a horse for 'my Lord Abbot' (Bede records that the Celtic Bishop Aidan 'always travelled on foot, unless compelled by necessity to ride'). The following are a few of the items listed in the Disbursements:

2,000 oysters	5s
salmon	4s
2 swans	9s 6d
12 teals	3s
12 lapwings	2s
12 partridges	3s
12 plovers	3s (presumably golden)
2 dozen fieldfares	1s
1 dozen 'small birds'	7d
2 sticks of roasting eels	6s 6d (there were 25 eels to a stick)
4 pipes of wine (420 gallons)	£10 6s 8d
3 barrels white herrings	18s 9d
3 pike	12s 8d
60 stone of cheese	£1
For working 14 wolves' skins	1s 9d

This is but some of the expenditure. It is interesting that an eighth of the expenditure of the Abbey went on wine and malt.

The inventory at the same time lists, among other things:

394 head of cattle	14 goats
2,659 sheep	50 swine
63 horses	

In the Fish House:

120 codlings
8 lasts of herrings (a last is about 10,000)
300 salt fish
3 barrels white herring

The Abbey had granges at Stakesby, Lathergarth, Whitby Laithes, Fyling and Hackness.

The inventory for the Abbot's lodging was incredibly lush. After a great list of gold, silver and copper vessels the Bursar says: 'and other items too numerous to mention'.

On 14th December 1539 all this was surrendered to the king, by Abbot Henry de Vall and his eighteen monks.

The property fell into the hands of the Cholmley family, the various members of which pulled the monastic buildings down for building stone, but suffered the abbey (bereft of its roof of course) to remain, probably as a sea mark. The nave fell in 1762, then the south transept a year later. The great west window and most of the west front went in November 1794. The massive central tower fell in an enormous cloud of dust on 25th June 1830, after a chimney-sweep boy had climbed it the previous day to pinch the weather cock off the top. On 16th December 1914 the abbey gateway and the west wall of the nave were hit by three heavy shells fired by the German battle cruiser *Derflinger* (which had the Crown Prince on board watching the edifying spectacle). Right up until 1920 farmers were still taking cartloads of stone away from the ruins for road making and other purposes. In 1920 the ruins came to the Ministry of Works.

As for what there is to be seen now: nothing of the Anglian monastery, the foundations of which have been covered in again, but there are gravestones of early Norman times which had been found on graves dug over the Anglian ruins. The foundations of the original Norman church, with its Benedictine plan of a five-apsed east end, have been uncovered. The east end of the later building, and north transept, are pure and lovely Early English, the west end Decorated, or fourteenth century. There is little to see of the monastic buildings. The very good little Ministry of Works booklet by the late Sir Alfred Clapham describes the ruins in detail.

The large and imposing private house south of the ruins was first built mainly of timber by Francis Cholmley between 1583 and 1593, and then rebuilt by Sir Hugh (who opened the alum works at Saltwick) in 1633–36. The north front was built about 1672 but was damaged by a tempest around 1800 and partially dismantled. Most of the south front of the house appears to be Victorian. The place is now used as a holiday home by the Countrywide Holidays Association, which is a Methodist organisation, and visitors to the house are not encouraged. The long range of stable buildings are a youth hostel.

It is said that in Raby Castle, Staindrop, County Durham, there are two panes of glass taken from the Abbey. One depicts a pierced heart surrounded by a rosary of beads and five Tudor roses, four of which have representations of nailed hands and feet, and writing which has been translated from the Latin thus: 'Hail most holy virgin, who art a red rose, and clothed in the garment of divine love above every other creature.'

On the other pane is a lovely picture of Mary at an upright weaving loom with the child Jesus holding her wool, and Joseph approaching with a bucket of water. The legend here is: 'Most holy mother, who with much care hath brought me up, as the tenderest of parents, by the labour of thy hands.' One other relic of the ancient Abbey survives today, and that is a custom of a pointlessness which arouses the greatest admiration. Every year, on Ascension Eve, the agent of the Lord or Lady of the Manor, has to cut some sticks and go down to Whitby Harbour and construct a woven fence which shall be strong enough to stand several tides. This is called the *Horngarth*, or *penny fence*. He must then sound a horn and cry out, three times: 'Out on ye!'

Various and imaginative are the explanations for this strange ceremony. The most popular is that three men, William de Brus the lord of Ugglebarnby, Ralph de Piercie lord of Sneaton, and a freeholder of Fylingdales called Allotson, on the 16th October in the fifth year of the reign of Henry II, were hunting a boar. The boar took refuge in the cave of a hermit near Whitby (in Eskvale) who barred the door so as to save the boar. The three hunters battered down the door and in their rage smote the hermit, to such effect that, a few days later, he died. But before he died he forgave the three hunters, who were arraigned before him by the Abbot, on condition that every year, for ever, they or their successors performed the strange ceremony described above. Major Turton, also Rev. J. C. Atkinson in his book *Memorials of Old Whitby*, however, surmise that the explanation is less colourful. They believe it was a hereditary duty of certain of the laity to build a hunting fence (such as we see built today by the baMangwate tribesmen of Zambia, and other African people) into which to drive the deer on the monastic lands, so that they could be killed for venison.

Hard by the Abbey ruins is the **parish church of St Mary**. This is a unique church, and even the least ecclesiastically-minded should go inside it. I always consider it in my own mind to be a whaling church. I believe that the extraordinary alterations done to it in the seventeenth and eighteenth centuries were paid for by the great wealth that was then flowing into Whitby in the form of whale oil. A mighty three-decker pulpit (all three decks of which are in use today) rears up amidst a sea of box pews – of such narrowness and height that the occupants are like frogs at the bottom of a well – they can all see the preacher standing high up above them like Moses on Sinai but they can't see each other. Have we come back here to the spirit of St Hild's little monastic cells, each monk or nun alone and undisturbed to meditate, pray, or go to sleep as he or she feels inclined? The pews are jammed together, and face the pulpit from all directions: the lord of the manor gazed at the back of the parson's neck – for his ornate gallery stretched across the chancel arch like a rood beam of old. Maybe in the minds of the people the lord of the manor had replaced the Rood. To make room for this vast wooden honeycomb the church had to be widened, until it is about as wide as it is long, and roofed with a great flat roof. In this we can surely see the hand of the shipwright: the great hanging knees up aloft might have come straight out of a Greenland whaler.

There are monuments, many, grand and various, and well worth examining. There is a grand chair in the chancel made from the wreck of the *Royal Charter* and presented by the widow of Wm. Scoresby Junior. (It was in the *Royal Charter* that he sailed to Australia as we shall later see.) In the antechapel under the tower is what I imagine to be the only specimen in the world of a funereal memorial inscribed with part of a letter to *The Times*. This is a letter of 9th February 1861, written by the vicar of St Mary's, describing a lifeboat disaster and hinting that some money might be useful to the widows of the departed.

'We have had a fearful storm today. Half a mile of our strand is already strewed with seven wrecks. Our new lifeboat but launched a few months ago was manned by the finest picked seamen in Whitby. Five times during the day they had braved the furious sea, and five times returned with crews from vessels in distress. A sixth ship was driven in behind the pier. The men, all exhausted though they were, again pulled out, but before they had gone fifty yards a wave capsized the boat. Then was beheld by several thousand persons, within almost a stone's throw, but unable to assist, the fearful agonies of those powerful men buffetting with the fury of the breakers, until one by one twelve out of thirteen sank, and only one is saved.'

Five thousand pounds was subscribed. The tomb of the twelve men lies near the footpath to the coastguard station. It may cast a little light on the character of the genus *fisherman* that one hour after the new lifeboat had capsized, a full crew had volunteered to man the old lifeboat which was brought out of her retirement. They were coxswained by Henry Freeman, the only one saved from the first lifeboat and a man who might have been thought justified in resting on his laurels for the remainder of that day at least. They rescued another ship's crew that day, and another on the day after. The crew of the ship that were to be rescued by the doomed crew were in fact got off safely by rocket apparatus. In that one storm seventy ships were lost on the Yorkshire and County Durham coasts. A detailed description of the two days' life-saving at Whitby is given in an excellent little book *The Ancient Port of Whitby and its Shipping* by Richard Weatherill, 1908.

This book gives an indication of Whitby's importance as a ship-owning and building port as well. In 1700, 130 vessels were owned in the port, two or three as big as 400 tons.

In 1790 250 vessels with a combined tonnage of 48,642.

In 1828 Whitby was the seventh port in the kingdom. In this year some of its ships were engaged in the emigrant trade to the Americas.

1835 there were 390 ships of a combined tonnage of 62,000.

1866 414 ships – 75,417 tons.

Many Whitby ships were engaged in the Baltic trade. From 20th December every year until the 1st of March it was the custom to lay these ships up, and so the harbour above the bridge was jammed with shipping (it was said that you could walk across the river on their decks) and the town was full of swaggering sailormen.

Whitby was a famous nursery of seamen: William Moorsom rose to be Admiral of the Blue, and served with distinction in China, Borneo and the Crimea. Luke Fox sailed from Deptford 15th May 1631 and tried (unsuccessfully) to discover the North West Passage. Francis Gibson was the author of *Sailing Directions for the Baltic* (1801) and he charted the coasts of New England. In Charles II's time there was another Whitby – in Tangier. Charles received Tangier with his wife's dowry, from Portugal. He sold Dunkirk in order to raise the money to develop Tangier and sent Hugh Cholmley, who lived up in the big house next to the Abbey, to build a harbour there. Cholmley took with him several hundred Whitby men, and they lived in a village which they built and named Whitby. A vast sum was spent on building a harbour mole which was continually washed away, and the whole operation was a fine fiasco and petered out completely.

CHAPTER 15

Whitby II. The Whale's Road

&

AND SO we come to James Cook, who was not strictly a Whitby man, but the town can certainly claim him, because it was in Whitby ships that he became a sailor, and in Whitby ships that he sailed around the world.

He was born at Marton, near where Middlesbrough was one day going to be built, in a two-roomed thatched cottage, on 27th October 1728, and in the church registry is:

'1728, Nobr. 3 James ye son of James Cook day labourer baptized.'

He learnt to read at a dame school. His father's master, a farmer named Skottowe, paid for young James to go to a better school. He left school to become a stable boy and then, as we have seen, at the age of sixteen was apprenticed to a haberdasher at Staithes. Haberdashery was not his forte, and he left to be apprenticed to John Walker, a Quaker ship-owner of Whitby. His first ship was the *Freelove*, a collier of 450 tons (single-decked, with a crew of 16 and armed with 8 nine-pounders. She was built in 1745 in Whitby and reigned until the mid 1800s). Cook appeared in the crew-list as 'servant' which was probably the equivalent of our Ordinary Seaman as opposed to Able Seaman. It is fascinating that the name of the first ship he sailed in was bowdlerised by several Victorian writers to *Brotherly Love*! *Freelove* was a little more than they could take.

In the depth of winter, when the ship was laid up, he lived in a garret in his master's house, and we are told that the ancient house-keeper, Mary Prowd, used to make a fuss of him and give him candles so that he could study. His master encouraged him in his studies of mathematics, navigation and so on. He moved to the *Three Brothers*, in the Norway trade, and became an A.B., and at the age of twenty-four became mate of the *Friendship*. After five voyages, in 1755, at twenty-seven, he was offered his command. He refused it and joined the Royal Navy.

He went to HMS *Eagle*, a sixty gun fourth rater, and a month after his posting was promoted to Master's Mate. The Master of a warship was the man who actually sailed the ship. The Captain was probably a gentleman who didn't know much about sailing and whose job was to maintain discipline and fight the ship. The Captain would tell the Master what he wanted the ship to do and it was the Master's job to make her do it. Cook served in several actions against the French, and in 1757 went as Master to HMS *Solebay*. In 1758 he sailed for Nova Scotia as Master of HMS *Pembroke*, and twenty-nine men died of scurvy on the way. Cook here came into his own as the superb navigator and surveyor that he was, for he played the leading part in surveying and marking the St Lawrence so that the British fleet could sail up it to attack Quebec. He was paid £50 as a bonus for this work. He also surveyed part of the coast of Newfoundland. After five years he returned to England and got married, but he really needn't have bothered for all he saw of his wife or she of him. However he did just find time in the intervals of his almost constant voyaging to sire five sons and a daughter.

Early next year Cook was appointed King's Surveyor, and off he went back to Newfoundland as Captain of his own ship, the schooner *Grenville*. He spent four years there, and was noticed by scientific authorities when he made some valuable observations of an eclipse of the sun.

Venus was to be in transit over the sun on the 3rd June 1769, and the Royal Society was anxious to send observers to view this from the Southern Ocean, and an enlightened government decided to help them. It was also desired to see if there really was a 'Great Southern Continent'. Tasman had already discovered 'Van Diemen's Land' and had just sighted New Zealand. What is significant now is that somebody had the sense to choose a commander for this expedition who was a practical working seaman. There must have been plenty of 'gentlemen' and people of noble birth, or men with friends at court, who would have given anything for such a command, but a farm labourer's son who had served for years before the mast in the dirty and dangerous collier trade was selected, and this selection was the cause of the astonishing success of the expedition and the two other circumnavigations which followed. Cook's ship-mates were to write afterwards of his almost uncanny skill at sensing shoaling water or the set and strength of currents and tides and their relationships with the winds. Anyone who has sailed an East Coast sailing barge with an old skipper will know what this means. It is almost impossible not to believe that there is a sixth sense at work here, and not one that can be developed at navigational schools or naval academies.

A Whitby ship was selected for the job: the bark *Earl of Pembroke*, a typical 'cat' or bark of the collier trade. The selection of the ship showed as sound a judgment as the selection of the man. She was renamed *Endeavour*. She was 106 feet long, 29 foot 3 inches beam and 386+ burthen, and was just over three years old. It seems incredible to anyone knowing how long it takes to prepare a sailing dinghy for a voyage across a boating pool, that HMS *Endeavour* was manned, victualled, equipped and commissioned in under two months! She sailed from Deptford on the 21st July 1768, put in at Plymouth to collect her 'gentlemen': ten botanists, artists and naturalists and their servants, and to complete her stores and take on more armaments and ammunition. She sailed from Plymouth on 26th August 1768 carrying 94 people, 18 months' provisions, 10 carriage guns, 12 swivel guns and a good stock of ammunition and stores of all kinds.

The newly discovered King George's Island was the place chosen for the observation of the transit, and to this Cook sailed, and had, as he wrote in a letter to his old master John Walker of Whitby 'an Extraordinary good observation'. He went on to explore the whole coast of New Zealand, establishing that it was two islands and not part of 'the Southern Continent'. Cook loved the lands which he discovered and visited, and after shooting a few of the inhabitants, he developed a friendly relationship with the people. 'We . . . learnt how to manage them without taking away their lives'. He never patronised or despised them. Even the Australian Aborigines, who went 'wholly naked, it is said of our first parents that after they had eat of the forbidden fruit they saw themselves naked and were ashamed; these people are Naked and not ashamed . . . These people may truly be said to be in the pure state of nature and may appear to some to be the most wretched upon Earth: but in reality they are far more happier than that we Europeans, being wholly unacquainted not only with the superfluous but of the necessary Conveniences so much sought after in Europe they are happy in not knowing the use of them. They live in a Tranquility which is not disturbed by the inequality of condition, the Earth and Sea of their own accord furnishes them with all things necessary for life; they Covet not Magnificent Houses Household stuff &c. they sleep as sound in a small hovel or even in the open as the King in His Palace on a Bed of down.'

After leaving New Zealand Cook explored the east coast of Australia for 1,300 miles and, after sailing round the world, anchored in the Downs on 12th June 1771. He was received by the king, commended by the Admiralty and the Royal Society, and promoted to Captain Commander.

Next time two more Whitby colliers were bought – the *Drake*, renamed HMS *Resolution*, 462 tons, and the *Raleigh*, renamed HMS *Adventure*, 336 tons. Lieutenant Furneaux commanded the *Adventure*. The fool of a man in charge of the scientists refused to sail this time because he disagreed with Cook about some alterations done to the rig of the *Resolution*. His party refused with him, and so some more scientists had to be scraped up. The two ships sailed from Plymouth 13th July 1772. Cook, like a sensible man, called at Madeira (as he always did) to take on wine, and at Cape Town to careen his ships and check his new chronometer. On his first circumnavigation Cook didn't have a chronometer, which was partly why he was chosen for the voyage: he was one of the few navigators competent enough to work out his longitude from a 'lunar', i.e. from observations made without a chronometer. But this time he had one of these useful instruments.

He sailed south, and for three summers probed the ice fields of the Antarctic, still looking for the fabulous 'Great Southern Continent', and for the winters exploring among the 'South Sea Islands', finding many new ones. He was the first man thus to sail from west to east round the world in Antarctic waters, and by doing so he disposed of the legend of the 'Southern Continent'. Australia was the only Southern Continent there was. It is astonishing, when we think of it, that Cook was able to keep his ship's company from mutiny in such a prolonged and arduous voyage as this. They were probing further into the southern ice than any man had ever done before, and sailing seas unknown to man. Yet for three years Cook kept them cheerful and, furthermore, in good health.

It was in this matter of health that Cook was one of the great innovators. He made it his first concern to prevent his crew from getting scurvy, and in fact was one of the world's first great 'food cranks'. Whenever he came to land he sent parties ashore to get fresh fruit and vegetables; he used malt liquor, *saur kraut* and lemon juice; he kept his crew warm and dry and made them keep themselves and their quarters clean. The two ships under his command got parted, and the *Adventure* sailed home alone, a year before Cook, with a beautiful Tahitian youth named Omai. The *Resolution* sighted England 28th July 1775.

On his return, again Cook wrote a long letter to John Walker, describing the whole voyage, both perils among the ice floes and visits to islands such as 'Huaheine and Ulietea where the good people of these isles gave us everything the isles produced with a liberal and full hand and we left them with our decks crowded with

Pigs and Rigging loaded with fruit. I next visited Amsterdam . . . discovered by the Dutch in 1642; it is one of those happy isles on which Nature has been lavishing of her favours and its Inhabitants are a friendly and benevolent race and ready to supply the wants of the Navigator.' Cook has been criticised for allowing his sailors to fraternise very much with the natives, particularly the female ones. But how else could he have kept them as happy as he did on these three-year voyages away from home? Cook loved the South Sea Islands and their inhabitants, and was obviously far happier there than at home. He met with 'Hospitality altogether unknown in Europe' practically everywhere he went, and even after he had convinced himself only too effectively that some of the Maoris were cannibals (they admitted to having eaten some of the *Adventure*'s crew), he could write: 'Nevertheless I think them a good sort of people, at least I have always found good treatment amongst them'.

He arrived at Spithead on 30th July 1775, having only lost four men and them not from scurvy.

He sailed once again from Plymouth on 12th July 1776, in his former ship *Resolution* which, having had one arduous voyage already, was destined to give him much trouble, and he joined the *Discovery*, yet another Whitby-built ship, at Table Bay on 18th October. He had Omai with him, one of the purposes of this voyage being to return him to his native land. Another, less altruistic, was to try and discover a way from the Pacific to the Atlantic through the Behring Straits.

The two ships sailed round the Horn into the Pacific, and to Tasmania, New Zealand and various islands. This time Cook had a great load of domestic animals which were presented to various islanders, and he left Omai (of whom more later) on Huaheine. He then discovered Hawaii which he named the Sandwich Islands, and travelled north to the Behring Straits (which had been discovered by a Dane). He sailed through them and convinced himself that a North-East passage was not feasible. He then returned to Hawaii and was killed, his death being the result of a stupid misunderstanding. After having taken Cook for a god and lavished unprecedented hospitality on both him and his crew, the natives stole one of his long boats. Cook went ashore and asked their king to come aboard as a hostage for the return of the long boat. A crowd collected and, thinking that Cook was going to harm their king, they killed him. They were terribly contrite afterwards and gave him a magnificent funeral ceremony, before he was in fact buried at sea by his own people.

The two ships, under Charles Clerke, again sailed through the Behring Straits, and were again defeated by the ice, and returned to England, anchoring in the Thames on 6th October 1780. It is very easy to make a case for Cook having been the greatest explorer the world has ever seen.

As for Omai, his progress through England was triumphant if sometimes hilarious. He was lionised by the great, painted by Sir Joshua Reynolds in the costume of a Tahitian prince (which he was not, being only a commoner), taken to Mulgrave Castle where he did much shooting – 'but he could never be induced to recognise distinctions between wild fowl and the cocks and hens of the farm-yard' – and consequently slaughtered many domestic fowl. When he was to go home he was told to take anything with him that he liked, and he chose a barrel organ, various 'electrical machines', some horses and a suit of armour, in which he appeared before his startled compatriots.

Another great Whitby man and a contemporary of Cook was Captain William Scoresby senior (1760 to 1829) and, like Cook, this man was a farm boy and was great because of his single-mindedness, minute attention to detail, willingness to innovate, daring and determination to master every facet of his trade. Scoresby was the greatest of the British whalers, and probably the greatest whaling captain who ever lived. This last statement would be most hotly disputed by the Americans, who despised British whalers (*vide Moby Dick* and *The Cruise of the Cachalot*), but the plain hard figures are that Scoresby, in thirty voyages in six different ships, captured 533 whales (over fourteen 'fish' per voyage – the average then was under four), yielding (with many thousands of seals and hundreds of walruses, also) 4,664 tons of oil and 240 tons of whale bone. This was by a huge margin the European record and it would be very surprising to see American records, taken from an authentic log book, to beat it. It is interesting that Melville, who was so par-ticularly scathing about British whalers in *Moby Dick*, sailed half-way round the world on his one and only whaling voyage before deserting her at the island of Typee, without his ship killing a single whale. It is a measure of Melville's skill as a writer that he was never actually in at the death of a whale. He wrote those marvellous descriptions of the fishery (the chapter 'Stubb kills a Whale' is a world master-piece of descriptive writing) from hearsay only. But of course his whaling was sperm whaling, in which the British hardly engaged.

Scoresby's enormous success was due to his many sensible inno-vations and insistence on choosing his own officers and crew (and of course success begat success, because he soon had the pick of all the seamen in England). Other whalers sailed as light as they could when they left in the spring for the whale fishery, so as not to stave themselves in when they hit the ice while trying to force their way through the floes. Scoresby, on the other hand, sailed his ship with a third of a full load, carrying water ballast in his bottom two tiers of casks, and he also paid great attention to the windward performance of his vessel in other ways, not caring how she went to leeward. This meant that his ship was 'far more manoeuvrable than his rivals', because she would really sail to windward, and would *stay*, or come about through the wind, efficiently: he could thus thread his way among the ice-floes without hitting them and get much further into the ice than anybody else, and earlier in the season. He invented the crow's-nest, new lances for finishing off whales, new harpoons, new ice drills, and a new type of blubber cask. He installed davits for the rapid lowering away of his boats, and drilled and drove his men much as Nelson used to do. He ventured further north than any other man, sailing, working and 'tracking' (man-hauling) his ship through the ice until he came to a great sea of open water and got his ship once within 510 miles of the North Pole. His son wrote in his Journal: 'Our situation was singular and solitary indeed. No human being, it was believed, was within 300 or 350 miles of us.' On this occasion, as on nearly every other, he quickly got 'a full ship' and was able to sail home long before the first of his more cautious rivals. One of his peculiarities was that he would not allow a 'fish' (which is what the whalers called whales) to be struck on a Sunday, and sometimes, after months of blank fishing, his crew would have the chagrin of watching whales blowing all around, and other ships launching after them, while they had to stand inactive, and were not allowed to launch the boats. Their captain made up for this though by treating them to a long divine service which they had to attend. But either in spite of or because of this restraint on Sundays, they always caught many more whales than anybody else, and Scoresby made a great fortune at the fishery, and owned his own ships for many years. For good measure he once brought back to Whitby a live Polar bear.

A big whale was worth a thousand pounds. The products were the oil from the blubber, and the whale bone which was made into corsets. Before the widespread discovery of mineral oil, whale oil was the most important form of lighting, and in places even street lamps were fuelled with it. The whalers sailed from Whitby, or other English ports, in the early spring, and when they reached the pack ice tried to penetrate it as far as they could as early as they could so as really to be on the spot when the ice had opened enough for whaling. (*Balaena mysticetus*, or the Greenland Whale, was the one they were after.) When the lookout in the crow's-nest sighted a whale, all boats were launched and either sailed or rowed, with as little noise as possible, to the point where the whale was last seen to blow, and when it surfaced the harpooner of any boat that could get to it would 'plant his iron', or fling his harpoon into the whale's back. There were no less than 750 fathoms of line attached to the harpoon, and as the stricken whale sounded, this would run out at such speed that water had to be constantly thrown on it to prevent it setting fire to the gunwale of the boat. Scoresby's son relates a horrific story of the line getting twisted round a harpooner's arm and the man being whipped overboard at such speed that he simply seemed to disappear into thin air. When a boat struck a whale a flag was immediately hoisted aboard her and everyone, on seeing it cried: 'A fall! A fall!' a cry which, like most English whaler's jargon, came from the Dutch. Other boats would converge on the 'fast boat', and as the whale surfaced other 'irons would be planted'. If the whale went on sounding, other boats would bend their lines to the first's. At last, when the whale was sufficiently exhausted, a boat would go right up to it and the dangerous process of killing it with a long sharp lance would begin.

When the whale was dead it was got alongside the ship and there, afloat in the water, the thick layer of blubber would be stripped from it like the peel from an orange, one man balancing on the whale's body as it revolved in the water, cutting a spiral, while others hauled the strip that he cut up on to the ship with tackles. On board the blubber was cut again into small bits and packed into the casks which practically filled the ship. This was unlike the practice in the American sperm whale fishery, where the blubber was 'tried out' on deck, and the resultant clear oil put into casks. The Greenlanders carried the blubber back to England and it was tried out on shore. The ships spent much of their time moored to ice floes riding out gales, or being hauled by their crews through narrow channels in the ice, the crews walking or 'tracking' along the ice, and channels had to be cut for them sometimes with ice saws. Often ships got 'beset' by the ice, and sometimes crushed, and sometimes squeezed right out of the water so that they lay on the ice like stranded members of the prey they were after, and whatever happened to them, and whether successful or not, it was certain that they never came back from a season without their crews having suffered great privations.

So many ships were lost that an elaborate code was worked out whereby any ship sighting a shipwrecked crew had to take it aboard, but thereafter was entitled to share the victims out fifty-fifty with any other ship she encountered, thus spreading the load of extra mouths to feed. Many a crew was lost for ever, and others made epic journeys over the ice dragging provisions in a whale boat used as a sledge. Scoresby's last voyage was in his own teak-built ship the *Fame*, 370 tons, when in 1823 he put into Orkney to take on extra hands (a common practice) and the ship went on fire and was totally destroyed. But the fishery was coming to an end by then anyway, and the old man retired. The whale fishery started in Whitby in 1753, and it is recorded that 2,761 whales were brought into the port before it finished. And William Scoresby's son was in his way as great a man as his father. He was less single-minded but more literate: so literate, indeed, that he published ninety-one works of one kind or another, and the best of his books should be rated very high indeed.

He made his first voyage to the Arctic, with his father, at the age of ten, and thereafter sailed regularly as a member of the crew. He was First Officer or Spectioneer (from Dutch *spek synder* – fat cutter) at sixteen. At twenty-one he was Captain of his own ship, the *Resolution*. He whaled after this, with a short spell in the Navy under the well-known Captain Bligh, for twelve years and then read for holy orders and became ordained.

He wrote what were perhaps the best accounts of the whale fishery and Arctic voyaging, ever written. His *Account of the Arctic Regions with a History and Description of the Northern Whale Fishery* has recently been beautifully reprinted by David and Charles. His interest was more general and scientific than his father's, although he was at the same time a very good whaling captain. One year when he was ice-bound by the coast of Greenland and could neither break out to open water nor find fish, he carefully surveyed a long stretch of the Greenland coast, being the first ever to do so, and made frequent landings out of scientific curiosity. He was convinced that the descendants of the old Norse settlers in Greenland would have survived, and indeed he found many signs of human occupation (certainly Eskimo), but no humans. He used to get impatient at his crew's lack of scientific curiosity: 'several ducks, partridges, and other birds that they had shot, instead of being carefully preserved and brought aboard, were, without scruple or care, coarsely skinned, broiled, and eaten on the spot,' he writes indignantly. When locked in the ice and unable to move, he made experiments with magnets, and a magnet that he made off Greenland will even now, in Whitby Museum, lift fourteen pounds. After he was ordained and was tired of being a parson, he sailed around the world to Australia, on behalf of the government, to test the behaviour of the magnetic compass in an iron ship. He wrote a book called *My Father*, which is a marvellous biography of that stalwart man. There is a nice bit in it when, owing to a government regulation, his father was told that he had got to have a surgeon aboard his ship. He found a totally untutored fellow and sent him to a real doctor to have him examined for a medical certificate. The man came back immediately – with the certificate. Old Scoresby asked him how the examination had gone so quickly and he replied 'Well I said to the doctor "the long and the short of the business is, if I can do no good, I'll do no harm." "Then," he replied, "you'll do better than half the doctors in England" and he at once wrote out my certificate.'

Scoresby, as a writer, at his best is superb. There is a description of a storm near the end of *Journal of a Voyage to the Northern Whale Fishery* which might stand by anything Conrad wrote, and the ending of this book (when he arrives back in England to find that his wife has died) is one of the most poignant passages in English literature: it is most astonishing that his work is not better known. It may be wondered how a man so sensitive could cheerfully bring about the deaths of so many vast and noble animals, but this is to forget the difference between his time and ours. At least in his day it was a fair fight between whale and man. Even now the Japanese with fast motor catchers, helicopters, and explosive and even electrocuting harpoons are doing what the old sailing whalers failed to do: exterminating Leviathan. Marvelling that the enormous whale did not more often use its strength to smash its puny attackers, Scoresby wrote: 'But, like the rest of the lower animals, it was designed by Him who "created great whales and every living creature that moveth," to be subject to man; and, therefore, when attacked by him, it perishes by its simplicity.' I wonder if he had ever read the work of Caedmon, his fellow townsman who wrote twelve hundred years before:

> To you shall the salt water
> abide in dominion,
> and all the worldly creation
> Enjoy prosperous days,
> and the ocean freight,
> and fowls of heaven;
> to you is sacred the cattle

and the wild beasts
in dominion given,
and all living creatures,
those that tread the land,
a race endowed with life,
these which the water bringeth forth,
throughout the whale's road, all shall you obey.

CHAPTER 16

Whitby III. Whitby to Fylingdales

꙳

UP to the middle of the eighteenth century Whitby was connected to the outer world only by sea: by land routes she was one of the most isolated towns of any size in the kingdom. In 1759 the first breakthrough in a terrestrial direction occurred: a turnpike road was built over the wild moors, to Pickering. By 1788 a diligence was going along it, to York, twice a week and in 1795 a bi-weekly stage coach began to run. By 1814 a road had been driven along the coast and there was a weekly stage coach to Stockton on Tees (£1 inside, 14s out), and by 1823 the *Royal Mail* ran thrice weekly to York. All this development of transport across the desolate North Yorkshire moors was largely paid for by the proceeds of the whaling industry. But by 1830 the whaling was finished. The Greenland whale had been so dispersed by over three hundred years of persecution by the ships of a dozen nations, that it was harder and harder to find. Alternatives to whale oil for illumination had been found (notably gas and mineral oil), and the British government had ceased to pay a bounty to encourage ships to go whaling. The isolated little town of Whitby had created great wealth by the industry (as witness still the rows of fine solid Georgian and Regency houses west of the river), and in 1800 it must have been a place of enormous activity. The banks of the Esk were packed with shipyards in full production, in winter the little town thronged with captains, spectioneers, harpooners and sailors busy spending the large amounts of money that they had earned in one of the most arduous, dangerous and romantic callings in the world. In spring the bustle of victualling, storing and equipping dozens of great sailing ships for the Arctic voyage, then the months of waiting – with no chance of any word from any of the fleet until the first ship came home – and then the stirring season when ship after ship sailed into the harbour – either flags flying from every mast and the ship well down to her marks with blubber, or no flags and that dreaded calamity – a' clean ship'. Not a barrel of oil to pay for the big capital outlay and the months of effort. And sometimes the dreaded news, carried by newly arrived crews, that such and such a ship would never return. Or else, worse still,

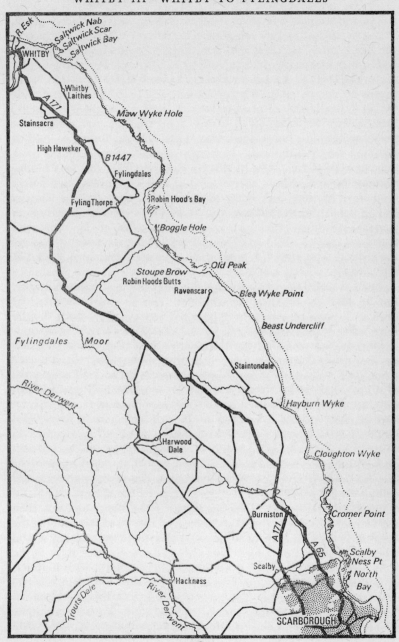

weeks and months and then years of waiting with no news at all.

But by 1830 it had all vanished. The shipyards had mostly closed, the last whaler had been sold into another trade, even the Whitby collier fleet was in the doldrums: larger ships were beginning to take the traffic and the once-great alum industry was nearly dead. A very severe depression set in. Then, on 26th May 1836 to the music of no less than five bands all playing at once (and not necessarily, we are told, always the same tune), to the reports of cannon, and in the presence of a vast crowd including ladies and gentlemen of the first fashion, the Whitby and Pickering Railway was opened with enormous rejoicing. It must not be supposed that this was a *steam* railway though. The coaches were drawn by horses, and before reaching Pickering they were uncoupled and the carriages allowed to run down the steep slope, and 'in order to gratify the company a speed of thirty miles per hour was allowed to be obtained'. Carriages loaded with water going *down*, hauled the coaches back *up* the incline, with a rope over a pulley. Charles Dickens rode on it in 1861, to visit Wilkie Collins.

This marvel of ingenuity did not solve Whitby's troubles, however, and in fact the company went broke. But it was bought up by another company and converted to steam in 1847, and Whitby began slowly to struggle back, helped partly by the jet industry.

Jet is a product of the Jurassic and has been described by geologists as fossilised drift-wood that has been altered chemically by stagnant water and subjected to enormous pressure. Some geologists have said that it probably originated from a tree resembling a Chilean pine, or Monkey-puzzle. It is much harder than coal, less easy to fracture, breaking in a conchoidal fracture rather than a cuboidal one as in coal. It is electric when rubbed, brown when cut and first exposed to the light, but weathers to jet black and can be brought to a fine polish. In the Jurassic cliffs it occurs in a layer called the Jet Rock, the best specimens occurring in the *Ammonites serpentinus* zone near the bottom of the Upper Lias. Much of it is picked up along the sea shore. If you find a piece of black stone, scrape it with a knife. If it is jet the scraped area will be brown. You will scarcely make a fortune by picking it up: a pound of it is only worth about 40p.

It has been used as an ornament from the very earliest times, having been found in Neolithic, Bronze Age and Iron Age barrows and burial places, worked into beads and ornaments, hundreds of miles away from its source in the Cleveland Hills. It must have been an object of trade. The Romans were very fond of it, and it has always been thought to have benign magical properties. Crosses carved in it are very efficacious against witchcraft and the evil eye, and according to the *Lapidarium of Marbodus* (see Hugh Kendall's excellent little Whitby Museum pamphlet *The Story of Whitby Jet*):

> The female womb its piercing fumes relieve,
> Nor epilepsy can this test deceive;
> From its deep hole it lures the viper fell,
> And chases far away the plagues of hell;
> It heals the swelling plagues that gnaw the heart,
> And baffles spells and magic's noxious art.
> This by the wise and surest test is styled,
> Of virgin purity by lust defiled.
> Three days in water steeped, the draught bestows
> Ease to the pregnant womb in travail's throes.

Unlikely as it may seem, jet came partially to the rescue of depressed Whitby after the collapse of the whaling industry, for, building up quickly after 1820, the jet mining and carving industry expanded until in 1870, fourteen hundred men and boys were employed. This was a large proportion of the working population of the town. The industry was given tremendous impetus by the death of the Prince Consort, after which Queen Victoria hung herself about with jet. In our century a rapid decline set in, and by 1921 only forty men were employed part-time. Now there is one full-time jet carver, and he works in the jet shop in Church Street, and just makes enough ornaments for his own shop. Horrifically, most of the 'Whitby Jet' ornaments sold in Whitby today are *plastic*. The decline has been mainly due to a change of fashion (after Victoria much lighter, less massive, jewellery was required), and to the importation of inferior foreign jet, which broke, or lost its shine, and gave jet a bad name, but more especially still to the imposition of purchase tax. The Whitby jet is still the best there is. Old men still prowl the beaches picking it up, and boys sometimes brave death from falling, or apprehension by the law, by hacking it out of its seam in the cliff face (this is not now allowed). Once it was mined extensively on the moors – there is a long line of spoil mounds, for example, on Hasty Bank above Stokesley, looking south towards Raisdale, and another lot above Roseberry Topping. If the right vision and skill were brought to bear on creating an entirely new style of jewellery, and if the iniquitous purchase tax were withdrawn from the products of handicraft industries, there might well be a useful revival of the craft.

Against all expectations, and contrary to the Government's

expressed policy of allowing, and indeed encouraging, the decline of Britain's smaller ports so that the traffic shall be channelled through the larger ones, the Port of Whitby is coming back into its own again. Towards the end of 1969 the biggest ship ever to enter the River Esk, the Russian timber ship *Spartak*, 1,800 tons, berthed at Endeavour Wharf.

The 700 feet of quayage of this wharf were completed in 1964, and the tonnage coming to it is expanding rapidly. Such are the doldrums in which the railways find themselves that, although lines are laid along the wharf and direct rail communication is provided to most of the destinations of incoming cargoes, the rails are rusting from want of use and huge lorries carry the goods through the over-crowded streets of the little town. Currently, a floating drill is taking cores out of the rock underlying the harbour, in order to ascertain whether it would be feasible to build a grand extension to Endeavour Wharf, thus providing more berthing accommodation for ships and a large Marina.

Whether we like these last oddly named phenomena or not, there is assuredly a great shortage of berthing space for yachts and pleasure boats right along the north-east coast. Whitby, in particular, is bad in this respect. Although perhaps the most beautiful place to lie with a yacht around the coasts of the British Isles, there is just nowhere to berth, and nowhere, really, to leave a boat at anchor in safety, without annoying other people. The Whitehall Shipyard tried to remedy this a few years ago by forming a kind of Mulberry Harbour up the river with concrete barges, but a spate came down and washed the whole conjuration, yachts tied up to it and all, under the bridge and out to sea.

If we cross the swing bridge over the Esk, and turn right along Grape Lane, past the house in which young James Cook lodged when a boy with his master Captain John Walker (the house is private, but the garret in which Cook slept is still much as he saw it, with many of its exposed timbers obviously out of old ships and put in by shipwrights), and then along the bank of the river, we come to Whitehall Shipyard, with a new 'Shipyard Club' with many flash bars with nautical-sounding names, and a lot of yachts of various kinds and sizes, either hauled up in the yard or at moorings on the mud or water.

Whitehall Shipyard is the successor to a yard that built whalers and wooden walls, and thereafter iron ships until 1907 when it closed down. No building was carried on there in the between-the-wars doldrums, but it reopened in 1943 for building ships' lifeboats (not to be confused, of course, with RNLI lifeboats which are quite a different thing), and also some 'keel boats', or Scottish-type decked fishing boats. A most ambitious scheme was then carried out of building a large slipway (still in use), and this was too much for the little firm and it went bust. In 1967 it was re-opened, and still seems to be feeling its feet. The 'Shipyard Club' is great fun and looks like being successful. The slipway is used for hauling out and repairing vessels and there is quite a bit of repairing work in the yard; some fibreglass yachts have been built but this activity seems to have lapsed, and yachts are hauled out and stored, and moored, and generally looked after.

Further up the river we come to a magnificent stone railway bridge, and over this we can walk (it is not used for its proper purpose any more) and can descend, past the gas works, to a little boatyard run by Mr Gordon Clarkson. Mr Clarkson, like his father and grandfather before him, and probably even more remote ancestors, builds cobles which are famous among fishermen all along the Northumbrian coast. He also builds excellent motor yachts with decks and cabins on similar lines to the coble (at least if not on the same lines with the same no-nonsense strong construction).

We can walk on between the river and the railway until we get back to Whitby west of the swing bridge again.

Of other things to see in Whitby, do not miss the Museum, which has good Cook and Scoresby exhibits, relics of the whale fishery and many items from far-off lands. There is an excellent collection of fossils from the Jurassic, examples of magnificently carved jet and some really impressive ships' models. Also some ghoulish head-hunters' souvenirs. We can spend hours walking about Whitby with pleasure and delight. In spite of strenuous efforts by the council vast hordes of holidaymakers do not infest the place – except for Whitby Regatta. This is a most splendid day, some time in August when the tide suits, with great events taking place on the river and people – largely pretty girls from Leeds – in colourful dresses, lining the banks, standing on every eminence and even at times sitting on the roofs. At night there is a firework display, and when all is over the swing bridge is opened and the fishing fleet – perhaps some scores of fine wooden keel boats, some local but most Scots – comes steaming through in line to go to sea and earn its living, with oil-skin-clad men standing silent on the decks. All the boats withdraw above the bridge to be out of the way for the regatta. The most picturesque part of Whitby is the jumble of steps and cottages on the steep slope between Church Street and Church Lane. It is a miracle that this has been allowed to survive. Further on along Henrietta Street are two fish-curing places, curing mostly fillets of haddock and kippers. What a pity the practice of filleting haddock for curing has come in: haddock on the bone is incomparably better.

As for writers on Whitby, Mrs Gaskell in *Sylvia's Lovers* gives a good description of the place. She lived at No. 1 Abbey Terrace in 1859. Mary Linskill (born 1840) wrote indefatigably for the SPCK, and produced many now somewhat forgotten novels about Whitby.

To leave Whitby, if we can bring ourselves to do it, we can either keep to the beach, at low tide, or walk along the cliff top. If we go below we see the Upper Lias shale exposed on the foreshore: the strata here are highly inclined and present a section of Alum Shale, Dogger and Lower Estuarine sandstone. The Dogger dips nearly to beach level and forms a terrace. You can sometimes find small tongue-shaped pockets of Dogger poking down into the Lias beneath. These are supposed to be worm burrows, and thus even in Jurassic times the humble worm was performing his beneficial office of mixing soil and subsoil. In the Dogger is a thin seam of brilliant coal. Hereabouts are many fossil plants including *Williamsonia* and *Taeniopteris vittata*. In places the Dogger has holes in it where the roots of Jurassic trees forced their way through to the Lias mud beneath.

At **Saltwick Nab**, which belongs to the National Trust, the alum shale exposed at low water is in the *Ammonites serpentinus* zone and there is an abundance of small *Aptychi*. There is a vast alum quarry above here in the cliffs. In the first sandstone bed above the Dogger as we climb up this are *Unio kendalli*, a big fresh-water mussel, and the footmarks of three-toed saurians have been found.

On Saltwick Nab, on 30th October 1914, the hospital ship *Rohilla* went ashore in a gale. Aboard were 229 people including five female nurses. The Whitby men tried to launch their Number One lifeboat but failed, and so dragged their Number Two, a smaller vessel, over the eight-foot seawall and across the rocks to the shore near the wreck, launched her and saved the five nurses and twelve men. A second journey saved another eighteen, but after this the lifeboat was too battered to be used again. Meanwhile, the survivors on board the *Rohilla* were clinging to the ship for their lives, for the seas were crashing right over her. The Upgang lifeboat was sent for, and was dragged on wheels through Whitby and lowered down the cliffs, but launching was found to be quite impossible. The boats from Scarborough and Teesmouth were then towed along the coast by tugs, but they found it impossible to approach the ship under oars alone. Finally the new motor lifeboat from Tynemouth arrived under her own steam and managed to save all the remaining men, the last of whom had been clinging to the sea-swept wreck for fifty hours. The Tynemouth boat had to pour oil on the troubled waters before she could get alongside.

I cannot recommend walking along the beach though from Whitby, other than just to go and look for fossils, because the rocky beach is narrow, the cliffs steep, and we are liable to be beset by the tide. A better plan is to climb the 199 steps from the town leading up to St Mary's (or walk up the 'Donkeys' Path' beside them) and proceed along the cliff-top. Above Saltwick Bay is a small holiday village, with a site for tents which, we are assured, is *sprayed against earwigs*. For me – camping would not be quite the same. Some way past the lighthouse is a hill, to the south of which are Whitby Laithes. These are stones marking the spot where Robin Hood's arrows fell when he was invited by the Abbot of Whitby to shoot from the tower of the Abbey to display his prowess. I've never been able to find them. At **Maw Wyke Hole** is a waterfall, and beyond it another streak of bright coal in the cliff face. This word *wyke* by the way, meaning one of the steep narrow clefts which cut the country here, is from the Norse *vik*, a sea creek.

If we cut inland, to the B1447 road, we find St Abba's Well, with a verse on it in dialect of the direst. If the frogs don't object we can taste of its waters. If we stick to the cliff-top we suddenly come to a most splendid view – that of Robin Hood's Bay (the bay not the town) with its beautiful sweep round to the bold headland of Ravenscar.

The town of **Robin Hood's Bay**, or **Bay Town** as its inhabitants call it, is an almost unbelievable little place. Like its smaller edition Runswick, like Staithes, and like part of Whitby, its houses cling to a steep, steep hill, so that you look out of your bedroom windows over the chimneys of the house below. By all means go and see Bay Town, it is one of the most amazing places in England. A motorable road, if one-in-three is motorable, goes down to the bottom of it, but I cannot plead too strongly for the casual tourist to leave his car resolutely at the top. The extraordinary charm of the place is quickly shattered by motor-cars, and the congestion down this narrow, steep hill can be terrible.

As we go down we find side paths striking off mainly to the left and sometimes to the right. These are the paths that must be explored. Here again we catch the whiff of whale blubber: many of the better-class houses in Bay Town (locally called 'Captains' houses') were paid for by money from the whale fishery. These houses, although not big, are solid and substantial, and seventeenth and eighteenth or early nineteenth century. Most of them have a back door on a higher street from the front door. They are jumbled together in a most fantastic fashion, and the little alleyways and steep stairs wind among them. Some have figure-heads in their minuscule gardens, but few have gardens. They have nearly all now been bought up by fairly wealthy people who holiday and weekend in them, or else live retired, or else make pots or paint pictures. Dame Ethel Walker kept her court here every summer until she died in 1950. Robin Hood's Bay was once a place of fishermen. There is no professional fisherman left here now.

As we wind our way about these extraordinary alleyways we will see a sad sight: houses cracked in half and busy falling into the sea. Bay Town is built on a foundering cliff, a slithering mass of boulder clay, and the wonder of it is that it has not slithered into the sea centuries ago. Much of it has in fact: it is said that 193 houses have gone over the cliff in 202 years. Old paintings indicate that the shore was much further to seaward a couple of hundred years ago than it is now. Some work has been done down below at sea defences, to stop the base of the sliding clay morain from being washed away, and currently it is being considered whether it is worth spending a quarter of a million pounds on saving the rest.

Why Robin Hood's Bay? There is a legend that Robin Hood, when in this vicinity, kept boats in readiness in the bay in which to make a getaway if too hard pressed on land. There is another tale that Richard, Abbot of Whitby, asked Robin Hood to help him to repulse Danish pirates. A hundred of these latter tried to climb the cliffs and Robin and his men rolled boulders down on them and shot them with arrows and killed seventy of them, losing seven of their own number. It was after this exploit that the Abbot is said to have invited the band to a feast and then watched them shoot their arrows from the tower of the abbey. Abbot Richard ruled from 1148 to 1178. This legend is related by Charlton in his *History of Whitby* of 1779.

Apart from Robin and his Merry Men, it is related in a letter written by Sir Richard Colmley to the Earl of Shrewsbury, that 'the men of Robynhodbay' drove off a marauding party of Scotsmen. Leland, in the reign of Henry VIII, wrote that Baytown was 'a fischer tounelet of twenty bootes with Dok or Bosom of a mile yn length'. In 1817 there were five big yawls here, called 'Five Man Boats', each carrying about 58 tons, 46 foot long, 16 foot beam, clinker-built, decked, with three masts setting four lug sails, each carrying five or six men and two or three small cobles carried on deck. These, in the winter, would sail out to the Dogger Bank, launch the cobles, and the men would go off in these, long-lining. These long lines were in 'pieces' of 60 fathoms, six pieces making one line, with a snood and hook every two and a half feet. There would be fifteen lines in each coble.

At about Christmas the big luggers were laid up, as the Bank became too rough for fishing, and the men got out their big winter cobles and continued long-lining inshore. When the herring season came along again, in summer, the luggers were got into commission again and would join the herring fleet, up north, or wait until the shoals got to the Whitby area, and then follow the herring down (*up* in seaman's talk) for the Yarmouth herring voyage in late summer and autumn.

Many men went whaling from Bay Town, but when this finished they put their money into trading vessels, each man buying so many shares in a new ship. In 1806 the Robin Hood's Bay Mutual Shipping Insurance Company was floated, and by 1867 was insuring £94,300 worth of Bay Town-owned shipping! At one time 174 ships were owned mainly by Bay men, some of them going up to nearly 300 tons and worth £1,700. Some of these were colliers, others traded to the Baltic, Mediterranean, and even to the Americas.

The people of Bay Town tended to belong to a few families: Duke, Bedlington, Todd and Storm being common names. Forty-three Storms are recorded as having died at sea. One winter day in 1843 the lifeboat capsized and six men were drowned.

There were many great rescues performed by Bay men. Ravenscar was particularly dangerous and it was even alleged (wrongly) that the masses of iron ore somewhere here must have deflected the compass needles of ships. The sailing ship *Visitor* was one famous wreck. She was a ship of 209 tons, one of her sixteen owners being a Bay Town man. She left Shields towards London on 16th January 1881, with Captain Anderson and five men. At four p.m. she was off Flamborough Head, the wind came in easterly with snow and she lost all her sails save her main top and main staysail. By two a.m. the next day she had managed to run back to Robin Hood's Bay and off there she dropped anchor. The ship foundered, however, and her crew took to the longboat, but in this they had no chance of getting through the breakers. The Bay Town lifeboat was imme-diately launched – but driven back with most of her oars smashed. The Whitby lifeboat was then dragged overland to the shore near the wreck, launched, and the Bay men waded and swam into the sea ahead of her to show her a clear way through the rocks. She managed to get through the breakers, alongside the longboat, and all the men were saved.

On 26 January 1860 ten ships were driven aground at Ness Point. Twenty-three carpenters were later employed to patch them up and many of them were refloated.

Bay Town *looks* as if it ought to be the haunt of smugglers, and there is no doubt whatever that it *was*. None of the old Bay Town people now will admit that their ancestors, not long ago, engaged in this trade (personally I should be proud of it), nor is it easy to persuade one of them to show you a piece of the lace which he or she possesses and which came into this country without troubling the Water Guard. But the facts of the case are well documented. The fact that the Major of Dragoons who had his headquarters at York stationed an NCO and six men permanently at Robin Hood's Bay speaks for itself. (He stationed two men at Sandsend, two at Hinderwell, two at Runswick, and four at Staithes. So Bay Town headed the list.) And in his reports he was constantly complaining that his men at Bay Town were being got at. On 6th October 1779 the excisemen captured 200 casks of brandy and gin, 150 bags of tea, a chest of blunderbusses and cartridges for twenty men near Robin Hood's Bay, but the smugglers attacked them and retook it all but a few bags of tea. When the revenue men entered Bay Town for the purpose of arresting men, they several times had boiling water poured on their heads from upper windows, and in any case one only has to look at the place to realise what a hopeless task it would be to find somebody who didn't want to be found there. Every house in the jumbled terraces has a 'smuggler's cupboard': a cupboard, up-stairs, on the party wall with the next house, with a thin wooden partition between it and the next house, where is an adjoining cupboard there too. It is said that a man, or a bag of goods, could be got from the bottom of the town through these cupboards to the top without seeing the light of day. There were dragoons stationed here as late as 1830.

Several of the big ships owned by Bay men were heavily armed and fitted out quite openly as free traders. There were many complaints by the captains of revenue cutters that they had come up with a smuggler at sea and, seeing that they were completely out-gunned, had had to sail away and leave her. During the latter half of the seventeenth century and for most of the eighteenth, the smugglers had their way almost completely, and if battles were fought the smugglers generally won them. But towards the end of the eighteenth century the Government decided that this was a battle it had got to win, and it sent vessels of the Royal Navy to help, and the free traders found things getting too hot for them and had to abandon their big ships and big guns and smuggle, if at all, by stealth. One of the greatest smugglers of this coast was George Fagg, commonly known as 'Stoney', owner and captain of the *Kent*, 200 tons, built at Dungeness, who had successfully held off both revenue cutters and naval vessels on several occasions, met his Trafalgar on 7th July 1777. He was sailing past Filey when he was hailed by two revenue cutters. He shouted 'Fire you . . . and be damned to you!' They did, and a battle ensued that Stoney, as usual, would have won, but for the arrival on the scene of two of His Majesty's frigates, the *Pelican* and the *Arethusa*. One of these quickly shot his mast through, he struck, and was taken into Hull a captive. The *Kent* was found to have sixteen four-pounders, twenty swivel guns, a big stock of muskets and blunderbusses, and plenty of powder and shot. She also had 1,974 half-anker tubs of spirits (nearly 8,000 gallons), and 550 oilskin bags of tea. Her mainmast was 77 feet tall, her main boom 57 feet long. The ship and tackle without the cargo were valued at £1,405. *Smugglers' Britain*, by G. Bernard Wood, is a mine of information on this subject.

Another channel of smuggled goods into the town are the strange streams that run beneath it all. The King's Beck, the biggest of these, runs into the sea just by what was the coble landing, and, if you have a torch, you can follow this and its tributaries up, in their underground windings, and note where holes that used to connect with the houses up above have been bricked up. No doubt these holes were used for drains – but for other things too. It is the fashion nowadays to cluck our tongues over the smugglers, and say what wicked men they were, but in fact they did nothing but good. The things they smuggled were all things that could not be produced in England anyway, such as tea, brandy, wine and Hollands gin, and the result of the smugglers' activities was simply to make these good things available to poorer people. No wonder that they had practically the whole country on their side.

Leo Walmsley, author of *Love in the Sun*, *Three Fevers*, and other novels, lived in a house down near the Bay Hotel, there is a plaque to mark the house, and this house, a typical one, was built in 1620. Higher up in the town is 'The Square', which is not square at all, where Wesley preached nine times. There is the plaque of an insurance company on a wall here – painted over in some horrible colour by the new owner of the house – how can people be so crass? People who lose respect for the past make a pig's ear of the future. Of other strange bits of Bay Town information: in 1893 a ship called the *Romulus* was driven ashore and her bowsprit went through a window of the Bay Hotel! The University of Leeds has its marine laboratory down near the landing in what was the coastguard station. The landing is called Fisherhead. One or two strange bow-shaped windows are said to be 'coffin windows', and in them the coffins of the dead were laid for people to file by and pay their last respects. Dead lemmings get washed up here from time to time – having, presumably, foolishly committed themselves to the deep the other side of the North Sea. The Black Plague hit Robin Hood's Bay in 1603, three years before it hit London on that particular occasion, so London is not first in everything.

Go, by all means, to the little old church of St Stephen's back along the Hawsker Road, whether you are interested in churches or not. This small place was closed down for years, as a big new church was built in Victorian times, but it was reopened in 1943 and is worth seeing. Firstly, there is a magnificent view across the Bay from its rough old churchyard, secondly it is full of box pews of 1821 in which the faithful could bow their heads – or abstain from bowing their heads – at the name of Jesus, as it suited their consciences, without being observed by prying neighbours, thirdly there are strange little objects hung up from the ceiling in the chancel, looking rather like bats. These are what is left of white gloves and garlands. These were carried by two virgins at the funerals of some girl who had died as a virgin. The last ones were carried at the funeral of Janey Levitt in 1859. There is a three-decker pulpit in this church, about half way up the nave, so that half the congregation had their backs to the east end and were thus not guilty of *East-worship*, and their backs to the table that had taken the place of the altar and thus not be guilty of *table worship*. There is a model of the SS *Pretoria*, built in 1900 for Whitby.

Fyling Thorpe, just inland, in the parish of which lies Robin Hood's Bay, is a charming stone village. Here is what is claimed to be the busiest shipyard in the world. It is Mr and Mrs Milsom's factory for making ships in bottles, helped by about twenty girls. Most of these models – over twenty thousand last year – go to America.

I must mention a most pleasant walk over the moors for anybody who would like to turn his back on the sea for a little while, and this is the 'Fish Road', 'Salt Road', or 'Robin Hood's Bay Road' which

crosses the desolate Fylingdales Moor to Saltersgate on the Whitby–
Pickering Road, and which is not a road but a cart track. Saltersgate has a well-documented history of smuggling, and the inn there,
once the *Waggon and Horses*, dates from 1650. High up on those
moors is a collection of vast silver spheres that look like an invasion
from another planet. These are components of the Fylingdales
Early Warning Station. This feeds information to Dewline (Defence
Early Warning System) at its operations centre at Colorado Springs,
to which it is linked by at least three cable or wireless routes. It is
planned to give fifteen minutes' warning to the United States of an
impending rocket attack by unspecified persons to the east. It is the
exact equivalent of the Roman signal stations along the 'Saxon
Shore', examples of which we have met, and another somewhat
decayed example of which we are due to meet at Ravenscar.

Fylingdales was Figelinge in Domesday. *Fygela* was Old English
for marshy ground.

CHAPTER 17

Robin Hood's Bay to Scarborough

❧

ROBIN HOOD'S BAY (and if I lived there I would say 'thank God!') has not got miles of yellow sand, but rock and sandy mud. The giant cliffs of Yorkshire here give way to low sliding mud cliffs of boulder clay overlying the Lower Lias, and Lower Lias fossils are to be found in the fallen boulders strewn about the bay. Competition among fossil hunters is here a bit keen though, and you are apt to see them grazing along the bottom of the cliff like a flock of sheep. The Bay is geologically important, being the axis of the Main Cleveland Anticline.

Mill Beck tumbles out at Boggle Hole, where is a charming youth hostel in an old water-mill. Over the cliff at Stoupe Brow we are told by Bigland in his *History of Yorkshire* that in 1809 a lady and two men were travelling in a post-chaise over Stoup Brow to Scarborough, and the driver stopped the carriage on the top of a steep hill and left the box for a moment. The horses ran away and fell over a hundred foot cliff of which forty feet was a vertical wall of rock. Neither passengers, horses, nor carriage were hurt. Bigland was shown the very place by a 'respectable person', who told him that the carriage rolled over three times. This story strikes me as being so unlikely that it is probably true.

In Robin Hood's Bay we can get beset by the tide, but can probably save ourselves by getting a foothold on the muddy sliding cliffs, but if we climb up them we may sink in places in quagmires to our knees. At Boggle Hole there is a road up, and we can walk along the cliff top, or, if we like, the old railway track, which is good for walking along or for horse riding. The enormous quarries alongside the railway track were brick quarries. We come to the Peakside Riding and Trekking headquarters, where, if we are footsore, we may perhaps hire a horse. This comparatively level area here between the steep cliffs inland and the sea is a sort of Shangri-la of a place, with a few fortunate farms with rolling green acres, growing oats and barley, or good grass. Inland the cliffs rise quickly to the moors and eight hundred feet above sea level, a terrain peppered all over with tumuli. The most notable of these are Robin Hood's

Butts, Bronze Age, 95 feet in diameter and eighteen feet high. A cinerary urn was found in them and flint knives and a bone pin. In 1961 a geological student found the bones of a *Plesiosaur* in the cliffs about here and the animal now resides at Manchester University. In the cliff at Ravenscar outcrop thin seams of coal.

Ravenscar was, as we have seen, part of the Dewline system of Imperial Rome. When the foundations of what is now the Raven Hall Hotel were being excavated the foundations of a Roman watchtower were exposed, with a stone inscribed, but in Latin: 'Justinian Governor of the Province and Vindicianus prefect of soldiers built this fort.' The stone is now in Whitby Museum. There is a model of what the fort probably looked like, in Scarborough Museum. This excavating was done in 1774, when a large private house, Raven Hall, was being built for a Captain Childs. The fort is believed to have been built in about AD 406.

The cliff rises dramatically at Ravenscar, and there is a bold headland jutting out into the sea called the old Peak, or South Cheek. This transposition from low crumbling cliffs to high bold ones is due to the Peak Fault, which has a throw of a hundred feet. The Lower Lias Shale gives way here, as we go south, to Upper Lias Shale right down at the bottom of the cliffs, surmounted by Dogger, and above this Lower Shale and Sandstone, capped with Oolite and this again capped with Upper Shale and Sandstone. We can climb the cliff just to the north of Ravenscar, and if we intend to continue south we had *better* climb it, for the beach beyond here is about the worst walking in the world. For four miles to Hayburn Wyke, the beach, when there is a beach, is piled high with boulders, large and small. At times it is necessary to clamber over boulder piles as high as a house. These boulders are slippery with seaweed and covered at high tide. There are a few places where, if you know them, you can clamber up the cliff, but there are many more where you could be beset by the tide and quickly drowned unless help came. I have walked this stretch of coast, but do not recommend it to the infirm. And of course to break a leg, or even twist an ankle here, would most probably be fatal. There is this you could be sure of – no one would ever come along and see you, and, owing to the shape of the cliffs, you would neither be seen nor heard from the deserted country up above and the tide would inexorably continue to rise.

The Raven Hall Hotel is large and grand, and has a golf course, but indifferent access to the sea. Fine views though. South of it is a strange never-never land, where tarred roads peter out into the grassland, and vegetation slowly recaptures its lost country, for here was an ambitious scheme, early this century, for 'developing' a seaside housing estate. The roads were laid down, drains and pavements made, but the hideous seaside 'villas' never came. This was to have been another Frinton. But it lacked a sandy beach: the child's delight and the nursemaid's boon.

At **Blea Wyke Point** it is just possible, if you know the way, to scramble up or down the cliffs. And here we may gain access, if we are athletic enough, to the strangest piece of country along the East Coast: the Beast Undercliff. This is a stretch of level land, three miles long, heavily wooded and having two small lakes in it. On one side of it the vertical cliff climbs up to the high country above, on the other it plunges down vertically to the boulder-strewn beach at low tide, or the thundering sea at high. A Robinson Crusoe could well live out his life here. He would have water to drink, plenty of wood to burn and build his hut with, rabbits and pigeons and seabirds to shoot and plenty of good level soil that could be tilled to grow the corn, the seed of which he would no doubt find in the lining of his pocket. He could fling his fishing line from his cliff-girt world into the very sea itself and haul out cod or haddock. He would practically never be disturbed. Very few people ever visit the Lost World of the undercliff. You can lower yourself down to it from above, or in places clamber up to it from below, but it is not an easy place to get to. It is, perhaps, one of the most richly fossiliferous stretches in England, but I don't suppose our Robinson Crusoe would be very interested in fossils.

But whether along the cliff top, or risking our lives below, when we achieve **Hayburn Wyke** we have come to a splendid place. There is a delightful little bay here, accessible by steep path from the top, there is shingle and easy walking, just above the shingle, in the Lower Estuarine Beds here, beautiful plant fossils can be found, and up above the Wyke itself is beautifully wooded with fine trees. Here too we can refresh ourselves, at the most excellent Hayburn Wyke Hotel: a place that I can most unreservedly recommend.

The rock beach south of Hayburn Wyke is as difficult as that north of it, and even more quickly covered by the tide, and I must strongly recommend the cliff top. For one thing, from an eminence near the cliff here one gets the most splendid views, not only out to sea and along the cliffs, but also inland towards the moors. At **Cloughton Wyke** is an easy path to the little bay below. At Crook Ness, half a mile south of the coastguard station, is a concrete path down the cliff, with a fine beach, part rock part clean sand, below.

At Cromer Point is a fine rock formation (I can recommend walking along the beach from here on), and a place called Sailor's Grave, and beautiful places for lighting a fire with driftwood, in the shelter of the fine cliffs, and cooking a meal. North of the rugged rocks of Scalby Ness a sewer disgustingly and wastefully utters its contents into the sea, and then we come to the vertically-sided Wyke that carries the Burniston Beck, and Sea Dyke, to the North Sea. We have suddenly arrived at **Scarborough**.

Half a mile up the beck is a youth hostel, and Scalby Manor which is a hotel. Along the beach is Scarborough's **North Bay**, which has every delight, including a large miniature railway (if you can have large miniatures), a water chute, a great model railway, a Chinese (or is it Japanese?) garden, boating lakes, children's playgrounds of every kind of elaboration, miniature naval battles, a splendid little zoo and – most important of all – PERFORMING DOLPHINS! There is just nothing on the land or the sea to beat a dolphin.

Scarborough's publicity department modestly claims that their town has *everything*, and really it is very hard to argue with them. It has two most splendid beaches, one sheltered from the north and the other from the south, it has a busy fishing harbour, a commercial harbour, a spa with some of the filthiest-tasting water this side of Droitwich, a ruined castle, a large fresh-water lake, a whole street-ful of Original and Only Gypsy Lees to tell your fortune, which I am told is always encouraging, bingo to satiate the most extravagant appetite, theatres, revues, comics with noses of the most rubicund, dances and concerts and donkeys galore. It is, indeed, very hard to think of anything that Scarborough hasn't got. And it has what is certainly the finest natural setting of any seaside resort in Britain, for wherever you are, you are sure to see the backcloth of that wonderful Castle Hill, with its castle on top of it, and one or the other of those two sweeping and magnificent bays.

Castle Hill is a result of two most spectacular geological faults, resulting in a great bluff of rock, Oxford Clay below but protected by Calcareous Grit and Coralline Oolite above, jutting out into the sea, with very steep slopes below, and vertical cliffs above, and cut off from the mainland, as it were, by a deep dry cleft. This place was an obvious choice first for a Roman signal station, and next for an Anglian, Norse and then a Norman castle. Scarborough gets its name from the Norse – probably from *Skarthi* – the hair-lipped, according to Prof. Moorman.

The bluff is just under three hundred feet high, and more than half of its perimeter needed no fortification at all, being vertical cliff. The Romans built their tower at a point from which the coast could be commanded for many miles in both directions. Before they had come there was a settlement there of late Bronze Age people (some say Iron Age), for bits of horse furniture, pottery, pins and bronze tools have been found there. It is impossible not to believe that Iron Age people settled there also, knowing their predilection for making settlements on such sites. The Roman signal tower was built at the end of the Roman occupation, when Roman Britain was being hard pressed by Anglian invasion: the Roman Dewline had a very short life.

There is not much evidence of Anglian occupation (except a chapel) but in King Stephen's reign the castle was already begun, and before the death of Henry I in 1135, William Le Gros, Earl of Albemarle, had already built a castle. Le Gros defeated the Scots at the Battle of the Standard near Northallerton, and thus became top dog in the North. Henry II attacked and captured the castle, and kept it in hand, and since then it has always been a royal castle. The King pulled down le Gros's gate-tower, and between 1158 and 1168 built the big keep, which still survives. He built a bank and a ditch east of the keep, thus making an inner defensive box. King John came here four times, and improved the place greatly, and Henry III and Edward I carried the work further. It was under them that the existing gate was built.

The castle has withstood, and has failed to withstand, many attacks. The unpopular favourite of Edward II, Piers Gaveston, was put in charge of it, the barons didn't like him, and in 1312 they besieged the castle, it surrendered, and Gaveston was taken off to Oxford where he was beheaded. In 1343 the barbican was built, defending the drawbridge over the natural chasm formed by the two faults. In 1536 the castle was besieged by Robert Aske and defended by Sir Ralph Evers. Aske was leading an army in the Pilgrimage of Grace, Evers was defending for the king: the castle got badly bashed about by cannon fire but the garrison held. In 1653 another attempt was made on it, this time temporarily successful. Thomas Stafford, who had royal pretensions, being descended from Edward III, angry that Queen Mary should have married the king of Spain, captured the castle by simply walking into it with thirty companions disguised as peasants and proclaimed himself Protector of the Realm. This did him no good for within a week the castle was taken away from him by the Earl of Westmorland and he was beheaded on Tower Hill.

But it was in 1644 that Scarborough Castle's adventures really began. Sir Hugh Cholmley, whom we met at Whitby, was its governor, at first under Parliament, but he suddenly decided to declare for the king. From February 1644 to July 1645 he held out with a small garrison against the Parliamentary army under Sir John Meldrum and Sir Matthew Boynton. Sir John, we read, ascending a rock to reconnoitre, upon a sudden: 'had his hat blown off, which he labouring to recover, his coat was blown over his head, and striving to get it down, the wind blew him over, head foremost down the cliff.' This spectacle must have caused the Royalists considerable edification. Meldrum, however, was a valiant officer and led several assaults against the castle; in the last he was mortally wounded. Sir Matthew Boynton took over the command, and on the 25th July 1645 the garrison surrendered, obtaining honourable terms and were allowed to march out with banners flying and drums beating. Only scurvy and starvation had beaten them: the castle had withstood repeated attempts at storm and escalade, and the pounding of cannon, including a battery on Peaseholm ('Roll Egg Hill'), guns in St Mary's church, and one very big cannon: a thirty-six pounder.

The House of Commons voted £5,000 for the repair of the castle, and put another Boynton, a colonel, in command of it. Sir Matthew Boynton had died. This man, as Sir Hugh had done before him, rashly changed sides and declared for the king. Parliament, having had enough of attacking Scarborough Castle, offered him a cool £4,000 if he would surrender. He would not. They then shot a printed order into the castle to the soldiers, offering them a thousand to divide between them if they would surrender. They would not. So another siege commenced, led by Colonel Bethel with his headquarters at Falsgrave, and on 15th December 1648 Colonel Boynton capitulated. Hundreds of skulls, many with musket balls in them, were once dug up from a place called Charnel Garth, which was in the grounds of that grandiose piece of nineteenth-century Gothic building over the road from St Mary's. This is now a children's home, but empty at the time of writing.

Then, after the '45 Rebellion, the castle was re-fortified, and barracks for 120 officers and men constructed. These were knocked flat on 16th December 1914 when the German battle cruisers *Derflinger* and *Von de Tann* fired over five hundred shells into Scarborough, on the same voyage in which they paid similar attention to Whitby Abbey and Hartlepool.

For the rest, George Fox was immured for a year in the castle, under the most cruel conditions, for being a Quaker, and then released. Scarborough seems to have been a place for early Quakers, incidentally: one Richard Sellars was caught by the Press Gang between Scarborough piers and taken aboard a man-of-war. 'Take the Quakerly dog away and put him to the capstan!' ordered the captain, after Sellars had been flogged, but work at the handspikes he would not, and was flogged again, and put in irons. But however hard the officers were on him the ratings and petty officers were kinder, and eventually the entire crew refused to flog or torment the poor Quaker further, and the captain had to let him go to avoid a mutiny. Sellars then agreed to do work on the ship if it had nothing to do with killing. The ship engaged the enemy and the Quaker distinguished himself in valour and smartness, all was forgiven, and he was eventually put ashore and given his freedom.

But, back to the castle, what do we see when we actually go there, and pay our 9p over to the Ministry of Works? We enter the barbican, which is a small castle in itself: a foothold on the mainland, as it were, but capable of being cut off, if it fell, from the main fortifications by two drawbridges, now replaced by arches of stone. Over the defended bridges, with their deep dry natural moat beneath, we find ourselves confronted with the massive donjon, or keep, of Henry II, a splendid piece of high Norman architecture, though split in half by time (and possibly the Roundheads). The stone for this came from Hayburn Wyke. To the south of the keep there is an inner bailey, with a well in it 7 feet in diameter, 177 foot deep, and for the first 68 foot lined with stone. It is a strange well, for after going down beyond its masonry lining it becomes a square for 20 feet, then is round for the remainder of the 177. When it was excavated it had buried in it iron cannon balls, pottery, forged farthings of Charles I's time and moulds for forging silver coins. Someone had evidently been earning an honest living in the castle and had had to throw the tools of his trade precipitately down the well out of sight.

Keeping on the northwards we can follow the curtain wall until it peters out on the brink of the vertical cliff, and walk out to the headland, follow the cliff edge round until we come to the remains of the Roman signal station with the medieval chapel superimposed. This is a little hard to decipher, until we realise that the signal stations along this coast were all quite regular in shape: a square within a square – the outer square being a *foss* and *vallum*, the inner a multi-storied tower. The foundations of this can clearly be seen, but they are cut into in an eccentric manner by the foundations of first an Anglian chapel of about 1000, and then a Norman chapel built by William le Gros. Harold Hardrada apparently destroyed the Anglian chapel when he sacked Scarborough so thoroughly in 1066 that it didn't even have a mention in Domesday Book. There is a well just north-east of the signal-station-cum-chapels – Our Lady's Well. This was considered to be miraculous, in that it had water in it at all (being right near the edge of a precipitous cliff – and the water was ten feet from the surface), but without wishing to be iconoclastic, my own belief is that the presence of pervious coralline oolite and calcareous grit on top of impervious Oxford clay might have had something to do with this.

We continue our walk along the cliff edge, and come to the southernmost point where we encounter the curtain wall again. Here was, but is no longer because it has fallen down the cliff, a tower that some people say was Cockhill Tower and some say Charles's. It was supposed to have been in here that poor George Fox was incarcerated. Walking along inside the curtain wall, which has been so very much knocked about in various campaigns, and patched in red brick after the '45, we come to a sally port, then a large building called Mosdale Hall, which was probably started in King John's reign but completed about 1400 when John Mosdale was governor of the castle. It has the general form of a medieval hall and offices. After the '45 rebellion a huge brick barracks was built in it and it was this that was completely destroyed by the Germans in 1914. If we clamber up on the curtain wall here (which is disallowed) we get magnificent views over Scarborough – and they *are* magnificent. We really have to agree with everything the publicity department says about the place.

Sortieing again from the Barbican we can walk down the hill towards St Mary's church, and go into the little graveyard over the road from the church, to its east, to pay our respects, after so much militarism, to that most peaceful person Anne Brontë. She died on 28th May 1849, in the presence of Charlotte, at No. 2 The Cliff, Scarborough (pulled down to make way for that Babylonian extravaganza the Grand Hotel) and here is her simple grave. The church is large and interesting. It was much knocked about in the Civil War, when artillery was fired from its east window and counter-fire completely destroyed the east end.

A most pleasant walk now is up to the castle gate again, and turn right down a good path that slants down the Castle Dykes, outside the curtain wall, to the Harbour. There are two harbour basins, one the Old Harbour, with its West Pier given over to a fish landing, with a big fish auction and a large fleet of keel boats, trawlers and seiners, and a few big cobles. Coasters and small ships discharge timber and other incoming cargoes on Sandside, to the north of the Old Harbour. There is 500 feet of quayage here, four large mobile cranes, two belt-conveyors for grain, timber clamps capable of discharging up to a hundred standards of timber a day, but no storage facilities. Occasionally some barley is exported. The entrance to this harbour, which is an easy one, is 70 feet wide with about 15 foot draught at high spring tides and 12 at neaps. The harbour dries out. It is controlled by Scarborough Borough Council, and since 1964 has made a profit.

Above the harbour, steeply up the hill, run *The Bolts*, narrow stepped passages, equivalent of *The Scores* of Lowestoft and *The Rows* of Great Yarmouth. The East Harbour is for yachts, mostly, and various working boats or fishing boats that have been put out of the way.

The Old Harbour was built in the thirteenth century. The East Pier was completed in 1815, the West Pier in 1817. There is a yacht club in the base of the lighthouse.

Travelling south we pass the Futurist Theatre at which Mr Ken Dodd is the presiding genius when it is not occupied by the egregious 'Black and White Minstrels', and the rest of Scarborough's 'golden mile'. We can turn inland (there is a cliff railway to take us up) to look at the museum, which is in a splendid building, purpose-built for this job in Victorian times, and the art gallery, wherein is a splendid portrait of that magnificent soldier Sir Hugh Cholmley, who held out so long in Scarborough Castle, by Peter Lely, and a fine fellow Sir Hugh looks too. Scarborough has had several good painters: H. B. Carter in the 1830s and '40s painted nice shipping scenes, John Dunthorne (1793–1832) was assistant to Constable and painted well in his own right too, in a Constable-esque manner.

Certainly go along the Crescent a few yards and look at 'Woodend', the house in which the Sitwells led their aesthetic existence. This is now a natural history museum, of strong local interest, there is a vivarium which has, amongst many other creatures, a tankful of *blind cave fish*: almost as intriguing as dolphins – although nothing like as intelligent. What do they *think* about? There is a Sitwell Room, full of relics of the three illustrious siblings. Sir George Reresby Sitwell, their father, was M.P. for Scarborough in 1885 and 1886, and again for three years after 1892. He witnessed the coronation of the Tsar and captured a ghost at the headquarters of the Spiritualists, in London, in 1880, but history does not relate what he did with it. Osbert wrote *Before the Bombardment* about Scarborough,

Sacheverell *All in a Summer Day* and Edith much poetry. Edith and Sacheverell were born at Woodend.

Back to the shore, and we must notice the great Valley Bridge, and the even more spectacular Cliff Bridge, 414 feet long and opened on 19 July 1827, and then we must make the plunge to the Spa. There are many steps, but for the halt and the lame a cliff railway. Smollett made Humphrey Clinker grumble about the arduous ascent. He would not have to grumble now. The Spa is a vast building, and in it in the winter time you are liable to find yourself caught up with several hundred members of the Union of White Collared Workers who are having their annual conference. In the summer there is everything from all-in wrestling to Old Time Party Nights.

The Spa water was discovered by a Mrs Farrow in 1620. Various buildings were erected over the spot, the fame of 'The Waters' grew, on 17th February 1836 the Spa (always, of course, pronounced – and indeed sometimes spelt – *spaw*) was blown by a gale into the sea. In 1860 Sir Joseph Paxton, the architect of the Great Exhibition, remodelled the building. On 8th September 1876 the place burnt down, but was rebuilt. Sir Edwin Cooper added to it in 1913. In the 1920s a typically 1920s addition was made. The Germans shelled the Spa when they shelled the castle.

And what of The Waters now? They are completely unregarded. If you go down on to the beach, beneath the ice cream kiosk that stands on the promenade at the north end of the building, you will find a small niche of a classical character in the prom. wall, and this has a piece of rusty pipe sticking out of it, and out of this issues a dribble of water which runs away on to the beach un-drunk and unregarded. It tastes quite disgusting.

Pre-Raphaelite-lovers will wish to cut inland here to visit St Martin's Church, wherein the glass is all by Morris and Co and there is an *Annunciation* by Rossetti.

On 12th August 1688 the Mayor was tossed in a blanket, by the orders of one Captain Ouseley. Bartholomew Johnson, born 1710 and died a hundred and four years later, was for seventy years a town wait, and played the cello on his hundredth birthday. John Owston was coxswain of the lifeboat until he retired in 1912. He received a pension and a gratuity, two silver mounted pipes from King Edward, many medals, and once, in October 1880, he launched five times to different vessels that had driven ashore in a tremendous gale, and got every one of their crews off, twenty-eight men in all.

And what can be found inland from Scarborough? Well, there is Scarborough Mere, with very good coarse fishing and speedboating. Just above it is a motor-cycle racing circuit. Above that again Oliver's Mount, with the War Memorial, from which the most magnificent view can be had of a magnificently sited town.

Inland further is the most beautiful countryside imaginable, with big forests, moors, and steep-cut dales. Botanists can look here for rare plants such as Dwarf Cornel (*Cornus suecica*) on the north-facing slopes of the Hole of Horcum (the southern limit of its range), Yellow Star of Bethlehem (*Gagea lutea*) at Yedmandale and found nowhere else, May Lily (*Maianthemum bifolium*) near Hackness on north-facing rim of the valley.

Above, Robin Hood's Bay; *below*, the coast at Staithes.

Above, Scarborough Bay from the south; *below*, Filey Brigg.

CHAPTER 18

Scarborough to Bridlington

❧

South, past a lush 'residential area' if we are on top of the cliffs, and we come to White Nab, where a sewer discharges into the sea (surely it is time we started conserving instead of wasting all this potentially valuable NPK?), and we come to a weird cliff landscape of slithering mud and stricken trees, and rocks called Perilous stand out to sea. Osgodby Point bars our progress along the beach except at the lowest tide. Around it **Cayton Cliff** is well wooded and pleasant, although very muddy in wet weather. There are signs up to tell us to keep out or we shall be devoured by guard dogs, but I have never yet encountered any of these ferocious animals. Like Black Shuck, the Demon Hound of East Anglia, I believe they exist chiefly in the imagination. The cliffs here are occupied by NALGO: the *National Association of Local Government Officers*, who have a holiday camp at the top of them.

Cayton Bay is a fine sweeping inlet, with a good beach, somewhat dangerous bathing (if we are to regard the many notices), sundered blockhouses of the two last world wars, a most handsome water pumping station, and Kellaways and Hackness Rock cliffs capped by Lower Calcareous Grit. At the southern end of the bay a notice warns us that we cannot get to Filey along the beach at any state of the tide. Nor we can, and so we had better climb the cliff here, for the Calcareous Grit forms a vertical escarpment at the head of the cliffs (there is a footpath up Yon's Nab). Keen geologists, however, might go on along the rocky beach at low spring tides to look at the fossil plant bed in the Lower Estuarine Series at the foot of North Cliff. On top of Gristhorpe Cliff is a caravan site charmingly named 'The Flower of May Caravan Site'. At **Gristhorpe** was dug up an oak coffin, with the skeleton of a man inside, and weapons and ornaments of bronze, flint implements and those of horn and bone and wood, and a basket made of bark. The objects found are in the museums of York and Scarborough. The man was six foot tall, round-headed, and had a cloak of animal skin.

If we like to cut inland a mile and a half here we can have a pint at the Ox Inn, **Lebberston**, where the landlord, Mr Ernest Peel, has a museum of 'bygones' including several things for which no-body yet has suggested a purpose. What *were* those overshoes made of wire-netting used for? He also has a marvellous collection of walking sticks.

We are coming now to Filey Brigg, and the only place where in fact we cannot walk along the rocky beach at low tide is for a short distance just north of this. From the top of the cliff, a little further, we look down upon the Emperor's Bath, which is a beautiful rock pool, filled by the sea twice a day and retaining its water at low tide, clear and deep and blue, with a natural amphitheatre of benched rock above it, and if a Roman Emperor didn't bathe in it one should have. Whether one did or not, the small boys of Filey throw pennies into it and then dive down to the clean sandy bottom to pick them up again and have done, we are told, for generations. We can easily get down the cliff to it. Here, too, somewhere, there was a chalybeate spring, but I have never found it. Up above, on this sharp jutting headland, was yet another Roman signal station, foundations just by the modern coastguard lookout. This was excavated in 1857 and again in 1923, and socket stones for pillars were removed and placed in Filey's Crescent Gardens.

Filey Brigg is a most dramatic feature of the coast. A ridge of Lower Calcareous Grit stretches a mile out into the sea, like a great breakwater. At low tide on a calm day you can walk right out to the end of it, and many people fish off it, but in a northerly gale it can be a dangerous place, with huge waves crashing right over it, and many an unwary person has been washed off it and drowned. It is not the place to play King Canute on. It has been a graveyard of ships: many a coble in sailing days was overturned in the big tidal overfall at the end of it. There is said to be an artificial pier of stone running south from it, called by fishermen the Spittal, and built by the Romans, who made a harbour here. As it is, the **Brigg** shelters Filey Bay from the northerlies and is thus a great help to the fishermen.

The old sailor's saw has it:

> When Flamberry we pass by,
> Filey Brig we mayn't come nigh,
> Scarborough Castle out to sea,
> Whitby three points Northerly.

Walking westwards from the base of the Brigg, down under the cliffs towards Filey, we find the Boulder Clay of the cliffs (which is protected from the sea by a ledge of Coralline Oolite) carved into

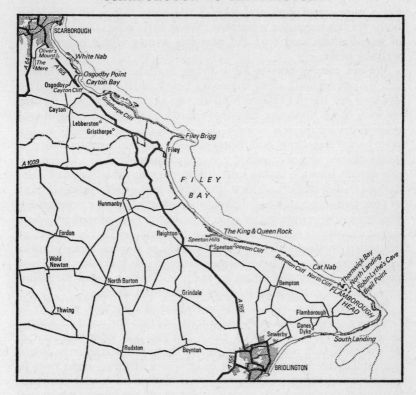

fine *arêtes*, or ridges and furrows, by the weather. There are fossils down below. Filey Sailing Club has its being in a little Wyke called Wool Dale, and then we come to that glory of Filey – the Coble Landing. Here, hauled up on a wide concrete ramp is as fine a bunch of big fishing cobles as you can find anywhere. Brightly painted, with the flags and banners of marker-buoys rearing up from their raking prows like battle standards, their superb sweeping lines and somehow very medieval-looking transom sterns, they look absolutely beautiful. Filey is the High Temple of the Coble Cult. Early in the morning, often soon after midnight, these vessels are hauled down the beach by big tractors, shoved out into the breakers, and off they go, big diesel engines thumping, to the fishing grounds. In the winter they go long-lining, in the summer lobster and crab potting, or drifting for salmon. After daylight, back they come, turning round to face the sea if there are any breakers, hauling out their big rudders and backing in to the beach where the tractor awaits them. The tractor advances into the waves, pushing an axle with two big wheels before it, two of the men in the coble jump out into the water, which often comes up to their waists, and, putting their backs to the coble, jockey her on to the axle, the tractor then hauls the laden boat out. Often, when winter long-lining, these boats are laden deep in the water with cod and haddock. In the summer they come in with good loads of crabs and lobsters. A crab in the North Sea, incidentally, has to spend its life walking north. This is because the mean set of the tides is southerly, and if a hen crab just stayed where she was born and laid her eggs there, they would be washed further south, and – the mean set of the tides in the English Channel being easterly – all the crabs in the sea would end up in a great heap off Dungeness. So as soon as crabs can walk they do so, and proceed north until when they lay their eggs the larvae will be washed by the residual current southward to where their mother was born. Thus the crab population remains static in the sea. A crab tagged and released at Whitby was caught at Fraserburgh a year later.

Filey has a really great fishing tradition. Strangely, on this harbourless stretch of coast, many big decked keeled boats were owned in days gone by and hundreds of cobles, large and small. As at Robin Hood's Bay there was a big fleet of fifty to sixty-ton yawls, each carrying two cobles on deck, ranging far out into the North Sea to shoot long lines. The cobles would be launched and each boat, with two men and a boy aboard, would shoot *nine miles* of line. Halibut used to be hooked up to a weight of twenty stone! Of course the trawlers killed it all by raping the beds with their heavy ground tackle, and they are taking the destruction further now with the comparatively new 'bobbin' trawls, the ground ropes of which are of such a nature that they can trawl over rocky ground, where before the fish – and the long-liners – had it their way. In the herring season the whole fleet used to sail for Great Yarmouth. There is a fine independent race of fishermen at Filey, and some of them are to be found, when ashore, not a hundred miles away from the Station Hotel. Unfortunately 'progress' (which so often means progress to the rear) has knocked down most of the old fishing streets that were so beautiful. There are still a few old cottages around Queen Street and Church Street that progress hasn't got yet, but most of Filey is modern and – let us face it – pretty dull. But the inhabitants are not dull and the siting of the place is beautiful. The great cliffs break here, for the River Derwent once ran into the sea where Filey is. A mass of glacial drift blocked the river and caused Lake Pickering to form, and the river now runs, improbably, west instead of east, and takes a great deal longer to get to the sea than it did before. There is a deep ravine through the boulder clay between the town and the parish church to the north, and this was once the boundary between the East and North Ridings (it isn't now). So that when a man was sick a'bed, and someone said 'I fear a's bound for North Riding', the words had a very ominous ring about them. The church is worth seeing for many reasons. It is Norman and Early English, with enigmatic pillars obviously once designed to support a west tower but never built on and a central tower instead, and there is much of interest but a good little church guide for six pence which nobody should boggle at. In the south aisle is a tablet to the twenty-nine men of Filey who were drowned at sea and whose bodies were never recovered between 1901 and 1948, and this does not include men lost in the wars. Between 1879 and 1896 thirty-nine local men were drowned and not recovered plus 'seven Strangers'. There is one class of people, generally unhonoured and unsung, that should not be neglected when discussing Filey. And that is the band of indomitable ladies, widows many of them, who work all winter in the 'bait sheds' putting mussels on the tens of thousands of hooks on the long-lines. They work extremely hard, for very little, and without them the coble fleet would not be anything like it is.

Charlotte Brontë used to lodge at Cliff House and wrote many letters. What else is there to say about Filey? It was Fucelac in Domesday, *fugl* O.E. for fowl, *lac* or *ley* pasture. At the conquest it was one of 154 manors handed over to Gilbert de Gant, younger son of Baldwin, Sixth Earl of Flanders, and a nephew of William the Conqueror. De Gant had his headquarters at Folkingham, in Lincolnshire. His son, Walter, proved a great leader, as an old man, at the Battle of the Standard. This was fought on 22nd August 1138, against David King of Scotland, who had come down with 26,000 men, and it got its name because the English knights and cavalry dismounted, when hard pressed, and rallied round the standard, and so won the battle. As we have seen, William Le Gros of Scarborough Castle was the English leader.

Unless you simply love *sand*, the walk southwards from Filey for a few miles is a bit boring. True there is Mr Billy Butlins, at Hunmanby ('The House of the Hound Man'), with a vast equipment and every delight. **Reighton** (where is a Saxon church) was the home of the great geologist Hugh Edwin Strickland, who was killed in battle as it were: run down by a train while examining the fossils in a railway cutting. Thomas Strickland carried the banner of St George at Agincourt. Talking of geology – at last we have left the tremendous Jurassic exposure, which we have followed all the way from the Tees, and reached the Cretaceous. We are coming here to a superficial moraine, covering the cretaceous, dumped by the great glacier from Scandinavia combined with one from the Tees, so there is a confusion here of dirt and rocks, but very soon, at **Speeton**, we come to the first of the mighty chalk bastion that makes up **Flamborough Head**. Here the cliffs fall vertically down into the sea at high water, and leave the merest strip of chalky boulders at low, and indeed there is a place under the Bempton Cliffs where whether at high or low tide nobody but a fish may proceed. From here to Bridlington we stroll along the beaches at our peril, unless we are very aware of the state and behaviour of the tides. The various rescue organisations get tired of retrieving inattentive holiday makers from the rising tide. And these chalk cliffs we have come to are magnificent. Now in these cliffs guillemots, razorbills, kittiwakes and even puffins breed, and lately a few gannets. There are few places in England, I believe, on the mainland at least, where such a plethora of birds may be observed. As you approach the cliff-edge, from April on, a great cloud of beautiful white and white and black shapes takes the air, with wild cries; others in their hundreds continue to sit resolutely on their tiny ledges, eggs drop in scores to the sea below – the birds are fantastically clumsy with their eggs – of course most of them hatch the eggs out by balancing them on their webbed feet – and any disturbance is apt to send the egg crashing down below when the parent bird looks stupidly after it as if wondering what has happened. Most of the eggs are pointed in shape – supposed to stop them from rolling. It doesn't. For the next seven or eight miles there are myriads of these birds. To look down on them, from the dizzy height of the cliff, is like looking at a cup of tea full of swirling tea-leaves – they circle and counter-circle about until you are dizzy and must take a grip on yourself to stop from joining them.

All these birds are now left in complete peace, and, like every other species which have no natural enemies (including man) suffer from the most ghastly overpopulation problems. Birds are driven to nest on ledges where hardly a bat could find *lebensraum*. It was not always thus. Up to 1954 when a law was passed to stop them there were the 'climmers'. The climmers were men employed on the farms at the cliff-top, who, every year, starting on 14th May, used to take leave of absence from their masters before haymaking, and lower themselves over the edges of these cliffs to collect some of the eggs. Each climmer had his own stretch of coast (the rights were vested in the landowner at the top), and these stretches were jealously protected, and honourably respected by brother-climmers, and the climmers would harvest the eggs on their stretches in such moderation as to ensure a good supply of eggs next year. If they hit a particular section of cliff a bit hard – they would 'fallow' it next year and not 'clim' it at all. The eggs they sold, and they were very good to eat (they sold in London hotels for enormous prices – as 'plovers eggs').

The climmers operated thus. A team of three men would set forth to the cliff top, secure a safe anchor a few feet back from the cliff top, and from this secure their main rope. Two men would remain up above, to haul the climmer up or lower him down according to his signals. The climmer himself, generally (we may gather from old photographs) a portly gentleman in a bowler hat (this necessary of course to bounce off pebbles) would lower himself over the cliff edge, with a second, lighter rope in his hand for signalling. Down he would go, down the vertical cliff face, and with great skill he would swing himself to and fro, often for amazing distances, to pluck the eggs off isolated ledges. The parent birds, meanwhile, screamed and dived at him, but of these he took no notice. Very often there were overhangs, and under these the climmer would swing himself, and sometimes climmers would drive pegs into the chalk, in order to provide themselves with hand-holds in such positions.

Into his satchel he would put the eggs. If he wanted up or down he would send up signals of so many tugs on his signal rope. These cliffs are four hundred feet high in places, and quite vertical, so climming was not a job for the faint-hearted. When his bag was full he would come up. In a good day he could take two to three hundred eggs.

Nowadays, with bird protection having reached a stage when it is no longer sensible or discriminatory, climming has been made illegal. This is a great pity, because a natural control over over-populated species has been eliminated (always a bad thing), some honest men have been done out of part of their livelihood, and an activity demanding great courage and breath-taking skill has been killed. So long as the system of privately 'owned' cliff stretches operated there would never be any danger of over-exploitation. The climmer thought of next year, and would never over-harvest his pitch. The birds would always lay again.

Another activity which grew up in Victorian times connected with these birds was one of the most unpleasant things the English have ever been guilty of. It became a practice for large mobs of 'sportsmen' from the cities of Yorkshire to descend on this coast in the laying time, hire cobles, and have themselves rowed or sailed along under the cliffs, from which vantage point they would blast off at the myriad flying birds above their heads with shot guns, killing and maiming hundreds. Mostly, they didn't bother to pick the birds out of the water: killing or wounding was enough. The climmers loathed this 'sport' of course, for the birds were killed and frightened to such an extent that they began to desert the cliffs. Thank God, and to the eternal credit of a few old Victorians including the parson of Flamborough (who wrote poems about it), the practice was at length stopped. Of course – how should the *hoi-polloi* of the wool towns know better – when their masters lined up every year to slaughter thousands and thousands of fat driven pheasants in the 'butts'? They were only copying their 'betters'. But *ugh*!

Now there are the Speeton Cliffs and the Bempton Cliffs and the North Cliff and the South Cliff, and there are Smuggler's Bay, and Church Bay and the North Landing, and the King and Queen Rocks, and the Breil and St George's Hole, and the Adam and Eve Rocks, and the Adam and Eve Rocks were once called 'Cole and Lampurgh', after two noted geologists who opened up this coast. Eve and the King recently collapsed. There is the Common Hole, the Pigeon Hole and the Kirby Hole. The study of the chalk cliffs of Flamborough can be a lifetime's work. There are caves that you can walk into at low tide, until you cannot see the light of day. There are caves that you can row a boat into at half tide – if you dare. There are isolated stacks and half-tide islands. R. D. Blackmore (*Lorna Doone*) wrote a novel about this coast, *Mary Aneley*, in which Robin Lyth was picked up abandoned on the beach as 'a pretty boy'. He grew up and became a famous smuggler. There is Robin Lyth's Cave still to be seen, just east of the North Landing, and like Lorna Doone herself, or Margaret Catchpole in Suffolk, nobody seems to be quite able to separate fact from fiction. Robin Lyth took refuge in his cave from the Preventives, the tide came up and he was forced to cling against the roof of the cave until it went down again, subsisting in a trapped pocket of air.

At a place called Cat Nab we come to the north end of that impressive artefact – **Danes Dyke**. This is a very large fosse and vallum, or ditch and bank, dug right across the Flamborough peninsula to defend it against the rest of the world. This is popularly supposed to have been dug by the Danes but it certainly wasn't. In 1879 General Pitt Rivers (*née* Lane Fox) excavated part of it and found eight hundred worked flints, and the chips that had been struck while working them. It is thought that this giant fortification is Early Bronze Age. The name Danes has been derived from *Dinas*, Welsh for fort. The northern part of the Dyke is all artificial, and is about twenty feet deep and sixty wide. The southern part follows a natural wyke, which has been improved by art. The whole makes a delightful walk, and has recently been footpathed and turned into a 'nature ramble'. Inside the Dyke, the country has been called 'Little Denmark', but this appellation strikes me as being foolish: the people who live at Flamborough are no more Danish than any other people living along the East Coast. There is a legend that in the time of the Danelaw the lord of Flamborough was supposed to pay a yearly tribute to the King of Denmark. As this monarch found himself no longer able to collect the tribute the lord contented himself with, once a year, firing an arrow out to sea with a gold coin on it.

This land of Flamborough Head is a very special place – a high windswept plateau, with a feeling of wildness and remoteness about it, and the smell of the sea. Before the cars and caravans it must have had an irresistible charm, and on a misty day in autumn to wander along the tops of the mighty cliffs, with the rolling sea lost below on one hand and the rolling open countryside fading away on the other is still marvellous. **Flamborough** village itself (probably from the Norse for arrow – *flame* – but Domesday has Flaneburg) was once a fishermen's village *par excellence*. It had the enormous advantage of lying between the two coble landings – the North and the South, and so from whichever way the wind was blowing one of these landings would be sheltered and it would be possible to launch cobles from it. Pennant, in his *Tour to Scotland*, was at Flamborough on the 3rd of July 1769 and wrote that there were a hundred and fifty houses in Flamborough 'all of fishermen few of whom die in their beds'. It is still a pleasant village, or small town, with enough pubs to satisfy the most bibulous – one of them called the *Royal* Dog and Duck – because of the fact that their Serene Highnesses Prince and Princess Louis of Battenberg visited it in 1900. The church is interesting (although much restored) having a rare screen and other early fifteenth-century woodwork, a rood loft (one of two left in Yorkshire), an original Pardon of Charles II to a Roundhead, a brass of Sir Marmaduke Constable, who was born in 1443 and commanded the Third Division of the English at Flodden at the age of seventy, and a monument to a man who had his heart eaten by a toad that he had swallowed. On top is a 'weather fish', like the one at Filey.

Prince James Stuart landed here in 1406, and was promptly captured and handed over to King Henry IV. The latter kept him for nineteen years, when he was freed to become James I of Scotland, and married Lady Joan Somerset, daughter of John of Gaunt. From this marriage descends the royal family of England.

The little place is much dominated by two grandiose chapels, one of the Primitive Methodist connection of 1874, big and Byzantine, the other just as large, of 1889, very ugly, and now disused. In the square in front of the first is a little memorial to the three men of the coble *Three Brothers* who were lost trying to save the crew of the coble *Gleaner*, near the West Scar, in the gale of 5th February 1909.

The **North Landing** is much backed up now by a large caravan site, stretching to Thornwick Nab, but this does not spoil the beauty of the cliffs and sea, which here is quite superb. Thornwick Bay is a wonderful place, and so is North Landing itself. Here the heavy, beamy, deep-draughted cobles peculiar to this place (rather ugly compared to the graceful vessels further north) are hauled up the steep concrete ramp by an engine. The cliffs descend towards Flamborough Head, being there only about two hundred and fifty feet. The Head, nevertheless, is grand in the extreme. To sail close to it, up or down the coast, is always exciting. The lighthouse, with its lantern 214 feet above the sea, was built in 1806, to replace the old chalk one built by Sir Richard Clayton in 1673, and still standing. Before the new lighthouse was built, ships were wrecked at the rate of five a year: 174 in 36 years. Sailors used to call the seabirds 'Flamborough Pilots', because, in a fog, their screaming acted as a warning to keep away.

We can follow the cliff around to the **South Landing**, and here was a lifeboat station (as indeed at the North Landing) but the boat was withdrawn in 1938. Most of the fishing now is done from the North Landing, but at least two families still keep cobles at both. At both Landings, incidentally, the beach and slope up the cliff is entirely composed of sea shells: memorials to the billions of shellfish which have been used as long-line bait. In 1895 there were 80 small cobles and 30 large ones fishing from the two Landings; now the number has dwindled to very few, and many of these are laid up in winter. When the caravans come in the cobles are apt to go out: men find easier ways of earning a living.

It would be unthinkable to mention the fishing of Flamborough without telling about the two famous cod. One of these, taken in 1893, had no less than 59 hooks in its belly, baited with whelks. The other, and more famous, had: a six-inch wooden doll in a woollen dress, a pair of unbroken spectacles, and a coral necklace. Flamborough fishermen had many special customs in days gone by. One was 'Raising the Herrings'. Women dressed as men would go about the village with music and singing, visiting neighbours. Another was the famous Flamborough Sword Dance.

A word about the geology of the chalk cliffs. The Speeton Cliffs are Lower Chalk, with high up the 'Black Chalk' or *Belemnitella plena* zone, Grey Chalk lower with no flint but lots of manganese, chalk marl at the base with pink bands and *Holaster subglobosus*. Speeton Hill of course, just north of the village, is the northern scarp of the chalk, where it begins as it were. Under the landslip near Speeton Gap is Red Chalk or Hunstanton Limestone, with *Belemnites minimus* and *Terebratula biplicata*. Lamplugh gives us the following fossils in the Lower Cretaceous:

Upper: *Belemnites semicanaliculatus*.
Lower: *Bel. jaculum.*
       Ammonites speetonensis
       Meyeria ornata
       Ammonites noricus.

In the Upper Cretaceous (seen well from Sewerby to Danes Dyke south end) we have the Upper Chalk, soft and no flints. Numerous sponges and marsupites, also *Belemnitella mucronata*, and bands of Fuller's earth. Beginning at the High Stacks working north we get Middle Chalk, with flints and *Ananchytes ovatus*. At Thornwich is the *Inoceramus mytiloides* zone.

Just inland from the lighthouse there is a small monument to the famous fight of the *Bonhomme Richard*, which occurred within sight and sound of Flamborough Head. On 23rd September 1779 the great American sailor (*not* the 'renegade pirate') John Paul Jones, arrived off Bridlington Bay with a small fleet consisting of his own ship *Bonhomme Richard* (6 nine-pounders, 16 new twelve-pounders, 12 old twelve-pounders and a battery of new eighteen-pounders), the *Alliance*, an American frigate commanded by a Frenchman, the *Pallas*, a French frigate, the *Vengeance*, a French brig, *Le Serf*, a captured British cutter manned by Frenchmen and Americans, and two French privateers, the *Mossieur* and the *Granville*.

They sailed into the bay, then decided to beat to windward round Flamborough Head going north. When off the Head they sighted a prize to make their mouths water: no less than seventy British merchant ships, coming back in convoy from the Baltic. But unfortunately for the Franco-Americans, the convoy was guarded by two British frigates, HMS *Serapis* of fifty guns and HMS *Countess of Scarborough*. The *Serapis* overwhelmingly outsailed and outgunned the *Bonhomme Richard*.

The wind had backed round by then to light south-west. The merchant fleet fled to the northward to get under the guns of Scarborough Castle. The two escorting frigates lay between Paul Jones and his prey. His two French privateers sailed out of his command and were not seen again. They saw this was to be no easy pickings. The *Alliance* and the *Pallas* kept their distance, but the *Pallas* soon engaged the *Countess of Scarborough*. 'Just as the moon was rising,' afterwards wrote a British midshipman, 'the weather being clear, the surface of the great deep being perfectly smooth, even as in a millpond' the *Bonhomme Richard* closed with the *Serapis* and gave her a broadside. Alas! Two of Paul Jones's new French eighteen-pounders exploded, killing their crews, and the rest of the gunners refused to fight the remainder. At one bang he had lost his main armament. The *Serapis* now had her turn, and poured broadside after broadside into the enemy, causing terrible damage, but Paul Jones, by consummate seamanship, manoeuvred his crippled ship so as to cross the T of *Serapis*, gave her another broadside, and closed in and grappled – making the two ships fast together with his own hands he whipped a loose forestay of *Serapis* to his own mizzenmast. The *Serapis* dropped her anchor in from fifteen to twenty fathoms of water three nautical miles east by south of Flamborough Head. 'Flamborough reapers, homegoing, pause on the hillside; for what sulphur-cloud is that which defaces the sleek sea; sulphur-cloud spitting streaks of fire?' Spectators flock to the Head. For two hours the two great warships lay locked together, the gunners of *Serapis* having to work their guns by pushing their loading-staves right back into the enemy gunports.

Meanwhile the *Countess of Scarborough* engaged the *Pallas*, and the *Pallas* quickly prevailed. The *Countess*, dismasted, struck her colours and the two ships were out of the battle. As for *Alliance* – she 'played the roll of a madman!' She scampered about the sea, and whenever she did come near the locked protagonists she would pour a broadside into the wrong ship! It seems certain that her captain had the idea of scuttling *Bonhomme Richard*, then taking the crippled *Serapis* and returning to France the victor. It is certain that he hated Jones, and was resentful of being put under the command of this colonial upstart.

By bad luck about the only guns that Jones could bring to bear, in the position the ships were in, were his useless eighteen pounders. He himself helped to drag a gun over from the other side and helped to fight it with his own hands. Jones always prided himself on his gunnery, and the standard of gunnery aboard his ships. *Serapis* meanwhile poured shattering broadside after broadside into her enemy, until her guns got too hot to use, and Captain Perron longed to be able to turn his ship round to use the guns on the other side, but he could not. At ten p.m. the English tried to board, but were repelled. The Continental flag was shot down and Pearson shouted to Jones: 'Has your ship struck?'

'I have not begun to fight!' yelled Jones, and nailed his colours back to the mast.

But a battle was going on overhead that was ultimately to decide the conflict. The French marines and other sharpshooters that Jones had ensconced in his fighting tops and rigging were steadily picking off their English counterparts. The time came when they were able actually to leap into the rigging of the English and take possession of it. Then they quickly cleared the weather decks of the *Serapis* of the enemy: no man dared come on deck from then on. But all the *Serapis* guns below the weather deck were able to fight on and the *Bonhomme Richard* became a shambles of blood and match-wood – so much so that some of Jones's officers tried to surrender – one actually tried to tear down the Continental flag but Jones prevented him. Victory in war comes to the side that can hang on just that little bit longer. When all seemed lost a Scotsman named William Hamilton dropped a grenade down a hatch of *Serapis* which set alight a great quantity of powder that the powder monkeys had brought up from below, there was an explosion that did great carnage, and, at five minutes past ten, when every man of Paul Jones's crew must have thought they had lost the battle, Captain Pearson hauled the ensign of his ship down with his own hands. Shortly after this the *Serapis*'s mainmast crashed over the side.

The firing ceased but not presumably the groans of the wounded. Captain Pearson stepped on board the *Bonhomme Richard* and handed Jones his sword. Jones handed it back again. Captain Jones invited Captain Pearson down into his cabin for a glass of wine. The cabin was nothing but splintered wood, but Captain Pearson was polite enough to ignore this, and the two commanders drank their wine and shared compliments. Paul Jones had taken 504 prisoners of war, including 26 officers RN and 18 masters of merchant ships. Out of a crew of 322 aboard *Bonhomme Richard*, 150 had been killed or wounded.

Prize crews were put aboard the two captured frigates, and for two days and nights the battered fleet sailed eastward. Then, at ten in the morning on 23rd September, the last man had to be taken off the *Bonhomme Richard*, and she quietly sank. Jones proceeded to Holland with the rest of the ships, and not long after this took service with the Russian navy.

Paul Jones was by no means a pirate. He was born a gardener's son on a big estate on the coast of Galloway, at thirteen went to sea, at twenty-one had his own ship in the West Indies trade, moved his headquarters to the American colonies and on 7th December 1775 accepted a commission in what the rebelling colonists called the Continental Navy. This flew the 'Grand Union Flag' – the Union Jack and Stripes, and recognised the sovereignty of the crown of England. Jones was a superb sea captain: many students think that he would have been the equal of Nelson had he had the same tackle. He had the same consideration for his men, and the same attention to training and preparation. Although he was a supreme fighting man he loathed war, and his one idea in attacking English shipping and coastal towns was to force the English to release American prisoners that had been taken from American ships and were not considered by their captors to be prisoners of war but simply pirates and consequently were being treated abominably. By capturing English sailors Jones forced the English to release American sailors in exchange. He is considered by the Americans to be the founder of their navy.

Well, we leave the ancient kingdom of Flamborough at the southern end of Danes Dyke, where was a large private mansion, now pulled down, and we can either walk along the cliff top here (Danes Dyke Farm is a fine brick fortress of a Yorkshire farmstead), or can keep to the beach among the fossil sponges which occur here in great numbers. In the spring numerous small falls of cliff occur here. As we have seen the Upper Chalk is soft, and crumbles, and the overburden of boulder clay on top of the chalk is apt to slip too. In the piles of loose chalk in new cliff falls we may look for fossils – but must take care not to become fossils ourselves. If one cliff-fall has taken place so can another. At **Sewerby**, in an old gravel beach below the boulder clay were the remains of the Straight Tusked Elephant, Leptorhine Rhinoceros, Hippo and many molluscs. About here a traumatic thing happens to the East Coast. The whole of the way from Marshall Meadows on the Scots border we have been travelling along a shore of rock. At Sewerby the chalk cliff retreats inland behind a mass of boulder clay, and we will see no more real rock until we come to the white cliffs of Dover except at Hunstanton. From here on the coast is to be low muddy cliffs, or sand dunes, or sea walls and marshes, and we say goodbye to the wild rugged rocks.

At Sewerby we may be startled to hear peacocks, and then we discover that Sewerby Park has a small zoo. The park is delightful, and the Hall itself a museum. There is a small archaeological collection, some pictures, and – wonder of wonders – the Amy Johnson Collection. This has the strongest period interest, and will bring back to English people who were newspaper readers in the 1930s the most vivid memories. To people of later generations perhaps it would be all one big puzzle.

And so we plunge into **Bridlington** itself, which at first glimpse seems to be a respectable and rather boring kind of a seaside resort, but on closer inspection proves to be very interesting. The harbour, which is tidal and dries out almost completely at low tide, making 'Brid' a dicey place to run for shelter to in a south-east gale, is nevertheless large and interesting. It has, besides a biggish fleet of 'keel boats' – some locally registered and some Scottish – a fleet of twelve of the oldest cobles left on the coast: each one, in fact, originally a sailing coble. That is, they were built for sail, in the days of sail, but now they sail no more: each one has, in fact, a diesel engine. Their appearance has been altered and somewhat spoiled by the addition of wash-boards above their gunwales, which heighten them unduly, but these wash-boards have been put there to adapt the cobles for the use to which they are now put. They are all, each and every one of them, employed, winter and summer, in taking out fishing parties, and the members of these parties must of course be kept dry, and so the raising of the sides is done to prevent a slop coming over. The hand-line fishing from Bridlington is very good, and Bridlington Bay is so wonderfully sheltered that it is seldom that the boats cannot go out. There is plenty of haddock and cod, and most of these boats spend a few hours of each day fishing especially for plaice and other flat fish. The people who hire them are generally roaring fellows from the West Riding cities, and to go with one of these parties is a pleasant experience. If anyone wishes to examine the lines of a typical big sailing coble of the pre-motor era let him have a good look at, for example, the *Sunflower*, at low tide. And be it added that these grand vessels, though old, are still as sound as the day they were built, and every year have to withstand a rigorous inspection by the Board of Trade. What a chance for the people of Bridlington to have a whip-round and rig two of them out with sail again (before it is too late) so that they could be kept as working museum pieces, taking parties out perhaps, and every so often could have a race for the edification of the populace. What a better way of spending money than on yet another dreary 'municipal garden'!

The other part of Bridlington of absorbing interest is the Old Town with the magnificent Church of St Mary, which has been said to be the finest building in the East Riding, next to Beverley Minster. So little do the inhabitants of the town esteem these things that it almost seems that they are hidden away and forgotten: the holidaymaker could stay in 'Brid' for a fortnight and never know they existed. One or two of the streets of Old Town have great charm (not because they have been preserved but because nobody has yet got round to pulling them down), and the priory church is magnificent. It was the church of an Augustinian Priory founded by Walter de Gant soon after 1100. The last prior, William Wolde, got himself hanged at Tyburn in 1537 for his part in the Pilgrimage of Grace. The great west end is superb (although the grand south-west tower is Victorian). The interior is vast and most impressive. There is a bread table inside carved with, amongst other fauna, a crane drinking from a jug, said possibly to have been the gravestone of the founder. All the modern woodwork inside is carved with little mice crawling up it, a circumstance which seems to intrigue everybody who knows about it. The Bayle Gate to the west of the church, is 1388 and well worth a visit. It contains a museum which in my experience is always locked. This, and the superb church seem, as I said before, to be entirely ignored by the powers-that-be of Bridlington. For visitors to Bridlington I cannot too strongly recommend *The Holidaymakers' Guide* by Johnson and Ingram, five pence and worth ten times as much.

Bridlington's commercial fishing fleet is suffering somewhat from the general overfishing of the North Sea, which has been exacerbated enormously by the invention of the bobbin trawl which is invading the last rocky refuges of the breeding fish. A few small cargo ships though are now beginning to use the harbour (some of them taking fertiliser to the Channel Islands), there is a growing fleet of yachts,

Above, Flamborough Head; *below*, Spurn Head.

The Boston Stump.

and there is a scheme proposed, by a Bridlington man named Dennis Alsom who has taken to Canada, to build a multi-million pound marina. If this is carried out, Bridlington is perfectly placed to become a northern Cowes, or Burnham-on-Crouch. The last time the harbour was enlarged was 1847.

Bridlington, which may seem so young and brash now as we survey its streets and streets of 'villadom', is an ancient and honourable town, and has much history. It had an author who wrote two hundred years before Chaucer: Robert the Scribe, a monk of St Mary's Priory. His *Dialogue* is in manuscript in the Bodleian and also at Durham. It has been translated into modern English by a Religious of the CSMU (Mowbray 1960). William of Newbury, born at Bridlington, wrote *A History of English Affairs* and was a successor to Bede. The thirteenth century Peter of Langtoft wrote a Chronicle in French verse, George Ripley, a famous alchemist, flourished at Bridlington in the fifteenth century. Saint John of Bridlington was prior there in 1362, canonised in 1401, and not every seaside resort has a saint. Edward II rested here after his defeat by the Scots at Byland, Henry V came to give thanks after Agincourt, Robert Fowler, a Quaker, built a ship here in which he and some companions sailed to America about 1657, none of them knowing how to navigate, and in 1871 the lifeboat was smashed and all its crew drowned.

On 22nd February 1643 Queen Henrietta Maria landed at Bridlington with arms and ammunition for her hard-pressed husband Charles I. Four Parliament ships were following her, and besides bombarding her ships in the harbour, they were ungallant enough to bombard her lodgings, wherefore Her Majesty was obliged to take cover in a ditch.

CHAPTER 19

The Coast of Holderness

*

WE now set forth for the vanishing land of Holderness. From here
to the Humber the coast can be described in a few words: it consists
of a low gently curving cliff of boulder clay, with sand – sometimes
rather muddy nondescript sand – between it and the sea, and the
sea is eating into it at an average rate of two yards a year. At least
two and a half miles of land on this forty mile stretch have gone
since the Romans left, and the following towns and villages are
known to have existed once but exist no longer: Sunthorpe, Wils-
thorpe, Auburn, Hornsea Burton, Ringborough, Waxholm, Great
Colden, Little Colden, Sand le Mere, Hartburn, Hyde or Hythe,
Monkwike (gone this last hundred years), Nesham, last heard of in
Stuart times, Northorpe and Hoton, all gone in 1396, Dimlington
which had a beacon and chapel, Turmaarr, went fourteenth century.
And last of all but not least Ravenspurn and Ravenser Odd: two
towns which, had they lasted, would have given Hull and Grimsby
a run for their money.

The fact is that the whole of Holderness was once sea, and the
northern shore of this sea was the chalk escarpment which we have
seen disappear beneath the boulder clay at Sewerby and which then
runs westward, a low steep ridge of hill, forming the south-eastern
face of the Wolds. In glacial times this whole sea was bunged up with
boulder clay, dragged hither from Scandinavia and the North of
England, and it is this soft clay which is now being eaten by the
sea, and which the sea has smoothed and stroked into the straight,
or gently curving, coast that we now see, and which ends at Spurn
Head. Over the sea the Dutch are busily engaged in making new
land. We are as busily standing by watching the loss of land we
have got.

Now the sands are pretty good at Bridlington, if you like sands,
and we can walk south with the sea on one side of us and the low
mud cliffs on the other. **Burton Agnes**, inland five miles, has a
fine hall, open to the public and worth a visit. At Auburn House,
where there are said to be foundations of an ancient village, they
charge people 25p to park a car, or they do if the people are

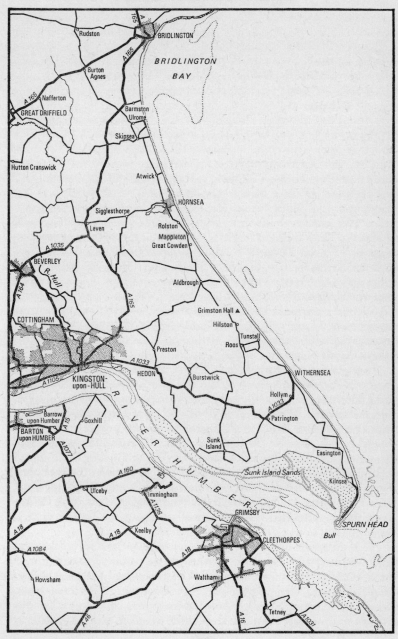

fool enough to pay it. The sands from here on are somewhat undistinguished, being pebbly and muddy and not meriting the hackneyed adjective 'golden' at all. At **Barmston** are caravans, a slipway for boats, the Black Bull Inn and a church with an alabaster effigy to (probably) William Monceux, who died in 1446. The Monceux were lords here for three hundred years and he was the last. At **Ulrome** are caravans again, and a tiny shop on the cliff-top, and a lake dwelling was excavated in 1880 – a wood platform 90 feet by 60 feet which had once stood on oak piles. Ulrome took its name from Ulphus, a Saxon earl of Canute's day. South of Ulrome, and right past Skipsea, is a shanty town, and this is the best possible use for most of this coastline. Each one of these shanties, or bungalows as their owners would prefer to call them, provides health and happiness for at least one family from the industrial cities. This coast is totally undistinguished. There are no rare birds or plants on it that might be destroyed. There is a fair enough beach to bathe from, launch little boats from, and for children to play on. It is an extremely safe beach. Why not just give the whole forty miles up to bungalows and caravans? It could be (is in a way) a poor man's *Costa Brava*. The bungalows need *not* be squalid. If we look at the equivalent on the Danish coast, at such places as Karrebaekseminde and Dragor, we realise that they can be an embellishment to the coastscape: if they are planned and built with natural good taste and looked after properly. **Skipsea** has an impressive mott and bailey west of the little village (Drogo built it – he was a Flemish adventurer who came over with the Conqueror and married the latter's niece, murdered her, and fled the country). The Albemarles then became lords of Holderness after Odo of Champagne. The castle was destroyed in Henry III's day. The church is in a circular churchyard. This was a Celtic custom, and the *Llans* that have named so many Welsh villages were circular enclosures containing shrines or churches. There was a British (thus Welsh) earthwork here. Many of the older buildings along this coast are built of random boulders from the boulder clay, each course being put in slanting, with the next one slanting the other way, herring-bone fashion. The rest is red brick.

The countryside here is very fertile, closely farmed, and a peaceful happy countryside. No tourists ever go there – why should they? There is nothing spectacular to see. The farms are of moderate size, prosperous, and the people are real Yorkshire country people, quiet and friendly. There is one phenomenon that exists in this country north of the Humber that exists nowhere else nowadays in

England. And that is a large tribe of horse-and-wagon-dwelling gypsies of a kind that has died out in the rest of the country. You will often find some of them encamped on a wide grassy verge in a country lane here, and they look like people from another age. The men and boys have long matted black hair, the women and little girls long dirty dresses, long hair also and gold ear-rings. They are obviously very poor, none of the men are sophisticated enough to pass the driving test, none of the children will be when they grow up, and so they seem to be bound to the *grai* and *vardo* – horse and living-wagon – for the rest of time. It speaks a lot for the tolerance of the Holderness country people that these gypsies are allowed to exist at all. If they wandered to the south of England they would be hounded to death, or driven into concentration camps like the New Forest Gypsies, whom they resemble. You will find the men and boys holding horses and ponies on long tethering ropes – letting them move along the roadsides to graze – and if you go up to any man and ask his name the chances are that it will be Smith – and the chances are only slightly less that it will be George Smith. The chances are that they don't own the horses they have with them. They go to Topcliff Fair every year and more prosperous gypsies there will *lend* them young horses, knowing that the horses will be carefully looked after, and returned in a year's time bigger and worth more than when they lent them. They never leave this small area of south Yorkshire, and other gypsies look upon them as people of an inferior race – in fact one hears it said that they are not gypsies at all – but came to Britain with the real gypsies as their servants. Their knowledge of *Romanes* appears to be slight.

Atwick had steps down the cliff, but they disappeared in 1969. There is a path up or down the cliffs about three hundred yards south though. In the village is the Black Horse, there was another lake dwelling here, and in some peat deposits the bones of an Irish elk were found. Just inland, in 1970, Texaco were drilling a wild-cat hole, in the hopes of striking either oil or gas.

After Atwick we quickly come to **Hornsea**. This was once a fishing village but is no longer: in fact there are no commercial fishing boats on this Holderness coast at all. It must be one of the longest stretches of English coast without one fisherman on it. In the Middle Ages Hornsea was a port, but just what sort of a port nobody can tell. It is probable that there was a pier and a considerable harbour of some kind. The Abbots of York had a charter in 1257 for holding a market here (that is they derived the revenues from the market that other people held here), and they had ship tolls, land tithes, wrecks, assize of bread and beer, market tolls and *chiminage* – a toll on all strangers passing through. They had gallows, tumbrils, a pillory and a prison to aid them in collecting all this, and several writs were taken out against the abbots at various times 'by reason of their oppression and rapacious tyranny'. When the Reformation came the Hornsea people, at least, must have viewed it with equanimity. Now Hornsea is a small holiday resort, quiet and unassuming, and as such places go, very pleasant. We can see here, as we arrive at the sea-front of Hornsea after having walked along the crumbling cliffs to the northward, how it is indeed possible to stem the inroads of the North Sea. Massive walls of concrete have been built, and these are holding, while the beach on each side of Hornsea continues to erode. What will happen if the erosion is allowed to continue and, say in a hundred years' time, the cliffs have gone back another two hundred yards, and the Hornsea concrete is isolated and undermined from the back, no-one can tell. Maybe by then the English people will be forced to do something about it. A negligible fraction of the 'dragons' teeth', or concrete tank obstacles, strewn round the coasts so uselessly in the Second World War would have been enough to have delayed the incursion of the sea very considerably, although it would take more than them to stop it.

Hornsea has a mere, 495 acres and the largest lake in Yorkshire. It is very reminiscent of a Norfolk Broad. The Mere is let to a family firm which runs it very sensibly, allowing people to put sailing boats on it (for 50p a day – or £2.50 a week), or to fish (for 25p a day). No canoes and no motor boats are allowed and as for the latter a very good thing too. Rowing skiffs can be chartered by the hour. There is a pleasant café and a sailing club, the members of which race Swordfish, Ospreys and Fireflies, and take it all very seriously. A roach of 3 lb 10¾ oz was taken from the Mere, claimed at the time to be a world record, a pike of 27½ lb, and there are good perch, tench and roach. There are herons, swans, grebes, Canada geese, cormorants and teal including goldeneye. The lake has pleasantly wooded banks, islands, and a path right round it which is well worth walking along. It belongs to Sir Marmaduke Strickland Constable. At one time there was a terrible legal shindy between the Abbot of Meaux and his brother of St Mary's, York. These two holy gentlemen engaged champions to fight for them, in a *jus duellum*, not once but twice, and on the second occasion the champion of Meaux, after having fought all day, began to yield and one of the justices (Roger de Thirkelby) stopped the fight and a compromise was arranged, which might well have been done in the first place. The main issue of dispute was the right of fishery in the Mere. Our anglers nowadays fling the fish they catch back as not being fit to eat. The old monks knew better.

The old part of Hornsea (near the Mere) still has old-world charm. The church is worth looking at, and there is a small museum in the Town Hall, but perhaps the most interesting thing to see is Hornsea Pottery.

In 1949 two brothers, both having recently been discharged from the army, started making studio pottery in their wash-house in Hornsea. They fired in an electric kiln with a cubic foot capacity – enough for a medium-sized bowl – and as it takes two firings to complete a pot (each of twelve hours with a cooling period of about two days) their output could not have been very great. Neither young man had done any potting before, nor had had any business experience. Now their pottery covers twenty-eight acres, employs scores of people and turns out a great range of very pleasant pots in large runs. Visitors are not so much welcomed as practically dragged in, or lured by baits such as no other business surely has ever set. There is a car park for *a thousand* cars, a large field specially for picnickers, a zoo, a large aviary, a pets' corner and monkey house, a lake with waterfowl, a large well-equipped playground for children, a café, and an enormous 'garden centre' with acres of flowering plants for sale, garden implements and all the rest of it. All these amenities are free, or practically free, and presumably such profit as there lies in them for the pottery comes from the 'selected seconds' that are sold to the visitors. (Presumably the café and garden centre pay for themselves.) It is really a most pleasant place, and a very good pottery, full of apparently very happy potters, and strikes one as being the very ideal of the sort of industry which should be developed in the countryside. In the little zoo there is a Japanese squirrel and over his cage is written 'Japanese Squirrel'. It is not necessary to read this, however, for over him is a mynah bird, and as you walk in, the mynah bird says: 'Japanese Squirrel!'

Just out of Hornsea, on the main road, to the left, is a most beautiful farmhouse and group of farm buildings: a superb block, comely, solid and comfortable. But it is broken and falling down. Surrounding it flood the council houses, or council-type houses, which tell us something about the taste of the age we live in.

Rolston Hall, two miles down the road and on the right, was once the home of William Brough, the Marshal of the High Court of the Admiralty. Captain Paul Jones used to fire at this house every time he sailed along this coast, because he considered Brough responsible for the ill-treatment of American sailors. There is said to be still a stone cannon ball in a field.

Mappleton, if it was famous for anything, was famous for having a carpenter's shop with a marvellous collection of name boards off wrecked ships on its gable. Now it is infamous for having allowed these to be pulled down.

After **Great Cowden** – the RAF and desolation. Then we have, inland, Bewick Hall, seventeenth century, and nearby the mounds of the castle of the de Melsas. There are de Melsa monuments in Aldbrough church.

If we are hungry when we arrive at **Aldbrough** we couldn't be hungry in a better place. For here is the George and Dragon, an ancient inn not long ago bought up by four local farmers who were tired of not having a decent place to eat, and turned into one of the very best eating houses in Yorkshire. The food is not cheap, but because the menu is large, the food fresh and of the very highest quality, the prices are very fair. There are also beds. (Telephone Aldbrough 230.) For the rest, in the church, upside down, is a circular sundial with VLF HET AROERN CYRICE FOR HANUM FOR GVNWARA SAULA written on it. (Ulf bade rear a church for the poor and for the soul of **Gunwara.**) In 1786 this church was 2,044 yards from the cliff edge. In 1895 it was 1,868 (a loss of 176 yards in 109 years). What it is now I leave the reader to pace out for himself. There is a good little church guide for 2½p.

South from Aldbrough we come to one of the rare long stretches of this coast un-caravanned. At Ringbroughs Farm – which we may take as a fairly typical farm of this area – fairly light, but good land, most of it tile-drained, cornland but some grass leys on which cattle are fattened in the summer, the cattle being yarded in the winter. The farm had sheep until recently but now has no more – we find huge gun emplacements left over from 1945. The first building we come to after this is a superb moated farmhouse, a gem of a place to live, which has been allowed to fall down while the former occupant lives in a new brick box with all the charm of a packing case.

Grimston Hall is now put to a grim purpose. The Hull firm of Reckitts has bought it, and uses it for experiments on animals. There are high fences and many grim notices.

Hilston is so small that it can hardly be said to exist, but there is a brand new church there with a rather good east window by L. C. Evetts of Newcastle.

At **Tunstall** there is a good church, and a caravan site and shop on the shore. It is melancholy walking along this shore, and seeing the cliff crumbling at place after place. And when the cliff slumps to the beach there are no hard rocks to break the force of the waves and save the cliff that remains. Just mud that quickly washes away and allows the sea to continue its deadly work. One day man will have to make a stand, and say 'Thus far and no farther!'

At **Owthorne**, which is now part of Withernsea, the church fell in 1816 and its remains are now far out to sea. It went over the cliff in 'an awful storm of unusual violence'. Many bodies in various stages of preservation were 'dislodged from their gloomy depositories and strewn upon the shore in frightful disorder.'

Withernsea had its pier washed away. It probably had a navigable creek running into the land, and in the bed of its little stream, six feet below the surface, the 'Roos Carr Images' were found, the work of pre-Viking Northmen. They are human figures of wood, with quartz pebbles for eyes, stuck into a little serpent-shaped boat and they are now in Hull museum. For the rest, Withernsea is a pleasant little resort of Hull.

As we approach **Easington**, if the wind is southerly our noses may tell us our whereabouts. For Easington was the first terminal built in England for natural gas. (Bacton, in Norfolk, was the second.) At present one 36-inch pipe brings it from 42 miles out at sea, but there is more to come. Easington, although not embellished by its gas terminal, is a beautiful little village, with some good old pubs, a fine tithe barn that looks about fifteenth century, a fine church, with the 'Easington Imp' on its tower arch (compare Lincoln Cathedral), an alabaster monument to Robert Overton, a friend of Milton and of Cromwell, Governor of Hull, who managed things so badly that he managed to get imprisoned by both the Royalists and Parliament. Easington had a haven in the fourteenth century: it is difficult to see where it was. In 1875 some trenches were opened in the cliffs, which exposed oyster-shells, pottery shards, and the bones of the short-horned ox, wolf and dog. These remains were Roman. A tip for the barmen of modern England – the Romans opened their oysters by nipping a piece of the two shells out with a pair of pliers on the wide edge of the shell and then inserting the knife into that – not trying to shove a knife-point into the hinge-end of the creature. I have tried it and it is marvellously effective. Shortly after Easington we come to a sea wall, running inland and cutting off Spurn. Whoever built it rather ungallantly excluded little **Kilnsea**, a minute village at the base of Spurn

Point. Poor little Kilnsea, now heavily be-caravanned and a mere scattering of houses, was once a fishing town, and had cliffs and a hill! The cliffs and hill have completely disappeared. In 1822 there were thirty houses only left, and a church. In 1831 the tower and half the church went over the cliff, and in 1852 the rest. In 1899 when the members of the East Riding Antiquarian Society wished to see the remains of the church they had to wait for the lowest tide of the year and then they found it 250 yards out to sea from the top of the cliff. The only thing saved was the font, now in the new church.

There is a café called the Bluebell and Bumblebee, once a pub, and the Bumblebee part of its name comes from another pub which went over the cliff. The café is currently for sale. It has a plaque on it which says that it was built in 1847, and was then 534 yards from the sea. It is now (1970) 270 yards (a loss of 264 yards). At very high tides and in gales the whole of Kilnsea is apt to get flooded, and the North Sea joins the Humber here. There are some massive, but badly planned and constructed, concrete sea-defences here, built in the 1914–18 war to protect the gun emplacements. They are proving quite ineffective, and the large masses of concrete are lying higgledy-piggledy, shattered and broken, on the receding beach. The Coastguard station has recently been moved here from Spurn Head. There are various other strange installations, including a beam of light which shines straight up into the sky from the garden of a bungalow opposite the Bluebell. This is meant to show the height of the clouds, but is much enjoyed by moths. The owners of the bungalow, Mr and Mrs Stinton, probably know more about Kilnsea and its locality than anybody else. Mr Stinton has prepared a very sensible-looking plan to *in*, or dam, the mud flats from the Spurn to Sunk Island, leaving a big deep water harbour for shipping where North Channel now is. This will help to provide more land for industry and agriculture. If the population continues to expand at its present rate, something like this will no doubt become necessary.

The market cross of Ravenspurn stood for centuries at Kilnsea after Ravenspurn had been drowned by the sea, then it was moved to Burton Constable in 1818, and thence to Hedon, where it still is.

And so we come to that strange vermiform appendix of Yorkshire, **Spurn Head**. For four miles we can walk down it, along the beach or along a tarred road, or if we pay 25p to the Yorkshire Naturalists' Trust, we can drive in a horseless carriage, with the sea one side of us and the Humber the other – shallow water if high tide – the

Kilnsea Clays if low – with sand dunes all about, and the remains of an old railway line showing sometimes from under the drifting sand. This railway line was put there by the military before 1914 to supply their fort on the end of the Spurn. For years, until the present road was built, it was the only land connection, and the lighthouse men and lifeboat men used to *sail* along it, if the wind was fair, using a rail trolley with a coble lug-sail. If the wind was against them they just had to push.

In due course we come to a towering fortress of the 1914–18 war: an artillery control tower with accommodation for officers and men, surrounded by a defensive wall with defensive embrasures. The place is open to the winds – and small boys – and the latter have wrecked it as much as they can. The ghost of a young subaltern haunts the north-east corner room. Opposite this, in an old bungalow on the Humber side, the University of Hull has its experimental station. Then we come to the Head itself, with its towering new lighthouse, and deserted old one standing now in the water with 'Explosive Store' painted on it, and half a mile of mostly subterraneous fortifications. There is a whole complex of gun emplacements, men's quarters and ammunition depots buried under the sand. The Coastguard has now left Spurn but there is a row of cottages, defying wind and weather, in which live the members of the only full-time professional lifeboat crew on the East Coast of Britain. Normally of course the mechanic is the only full-time salaried member of a lifeboat crew: the rest are all volunteers who generally fish in their working time. At Spurn there are no fishermen, and the place is considered so important by the RNLI that this full-time crew is retained.

As we stand at the water's edge on Spurn Head we see how fast the water boils into the Humber and out again, especially at spring tides. It reaches a speed of seven or eight knots which is formidable. The Bull lightship pitches at her anchors south-west, the Bull Sand Fort stands further out, and six miles away we can see the low Lincolnshire shore. Salt-caked trawlers come in from the distant-water grounds, heading for Hull or Grimsby, and big ships may lie at anchor waiting for the tide. South-east of us, at low tide, we will see the water boiling round the Stony Binks, which dry out at low water. At the lowest of springs it is possible to wade to them (but very dangerous).

Now somewhere about us, but nobody knows where, are the foundations of two lost cities. My guess is that they are to seaward – perhaps somewhere near the Stony Binks – or else further out, but my guess is as good as anybody else's. Spurn is a phenomenon of the sea – there is no hard-rock geological reason for its existence – it is merely a stroking-up of sand by sea and river-tide which shapes this bar of shifting sand and mud. The coast north of Kilnsea is retreating year by year and century by century. As it retreats my guess is that Spurn retreats too – walking westwards. If the sea broke through at Kilnsea, Spurn would disappear, very quickly, and simply form again a mile or two further west, to conform to the new coastline. If this happened the buildings on Spurn would crumble into the sea in a matter of weeks. I believe this is what happened to Ravenspurn.

The origins and the end of Ravenspurn are wrapped in mystery (as is its spelling). A skaldic poem tells us that Harold of England chivalrously allowed Olaf to carry away what was left of his army in 24 ships (all that were left out of 300), after he had defeated him, from *Hrafnseyrr* – the Raven's Tongue Land. William Shelford wrote that the Danes landed here in 867, planted the Raven standard, and founded Ravensburg or Ravenser, and this became one of the most flourishing ports of the kingdom, returning two members to Parliament, sending ships to the Navy, having an annual fair of thirty days. The place was mentioned twice by Shakespeare (Henry VI part 3, Act iv, Scene 7, and Richard II, Act 2, Scene 1). Baliol embarked from here to attack the Scots in 1332, Bolingbroke landed here in 1399 to become King of England, Edward IV landed here in 1471. Soon after the latter date the place was consumed by the sea.

Now there were two towns here. The first was Ravenser, Ravenspurn or other spellings. Early in the thirteenth century an island appeared out of the sea near it, and this was called Ravenser Odd. (Odd is Danish for a spit of land.) At first the Odd was but a desolate sandbank, but there was a law suit in 1273 in which the prosecution alleged that the Earl of Albemarle had built a town on the Odd, where no town ought to be, and that the town had already been there forty years. The facts that are known about the two towns are, briefly, as follows:

1251   Monks granted half an acre of ground at Od, near Ravenser, for fish house.
1273   A legal dispute concerning a chapel at Od.
1300   Edward I gave a grant of land at Ravenseodde.
1312   Ravenser empowered by king to raise a tax to repair its walls.
1315   Burgesses of Ravenserod had to pay king £50 for confirmation of their charters and 'kaiage' for seven years.
1326   King granted customs to port.
1335–6   Warships of Ravenser are referred to.

1336   William de la Pole left the town for Hull. He became the leading citizen of that town and his family afterwards Dukes of Suffolk.

1344   Ravenserode sent a representative to Edward III's Naval Parliament.

1346   One ship sent to the Siege of Calais (Hull sent 16).

1355   Bodies were being washed out of graves in graveyard.

1357   Frequent inundations are reported.

1360   Most of the merchants left for Hull or Grimsby.

1361   The town 'totally annihilated by the floods of the Humber and inundations of the Great Sea.' The Abbot of Meaux ascribed the town's disaster to 'wrongdoing on the sea, by its wicked works and piracies it provoketh the wrath of God against itself beyond measure.'

1390   All trace of town or towns gone.

1413   A grant of land for erecting a hermitage at Ravenscrosbourne.

1428   Richard Reedbarowe the hermit got a grant to take toll of ships to raise money for the completion of his light tower.

1538   Leland refers to Ravenspur in his *Itinerary*.

And with that muddle of different spellings and confusion between the two towns, we will have to be content. The rest is silence, or the murmuring of the sea.

The members of the Yorkshire Naturalist Trust administer the Head, exact tolls from cars, and try to keep other people from disturbing the birds. They catch and ring vast numbers of the latter every year. In 1968, besides birds of many other species, they caught Subalpine Warblers (in May and June), a Bee-eater in June, and for the first time in north-west Europe – a Spectacled Warbler (in October).

We now have the small problem of getting ourselves over the Humber. Unless we have a boat we will be constrained to go to Hull and either take the British Railways ferry, which is highly recommended because, up to date at least, the ferry boats are two splendid little paddle steamers, in which you can see the machinery working in the engine room. Alas they are now talking of building a bridge. Or we can go by hovercraft to Grimsby. Or we can go right round by land, going through Goole.

However we go, we shall probably go through **Patrington**, where it is worth looking at the fine church, the 'Queen of Holderness', and where the interesting parish records recommend the hanging of strings of onions around the necks of cattle to avert the cattle plague. We can if we like divert south to Sunk Island, which is interesting in being reclaimed from the salt. In the seventeenth century it was just sand-banks, in 1744 1,561 acres had been laid dry, by 1850 7,000 acres and by 1906 the present total of 9,601 acres. No doubt, in the ripeness of time, there will be more to come. The Humber is peculiar for its warp lands. The silt-laden water of the Humber is admitted on to the marshes through sluice gates, allowed to spread out over the land and deposit its silt before running back to the sea. This produces land of high fertility. On some of the warp lands are 'blow wells' where water bubbles up from the ground at a temperature of 47 degrees Fahrenheit, winter and summer. In the Humber itself there used to be 'whelps' and 'Barton Bulldogs'. These were quite furious springs of fresh water welling up from the sea-bottom amid the salt water. They have been somewhat abated by lowering the water table by pumping. Henry Empson, brother of William the poet, farms on Humber and is a great expert on 'warping'.

Hedon is on the way to Hull, and here we can see the Ravenspurn cross, the only thing left of that once important place. Hedon church is good (the tower is 130 feet high), the Town Hall has two maces – one said to be the oldest in England (reign of Henry VI). On the graves in the churchyard are names like Proom, Grimoldby, Droney, Gumbald, Dring and Thustinaway.

Burstwick is interesting to read about, if not to look at, because in a gravel pit there have been found rocks from Scotland, the Cheviots, Teesdale and Norway and fossils from Whitby, going to show from how far and wide came the glaciers which made Holderness. There have also been found there shells of Arctic species left over from one of the ice ages, walrus bones, and bones of elk, elephant and other animals which roamed Holderness in days gone by.

Kingston-upon-Hull, or **Hull** as nearly everybody prefers to call it (Hull is unique – Kingston is certainly not) does not really come into this book, but the nautically-minded will no doubt want to see the excellent Maritime Museum in Pickering Park. This has a fine collection of whaling stuff, including the best collection of scrimshaw work in the world. Scrimshaw was the art of engraving on whales' teeth or bone. The fish docks are also interesting, although the visitor may be disappointed by the small number of trawlers. The fact is that the distant-water trawlers which fish from Hull spend nearly all of their lives at sea. There were in 1970 71 wet fish trawlers, 20 all-freeze trawlers, one part-freeze trawler, one factory trawler and six seine-netters. The freezer trawlers tend to be vast, and most of them stern trawlers – hauling their enormous nets up ramps in the stern instead of over the side like their more old-fashioned sisters. Another bait for the nautically-minded is the great fleet of *keels* using Hull. The keel is a breed of river barge with a flat bottom but rounded chines, bluff bows and sterns the same shape – the stem and stern post apparently pushed in to give a snub-nosed appearance, evolved for carrying cargoes on the fiercely tidal waters of the Humber, Trent and Yorkshire Ouse, and also to penetrate that great network of locked waterways that reaches out over the countryside from the Humber, and takes in such places as York, Tadcaster, Leeds, Sheffield, Huddersfield, Lincoln, Nottingham, Burton-on-Trent. The typical keel was 62 feet long, $15\frac{1}{2}$ feet wide, 7 foot draught with a load of 100 tons. They used to have lee boards (heavy wooden fins, iron-bound, that hung down each side to act as a keel – in other words to stop the vessel slipping sideways when she should be sailing forwards) and big square sails – some of them square topsails setting over the course – some even, years ago, top-gallant sails – on their single masts. The mast was set in a tabernacle and could easily be lowered for a bridge and raised again by the normal crew of a man and a boy. When a keel entered a canal such as the Sheffield, where there were too many bridges for sailing, she used to put her 'gear' (i.e. mast, sail and rigging) ashore, charter a horse, and continue as a canal barge. When she got back to the tidal waters again she would leave the horse and pick up the sailing gear again. The keelmen called the long pole which they used as a punt pole a *stower*. There are still many scores of keels on the Humber but none of them sailing: all have motors or are used as dumb barges. There are still several wooden ones which were built as sailers. A Humber Keel Trust was formed some years ago with a view to keeping one of these beautiful vessels fully rigged and sailing, as an example to modern people of how their forefathers worked, but the people of the Third Port could not scrape together enough money to finance this modest venture. The Humber Sloop was a sea-going version of the keel, with much the same sort of hull but a fore-and-aft rig instead of the squaresail. The Billyboy was a yet larger and more sea-going version of the same sort of hull shape, and could have any one of a variety of sailing rigs.

Hydraulic engineers will wish to see the splendid Humber Tidal Model, run by British Transport Docks Board.

CHAPTER 20

Humber Estuary to Boston

❧

AND so, by land or sea, hover-craft, paddle-steamer, or bridge, we cross the Humber Estuary and arrive in Lincolnshire. A place simply not to be missed (although not anywhere near the true coast and therefore not really in this survey) is **Barton-on-Humber**. This was once a considerable port, and has two large and noble churches, one with important Saxon elements in it – one of the best pieces of Anglian architecture in the country. Barton is an extraordinary place, very beautiful, but see it now for it will quickly be ruined when the projected Humber Bridge gets going and it becomes virtually a suburb of Hull. There is a boatyard here, Messrs Clapson and Sons, which will find you a berth if you have a boat (or build you one if you haven't), and in this hurly-burly of an estuary it is not easy to find anywhere to drop a hook or pick up a mooring. They have moorings on the non-tidal River Ancholme as well as at Barton. The Humber is a desperate place for a yachtsman, incidentally. Fierce tides, heavy commercial traffic, and nowhere to get ashore in safety or comfort.

Immingham, a horrible place unless you like simply miles of oil pipes, puts Hull's nose out of joint by being, tonnage-wise, the Third Port nowadays. (Total tonnage in 1969 14,000,000 tons.) It is a huge tanker terminal, and iron and other ore port. It wasn't even thought of before 1900. The first sod of its dock was cut in 1906, the dock was opened by King George V and Queen Mary in 1913, and it is the deepest berth in the Humber. Besides simply lots and lots of oil it has a car ferry to Amsterdam and Gothenburg (the Tor Line) almost daily. Some of the Pilgrim Fathers sailed from Immingham Creek, for Holland, in 1608.

Grimsby was a fishing port in the thirteenth century and is one now. It has the edge on Hull with quicker rail and road communication with London. Its great days started when the Brixham fleet of sailing trawlers discovered that there was more fish in the North Sea than off Devon, and sailed round first to base itself on Boston, and then to move to Grimsby when the railway came to that town in 1848. The first Fish Dock was opened in 1856; in 1870 316 smacks

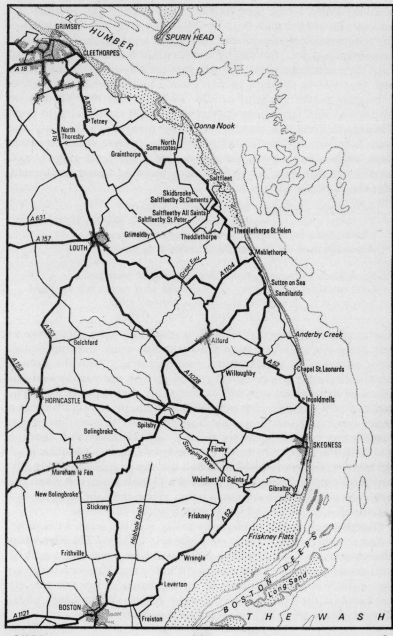

were registered at the port, in 1873 487, in 1877 531, in 1880 556 and in 1886 no less than 804. In December 1881 the death knell of the sailing trawlers was sounded: the *Zodiac* was launched, Grimsby's first steam trawler. (But sailing trawlers had had steam capstans to haul their nets since 1876.) Ice was first used by the smacks in 1858, and that was in the days of the 'Fleet Fishing', when the smacks belonging to one company would fish in a fleet and the fish be transferred into fast sailing cutters that would transport it to port. The smacks could then keep to the sea for months at a time, and the poor fishermen seldom saw the land. The biggest sailing trawlers were noble vessels: eighty or ninety feet long, ketch-rigged, and capable of keeping the North Sea in any weather, winter or summer, that the Lord liked to send.

> Sailing over the Dogger Bank, wasn't it a treat?
> The wind a'blowing east-nor'-east so we had to give her sheet;
> You ought to see us rally, the wind a'blowing free,
> A passage from the Dogger Bank to Great Grims*by*!
>
> So watch her, Twigger, watch her, the proper joobajoo!
> Give her sheet and let her rip – we're the boys to put her through.
> You ought to see us rally, the wind a'blowing free,
> A'sailing from the Dogger Bank to Great Grims*by*!

The trawler fleet, like that of Hull, is more and more going over to very large distant-water stern trawlers with quick freezing equipment on board. It is interesting, gastronomically, that the French have no freezer-trawlers – the Frenchman will not eat deep-frozen fish. The British customer will eat anything that is put before him, and can't tell the difference between a fish caught that morning in a beam trawl and one that was dragged about the bottom of the Barents Sea for four hours six months ago. Grimsby Fish Dock is said to be the largest fish market in the world, no less. Grimsby is an old town, and there is a ballad called the *Lay of Havelock* which tells how a fisherman named Grim rescued a Danish king's son when the latter was adrift in a boat when a baby. When the babe grew up and became rich, he rewarded Grim who founded the town.

Cleethorpes is part of Grimsby really and is a huge great ding-a-ding holiday resort. *There are performing dolphins!* **Humberston Fitties** is a vast caravan and shanty town, with a zoo and a mile of hard sand to traverse at low tide to get to the sea. Fitties comes from *fitty* – Old Norse for meadowland on the banks of river or sea. At the Fitties is the ramp of the Humber Mouth Yacht Club. Cleethorpes people are called 'meggies' or 'howletts'.

Tetney Haven was once an important place, for into this creek sailed keels and Billyboys galore to enter the Louth Navigation and be towed by horses up to Louth. It is to be an important place again, for oil pipes are being laid from here right out to sea, and they are to be picked up by some of the biggest tankers in the world, which cannot even get into the Humber, and which will lie out at anchor in the open ocean and discharge their oil. At Tetney Haven one man earns a living catching eels. At Tetney itself are blow wells, which form small lakes.

The shore now to Donna Nook, where I take it that the *coast proper* really begins, is desolate in the extreme. **Grainthorpe Haven** is a great place of saltings, marshes, miles of sand through which cuts a channel, and nothing else. And then we come to that splendidly named place **Donna Nook**. Nobody seems quite sure from where it gets its name, but the most usual story is that a ship was wrecked there with the name of *Donna* or something like it. At Donna Nook itself there is a coastguard station, and lanes going down, and therefore, in the summer sometimes, there are people. But the coast each side of it for several miles is likely to be quite empty of humanity (unless there may be some of the members of the Cleethorpes Ringing Group intent on capturing birds to ring) and if you want to be alone, here is a place to be by yourself. You can even indulge in that proscribed and manifestly wicked activity *camping in an unauthorised place* for many weeks before you are caught and dragged off to prison to expiate this fearful crime. At Donna Nook occurred an event that should be a lesson to all seamen not to flout the normal conventions of the sea. On *Friday*, that day of ill-omen when no good sailor would start a major voyage, on *April Fool's Day* 1966, *thirteen* men set sail in the *Anzio I*. She had had her name changed, from *Lochinvar*, and name-changing in ships is not a good thing in itself, unless for a very good reason. The *Lochinvar* was one of the earliest motor ships to be built – in 1909 – for the West Highlands passenger and freight service. She sailed from Tilbury on that inauspicious day, got as far as Donna Nook and came ashore there at about 11.30 p.m. A local farm worker saw her lights and went down to the water's edge and hailed her. Her crew answered, but there was nothing he could do. The coastguard rocket team came down and wading into the breakers shot their line, but it was too short to reach her. The Spurn lifeboat then arrived on the scene and tried to signal to the crew by lamp and by shouting, but realised that there was nobody left on board. The heavy sea that had built up had washed everybody off, and they were all drowned. There was a mystery (and still is) as to how the disaster occurred. The body of the captain was later recovered, in such a position that it was clear that he had been washed overboard some time before the stranding. The night was clear and nobody has ever explained why the vessel should have been put ashore at this point at all. The crew were mostly enthusiasts who had been working for Cable and Wireless in London and had left this organisation to take the ship to the West Highlands again and run her as a passenger service.

Just as the shore of Holderness is washing away, so that of this part of Lincolnshire is building up, and we can see this process in its various stages at Donna Nook. At the sea's edge at low tide is half a mile or a mile of sterile sand: sterile that is in that no rooted plants can grow on it. As we walk inland we eventually come to isolated plants of samphire (*Salicorria europaea*), residual skeletons in winter but green fleshy leaves in summer. This, incidentally, is very good to eat, either picked raw, or boiled, or pickled. The fleshy leaves are in fact filled with hard fibres, and when eating it one must pull the leaves through one's teeth to get off the flesh. In Lincolnshire and North Norfolk it is considered a great delicacy, and samphire sellers ply their trade with barrows in Boston, King's Lynn and other places. Where the plants of samphire grow a little blown sand collects. Further away from the sea we come to where tufts of grass have managed to get a foothold on the sand – just an isolated tuft here and there and then, further up, a more or less continuous patchy sward. The grass catches blown sand and grows through it, and catches more, and gradually builds up in height. Higher up still we see where this process has gone further and here we find *saltings* – areas of raised sandy mud, much cut by channels through which the tide rushes when it comes up or goes out again, and grown with a thick growth of grasses, sea lavender and other plants, covered by the sea only at high spring tides. Higher still are sand-dunes, on which men try to establish marram grass in order to bind the sand. Behind the sand-dunes is a sea wall, behind this the *delft*, which is the ditch from which the earth was taken to build the sea wall, and behind this the flat fertile land which would be flooded only at very exceptionally high spring tides if it were not for the sea wall. Obviously land is being built up, and, if the process goes on, it will be possible one day to build another sea wall, further out to sea, to enclose more land. At **North Somercotes** there is a very limited attempt at doing what seems so obviously the correct thing to do with these sand dunes: plant them up with conifers. The trees would do on a larger scale what the struggling samphire plants do lower down: trap and collect the sand which blows in from the sea beach at low tide when an onshore gale is blowing. Thorn fences have been erected in places to help catch and build up the sand.

We come to **Saltfleet**, officially a hamlet in Skidbrooke parish but the tail wags the dog: in fact the dog has almost totally disappeared. Saltfleet is a little village of great beauty and interest. In the first place it has what must be one of the finest inns in the whole of England. The New Inn is a huge building of mellow English-bonded hand-made brick, really Elizabethan, three storeys, Tudor gables, a jumble of red-pantiled roofs, stone flagged within, unspoiled without. It is a most superb building and a fine pub. Fortunately the landlord is a small farmer too, and a real local man, and has no intention of allowing this noble place to be snapped up, tarted up, or otherwise spoiled by city people. He has caravans discreetly placed at the back.

In the second place Saltfleet was once a port, and an important one, and a decayed port generally has an atmosphere about it. In fact it was once a great port, the principal port in the Roman province of Flavia Caesarienses, and from this place started the Fosse Way. In 1359 Saltfleet supplied two ships and 49 men to Edward III for the invasion of Brittany. In 1347 the existing fine manor house (now owned by the Ross family, which owns so much of Grimsby's fishing fleet) was built by the Willoughby family. Lord Willoughby is said to have entertained Oliver Cromwell and Lord Fairfax there when they were on their way to the Battle of Winceby. This manor house has two other claims to attention. One is that it still has some of the world's first wallpaper on its walls. The other is that on a window pane is scratched with a diamond: 'Robert Fox 1673' and a true lover's knot, and on another 'Jane Hardy 1673'. Sticklers for morality will be glad to hear that these fugitive lovers were subsequently properly married in Skidbrooke church.

As befitting an old port there are two fine warehouses in the village, and several good old houses and cottages, and there are old men who can still remember when the people of Saltfleet owned six good sloops of about sixty tons each, for carrying wheat and wool out and coal and timber and other commodities in. There were also five good pubs to provide beer for the men who sailed and worked these vessels. The sloops were mostly built at Thorne. The place exported chiefly wool and wheat and imported coal. The last load came in in 1935, and that was a barge-load of chalk, to be dumped at the mouth of Saltfleet Haven as part of the sea defence. Now there is a collection of yachts, some of them be it admitted rather ramshackle (but none the less loved by their owners for that), and it's rather a dangerous place for the inexperienced: it's easy enough to get *out* of, at high water, but not so easy to get into, being poorly marked from the sea. And if you fail to get into it, in an on-shore breeze, where else can you go? At low tide, of course, you cannot get into it even if you can find it.

The sea wall here now was built, and covered with grass sods, in 1853, and is still good and the individual sods can still be seen! The road here runs along a Roman bank, which indicates that the sea has not receded all that far in 1,500 years. There is a pump near Toby's Hill erected in memory of Trooper Fred Allen Freshnex, Imperial Light Horse, fatally wounded at the battle of Colenso, in the South African War. The church of **Skidbrooke** is a melancholy sight, a fine lonely medieval building, pigeons roosting inside, roof leaking on to the old rotting benches, and all palpably going to fall down. **Louth** is only a few miles inland, a very interesting town and one not to be missed. The last lock on the Louth Navigation incidentally, the entrance of which we have seen at Tetney Lock, is called Ticklepenny Lock. Louth is a very good example of a thriving agricultural market town, although no longer an inland port.

The people of Saltfleet, as of other parts along this coast, engage in various activities connected with the seashore. One of the most bizarre is performed by tractor drivers. When there are very low tides these industrious men drive their tractors right down to the edge of the sea (and it goes out a very long way) and hunt for stranded crabs. The crabs, big edible specimens too, get caught out by the tide being so exceptionally low and dig themselves into the sand. The tractor drivers see the little mounds of sand and jump off and pick the crabs up – and can often fill a sack with them! They are often beaten to it by the gulls, though, who know that the crabs are there and frequently peck them open first. There is good cockling along this shore, and until recently horse and cart trawling was practised for shrimps. The horse and cart would wade through the shallow water towing a shrimp trawl. What we in East Anglia call *pritching* – stabbing fish with barbed forks in shallow water – is here called *stunging*, and a *pritch* is a *stung-gad*, and the fishery is much practised. Another way of taking fish is to hang a baited hook from a willow driven into the sand at low tide. A cod or a skate caught on the hook cannot break the snood, for the willow wand is flexible and 'plays' the fish, and it can be retrieved at low water again. If you ask the people of Saltfleet if their ancestors engaged in smuggling they will tell you that the men of the place would go out and *fetch* the smugglers if the latter tried to go somewhere else.

South of Saltfleet, in the parish of **Saltfleetby** which is pronounced 'Soliby', the Lincolnshire Naturalists' Trust shares the foreshore with the RAF, and the latter uses it as a bombing range. Defying both is worth while, for here are miles and miles of saltings, of sand dunes, of wild lonely shore and beach. If the warning flags are not flying nobody will bomb you. This other Eden, demi-paradise, is so hemmed in with notice boards warning you of this or that, though, that the sea is nearly invisible.

At **Theddlethorpe St Helen** is a late fourteenth-century stone reredos (at the east end of the north aisle) with a crucifix broken off in front of it. At **Theddlethorpe All Saints** is a great church built of greenstone between 1380 and 1400, with a great screen. Near Bleak House, north of **Mablethorpe** and really part of that place, we come to a vast caravan town, and a new pub imaginatively called The Lively Lady after Sir Alec Rose's boat. From here we come to caravans, and bingo, and all the rest of it, crouching behind high sand-dunes, and then the concrete defences of Mablethorpe which cost two million pounds, and very fine beaches, and **Sutton-on-Sea** which is just part of Mablethorpe, and the bones of a ship stick out of the sand here, she was 126 feet long, and had fine lines fore and aft, and was ceiled, but more than this I cannot tell. South of **Sandilands**, inland from the long narrow golf course, is fine fattening grassland, still in ridge-and-furrow. The golf course is to the seaward side of the medieval sea bank here, showing a small increment of land. **Anderby** Creek goes under the sand-dunes through a tunnel, and here is a small row of houses built high up on the dunes, and so unoccupied during winter that I have seen a wild fox running along a yard or two from their front doors.

It would be wrong to go on from this part of the coast without telling of the flood disaster of 1953. After dark, on the terrible night of 31 January, watchers at Mablethorpe saw the breakers of the sea roaring over the *pullover*. (The pullovers of this coast are equivalent to the *gaps* of the Norfolk coast: low stretches on the sand-dunes over which it is possible to drag a boat). Great lengths of concrete wall collapsed and were used by the huge seas as battering rams to break down more. The sand-dune defences melted: at Sutton a five-hundred-yard gap was torn – and the country behind became flooded for miles. The rescue agencies, led by the army, got moving very rapidly. People and animals were evacuated by amphibious vehicles and assault craft. Louth became like a battle headquarters, and Louth and Alford were both crowded with refugees. After the water had receded the army took over and the roads were cleared while thousands of tons of slag were rushed from Scunthorpe by a ceaseless stream of lorries, night and day, racing to mend the gaps before the next spring tides. Forty-one people had been drowned along this short stretch of coast: seventeen at Ingoldmells, eleven at Sutton-on-Sea, one at Trusthorpe, eight at Mablethorpe and four at Saltfleet. After the battle was over the Lincolnshire River Board set about, with far greater vigour than hitherto, trying to establish better sea defences. Marram grass was planted on the dunes and *protected* from the feet of the ever-growing hordes of holidaymakers, thorn hedges put in, wooden groins pile-driven out to sea, concrete walls built.

Just north of **Chapel St Leonards** are two spoil pits belonging now to the Lincolnshire Naturalists' Trust and here be duck. Chapel St Leonards was all washed away in 1571. We now have caravans caravans all the way. There has been, in the last decade, what can only be called a caravan *explosion*. For seven miles now south, we will be in sight of caravans all the time, excepting where the housing is too thick for the caravans, and for this seven miles bingo is king. South of Chapel St Leonards an early Iron Age pottery was found, which specialised in making earthenware pans for salt-boiling, and it is said that at low tide wooden structures used to be visible which had been used for the brine boiling. In the Transactions of the Archaeological Society at Lincoln of 1848, is an illustration of one of these pottery kilns, with lots of rolls of clay ready for working (or perhaps props for supporting pots in the kiln which still, apparently, had finger prints on them which would have been identifiable by the Bertillon method used by the police. At **Ingold-mells** lived the patrician Reverend Joseph Charles Edwards, who existed in a lavish fashion and was well liked by everybody he didn't owe money to. He went bankrupt in 1867 having liabilities to the extent of £2,331 and assets, alas, of a paltry £90. When asked in court why, having no wife, he nevertheless has large drapers' bills, he replied: 'I tell you, Sir, it is a condescension for me to be examined at all by you. You are a buffoon.'

At Ingoldmells is a big church with Early English arcades and fine leaf moulding around the tower arch. There is also one of the biggest and oldest of the camps of Mr Butlin: so old now indeed that it stands in the same relationship to the others as Oxford or Cambridge stand to red brick universities. In the last war it was transformed for the duration into HMS *Royal Arthur*, a training camp.

Skegness, which is so bracing, got this description from the poster of the jolly bearded fisherman painted by John Hassall in 1908 for the GNER, for which service he received twelve guineas. It was to advertise day excursions from King's Cross to Skegness for three shillings, and the fisherman seemed to say: 'Skegness is so bracing'. And, as anybody who has been there in a winter east wind will tell you, it is.

Leland wrote: 'Skegnesse, sumtyme a great haven, toune, a four or five miles of Wilegripe. Mr Paynelle sayid unto me that he could prove that there was ons an haven and a toune waullid having also a castelle. The olde toun is clene consumid and eten up with the se. Part of a chirch of it stood a late. For old Skegnes is now builded a pore new thing. At low water appere yet manifest tokens of olde buildings.'

Well, Skeg, as its admirers as well as its detractors call it, has certainly risen from the sea again, and has a huge pier (built in 1881 and 1,843 foot long), and a mile of canal along which pleasure boats take passengers, and the fishermen of Skeg, finding it inconvenient to go fishing any more, turned to taking trippers out in boats, and from that to taking them along the dry sands in *dummy* boats on wheels. There is a noble stone lion outside the Lion Hotel. It is not true that it roars every time a virgin walks past.

There must have been a harbour here, as Leland says, for in 1430 a man was taken to court for damaging it. In 1856 6,000 tons of coal were landed here. In April 1887 a rorqual, a female, 47 foot long, was shot on the beach and sold to Mr Fulton of Hull by auction run by the local auctioneer. The auctioneer, and Mr Fulton, and Mr Fulton's son were then photographed standing on top of the dead monster by Mr Wain, the local photographer.

Skegness may have been the Metaris of Ptolemy – a walled station north of the Wash corresponding with Brancaster on the other side. Could it be that the Romans found it much easier to go north to their northern marches by taking boat at Brancaster and sailing or rowing across the mouth of the Wash than by the long and difficult route south of the Fens?

There was a time when Skegness was a small fishing port, the fishermen, chiefly named Grunnill, working cobles from the beach and keeping larger vessels in Wainfleet Haven. A Mr Grunnill, still alive, worked a splendid steam launch from here, named the *White Rose*, using her mainly for lining. He sold her in the coal strike of the 1930s, not being able to get coal to keep her going. Several sizeable smacks worked out of the Haven, beam trawling under sail, the last being the *Busy Bee*, the *Daisy* and the half decked *Harriet*. Now, *plus ça change*, a young man is having a go at fishing from this port again, in a powerful and well equipped motor coble from the Haven, fitted for trawling with an otter trawl. As the seals have been severely reduced in the Wash he stands a good chance of getting some fish.

South of Skegness there is a fine nature reserve: **Gibraltar Point**. The northern part of this belongs to the Skegness UDC, and the southern part to the Lindsey County Council but it is administered by the Lincolnshire Naturalists' Trust, and very well administered too. There is a well-marked nature trail, for people who like to be told where to go, and somehow the Trust manages to preserve sufficient peace for the birds without interfering too much with the rights of the citizen to move about in his own country. The greatest menace to birds has long been, not the man with the gun, but the bird watcher, who now moves about in such numbers that there are often more watchers than birds. The Trust has a field station here, in a house that was once the coastguard's but is now far from the sea, for the shore is accreting here, fast. It is estimated by about six feet every year. We can plainly see, near Gibraltar Point itself, where three banks have been thrown up by the sea, one in front of the other. In February 1968 the Steeping River cut itself a new mouth. Here is a great variety of habitat: sand, sand-dunes, marsh, salting, swamp and river. It is a very pleasant place. In the field centre lives a permanent warden, who, not contented with being surrounded by wild birds, keeps tame ones too, and has a very fine collection of both Norwich and Yorkshire canaries (the former a dumpy bird but a very sweet singer – the latter so slim that it can 'get through a wedding ring').

Abruptly at Gibraltar Point we come to the Wash proper. The tide-washed sand suddenly widens out from a beach at low tide of less than a quarter of a mile wide to one of three miles. We have come to a very peculiar and special land indeed. Or is it a land? Is it land or water? It is hard to decide. The Wash is one of the strangest parts of the English coast. It can be a place of mirages – of dead calm magic water broken by great stretches of sand – where sand banks a yard or two high look like mountain ranges – it can have so clear an air that the banded cliffs of Hunstanton, the bunches of big trees far inland in the Lincolnshire fens, and Boston Stump, all appear as clear and close as if they were coming in upon us. It can be, when a north-east gale is blowing, a raging hell of white water, and not for nothing is the sand bank in the middle of it known as the

Roaring Middle. But in the calm times of mirage it is most beautiful: the mirages here can compare with those of the Okavango Swamps or the Etosha Pan.

South of Gibraltar Point, where we are observing all these phenomena, there are two sea walls, the older one three-quarters of a mile inland of the other, and the land between is named the Outmarsh. It is a fairly recent inning. Three miles further in is **Wainfleet All Saints** – a very beautiful and interesting place indeed. Wainfleet just missed, in the Middle Ages, being one of the country's most important ports. It is supposed to have been the Roman harbour of Vainona: in 1800 men digging a cellar for the Angel Hotel found a Roman pitcher. In 1359 the port supplied two ships and forty men to the navy of Henry III for the invasion of Brittany. In 1394 a complaint was made that, whereas the channel into the port ought to be eight feet deep it was, in fact, only four. In 1457 the town was granted a charter of incorporation. In 1774 a report said that the harbour was almost completely silted up, but in 1829 it was reported that it was improving, and that the channel was six foot deep throughout. Now there is no traffic at all.

Wainfleet is said to have been killed as a port by the astute move of Boston in assuring that the great drainage system of the fens between the Steeping River and the Witham, should be made to drain south into the Witham instead of north into the Steeping – as it had been used to doing. Thus the water from it was employed in scouring out the channel of Boston harbour instead of that of Wainfleet. My own feeling is that Wainfleet declined because, when the wool export trade was finished, there was nothing else for it to do. Boston on the other hand had water communication with the whole of the English Midlands: keels could come up or down the Trent, along the Roman-dug Fossdike to Lincoln and from there down the Witham to Boston, and for centuries Boston was the main port of export for such commodities as Derbyshire lead. Wainfleet had no such water roads to the hinterland and so there was no money, or great urge, to keep its channel clear. Certainly here are the remains of a much greater place. There is a fine turreted building of 1484 (at least then founded), part of the school founded by William of Waynflete, who became Bishop of Winchester and founder of Magdalen College, Oxford. Here also is what I think the most extraordinary village street in the whole of England. It is called Barkham Street, and looks like part of early nineteenth-century Paris. It looks as though it got where it is by mistake somehow. Long may it remain there. There is a big old inn that I like to go to – like so many old inns called the New Inn – which, in the eighteenth century, was a furniture factory. The landlord will show you two chairs that he has that were made there. And, wonder of wonders, a small family brewery still survives in Wainfleet. It will be interesting to see how long it can retain its independence against the mighty molochs of Burton which will not be satiated until they have swallowed up every brewery – and pub – in England, and reduced all to dreary uniformity.

Now seawards of Wainfleet is the Wainfleet Bombing and Gunnery Range, which personally I cannot concern myself about, and the walk south along the shore of the Wash here is lonely and beautiful in the extreme. At low tide we can walk miles out over the sand flats, but remember the tide comes in pretty quickly. After all it has to cover here say three and a half miles of sand in six hours (the time it takes to flood), so it has to go at half a mile an hour. If we are right down at the water's edge at low spring tide – far out of sight of land if it is a hazy day – it is a little daunting to see the little wavelets advancing over the dry sand at this speed. We are all right provided that there is not a deeper channel inland of us. If there is we can be all wrong. But to walk along the foot of the sea wall is the most interesting, for here are the saltings, where the redshanks wheel about making their lovely eerie screaming like the lost souls of marshmen, and lapwings tumble about in the sky in that feckless way they have, and curlews bubble, and in the winter great rafts of wigeon feed along the edge of the mud, making their weird whistling noise (which you can reproduce so perfectly with the whistle off a Woolworth kettle), and in the winter, too, great skeins of pinkfoot geese fly overhead, winging in at evening to the stubble fields and old potato lands to feed, and out again at early morning to sleep in peace on the lonely sea. Here, as nowhere else in England, can we have the feeling of the world before man came and learnt the knack of interfering with every other living creature.

South of Wainfleet there are three successive sea walls, the innermost a medieval one. Opposite **Wrangle** we find, marked on the map, the Sailor's Home. This was a pub until a few years ago but is now a weekend cottage belonging to a Londoner. Lucky Londoner! What a wonderful contrast with Piccadilly Circus! At **Leverton**, in the church, is a memorial to Hy Pecham, 1597. He wrote *The Compleat Gentleman*. I regret I haven't read it: perhaps I should be a very different man if I had. The wide flat marshes here about, all well below high-water spring tides whatever the maps say, are extensively planted with cabbages and other brassicae, as well as corn. As we get further south we shall find more and more bulbs, firstly daffodils and narcissi and then vast fields of tulips. The motorist should avoid the tulip areas during the flowering season (May and early June) unless he likes driving bumper-to-bumper and inhaling exhaust fumes, for this has become an annual 'sight'. Personally I prefer the cabbages.

Freiston is so called because a colony of Friesians settled here (men not cows). **North Sea Camp** is a Borstal establishment, and is hard by the present mouth of the Witham, where this river joins the outflow of the Welland. Into the sea here drains a large area of England.

CHAPTER 21

Boston to Sutton Bridge

❧

MAN has caused the Witham and Welland to discharge at the same point: the new Welland mouth was cut in the 1930s. The idea is to concentrate the waters and thus enable them to cut a clear channel to the sea. Outside, in the Boston Deeps, we will often see ships, generally Russian, Dutch or German ones, lying at anchor waiting for enough water to get into the Witham. Out here too, in the Bar Hole, the Boston Pilot Cutter waits at her station. Here also we will see the Boston Prawners coming and going, going out to sea on the ebb and coming back generally on the last of the flood. These are fine little ships, nearly all old sailing smacks, some built at King's Lynn over the water, others from Essex. They now of course all have motors, and haul heavy beam trawls for the Pink Shrimp (*Pandalus montagui*) locally called the Prawn. It is fun to go for a voyage aboard one of these vessels. They leave Boston on the first tide of the day, generally between midnight and six o'clock in the morning, steam down the straight narrow 'cut' to the open sea of Boston Deep, then either keep down the Boston Deep or else cut through the Freeman into Lynn Deep, and shoot their trawls in from five to ten fathoms of water. They trawl for perhaps an hour, then haul, the strong arms of the three-man crew helped by a powered capstan nowadays. A big pile of shrimps and rubbish is dumped out of the cod-end on to the deck, the shrimps sorted out of it and boiled immediately in an old-fashioned copper built into the hold of the smack. Strangely, much salt has to be used for boiling – although the water they are boiled in is sea water. Sea water is just not salt enough. After boiling there comes a laborious business of riddling the shrimps in cold sea water, and picking over the catch carefully for creatures that are not shrimps. (There are often many hermit crabs, and it may be useful to know that the large claws of these creatures are very good to eat.) The boiled, cooled and picked-over shrimps are then packed into small sausage-shaped nets, and piled up on deck. While all this is going on of course the net is on the bottom again and catching more. This activity goes on for perhaps twelve hours, when the smack takes the last of the flood up

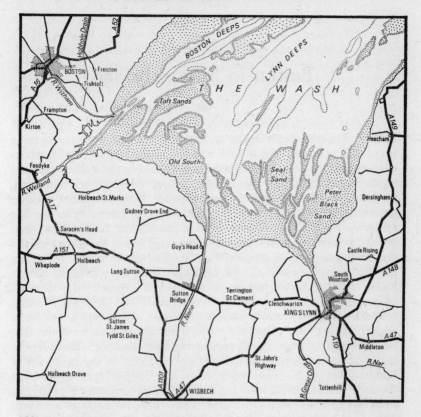

to Boston again. Shrimping in Britain is fifty years behind shrimping on the Continent. In Holland and the Friesland and Hanover coasts the whole thing has been worked out more carefully, and there we have the boom trawling – two booms, one each side of the vessel, which let down to lower two beam trawls into the water, and then lift, or steeve, up again when the trawls are hauled, thus lifting the cod-ends clear of the gunwale. The whole process of cooking and cooling the shrimps also has been much more carefully thought out, enabling the small crews to 'work off the deck', the much greater catches made possible by the two trawls.

Another great fishery from Boston is cockling, and here at least the English fisherman has thought of something new in the last few hundred years. He practises the illegal, but highly effective, 'ploughing out'. The 'sand-toppers' on cockle smacks (smaller

255

vessels than the 'prawners', and generally half-decked or welled), go down at about half ebb and anchor themselves in shallow water over the sands where their skippers know cockles to be. Now the old method of cockling, and the only one really allowed in the Wash, is to wait until the sands below the keel dry out, thus stranding the vessel. (The smacks have to be very strong to take the bashing of thus being 'shipwrecked' once a day – for that is what it amounts to – if there is any sea running the boats take a terrible bashing before they are high and dry.) Then, when the water has gone, the crews leap overboard and rake the cockles out of the wet sand with steel rakes, into specially made hand nets which latter are swished in the shallow water left by the tide to get the sand out. The cockles are shot into baskets, and the baskets carried back to the smack on yokes of the kind that one associates with dairy maids. Two men will thus take half a ton or even a ton of cockles before the tide comes back again to make the work impossible. They then have to clamber aboard and sit there, drinking tea and cooking up bacon and eggs, until the tide has come up high enough to float their laden boat, when they get up their anchor and off they go to Boston. But now, 'ploughing out' has come to make the job much easier. The only thing is – it has been made illegal by the Eastern Seas Fishery Board, the government body in charge of fisheries in the Wash, and if the officers of this organisation find you doing it they will take you to court and fine you. The method is – you drop an anchor far heavier than the one you actually need to hold such a boat. You then put your engine full ahead – and let the boat slowly turn herself around the anchor – the churning propeller only a foot or two above the sand. When you have made one revolution thus you veer out more cable – and make another. You continue doing this until you can do it no longer – because the tide has gone down further and you take the ground. You then wait for the sands to dry out and find all the cockles that were in the ground that you have thus 'ploughed out' neatly heaped up in a great circle. Of course the Dutch do the whole job hydraulically, at high tide, with practically no labour at all.

The other fishery of Boston is musselling. This was done once at low tide too, but as the mussels live in mud (a sort of slimy mud of their own making) it was a horrible job, and very laborious. A new mussel dredge has only recently been introduced which has revolutionised the business. It has an adjustable cutter blade in front, and can be dragged over the mussel beds at high tide, cutting out the mussels and leaving most of the mud. A smack can get up to seventy bags in a couple of hours like this. The mussels, unfit for human consumption because of the pollution in the Wash, all go for bait for the long-liners in the north of England. Those devoted women whom we met sitting in the bait sheds of Filey putting mussels on thousands and thousands of hooks were using mussels from the Wash.

Another industry has sprung up fairly recently from Boston, and that is pair fishing for sprats. Two boats work together, dragging a long net between them. There are about fifteen big 'prawners' fishing from Boston now, and twenty-four 'sand-toppers', as the cocklers are called, working as they do on top of the dried-out sand.

Well, here we are at the mouth of the Witham, by what is known as Clay Hole. We are constrained to turn inland and walk up-river towards Boston. The famous **Stump**, which in clear weather dominates the whole of the Wash (it is the tower of Boston parish church) is from here dwarfed, apparently, by electric pylons. It seems that Technological Man just has to have the last word: even the tower of St Botolph's church is not allowed its pre-eminence. But the pylons, although higher perhaps, do not have the same aesthetic quality. Technological Man loses in the end. We pass the pumping station that voids the waters of the Cowbridge and Hobhole Drains out into the Witham. Just beyond this is a small stone memorial to the Pilgrim Fathers. These worthy men tried to take ship here, to escape religious persecution by sailing to Holland preparatory to going to America. This was in September 1607. But, alas, they were captured and taken to Boston where, as we shall see, they were immured and made to stand trial. Just by this monument to one battle of the never-ending fight for freedom is a monument to another: a block house of the Second World War. We pass Woad Farm, by the hamlet of **Fishtoft**, and are reminded that the cultivation of woad, or *Isatis tinctoria* was practised around Boston until 1900. The people here did not dye themselves with it, as we are told their ancestors did, but cloth. It was a crop which took a great deal out of the soil, and thus was not grown for year after year in the same place. Hence the mills that were built for crushing and processing it were mobile, so that they could follow the crop.

At **Skirbeck** can be seen part of a dyke the Romans built to reclaim land. We then come to **Boston Docks**. These have seven acres of non-tidal water, and were built in 1882 and 1900 to the design of W. H. Wheeler. It is a busy little port now, benefiting like all other small ports from the intransigence of the London docker. It is an obvious port of entry for the East Midlands, now as it was in the Middle Ages. It is only a pity that now as then water communications with the hinterland are no longer used. Keels could be loaded alongside ships in the docks of Boston (thus eliminating shore storage) and navigated straight to any city in the Midlands or North of England. Instead the imagination of twentieth century man does not seem to be able to get further than the dangerous and grossly overloaded roads.

Boston comes from St Botolph's Town. A monastic establishment is supposed to have been founded here in 654. Skirbeck is known to have been a Danish settlement, and Domesday mentions it as having had two churches: it is assumed that one of these was St Botolph's in Boston. Very soon after the Conquest, Boston grew rapidly in importance as a wool-exporting place. Merchants from the Continent settled here to buy and export wool. On 30th January 1204 King John granted a charter to the town. Customs records between 1279 and 1289 show that Boston was the greatest port in the kingdom, exporting more even than London: in 1281 the total customs of the kingdom was £8,411 19s 11½d – of which Boston paid £3,599 1s 6d. The Great Fleet of Henry III had seventeen ships and 361 men from Boston: only Great Yarmouth had more. Boston was a walled town – in 1295 it had a grant to repair walls. In 1369 the town managed to wangle the Wool Staple from Lincoln: meaning that it was one of the few ports in England permitted to export wool. Boston also became one of the chief English centres of the Hanseatic League, vying with King's Lynn in this respect. In 1285 we know that the following imports and exports went through Boston: wine, timber, fox-skins, rabbits, silk, wool, cloth, raisins, figs, clay, pottery, sulphur, liquorice, sugar, salt, spices, ginger, pepper, honey, butter, cheese, tallow, almonds, rice, alum, vermilion, lead, wax, quicksilver and incense. When in 1287 a band of robbers disguised as mummers came and looted and robbed the town, it was said that in the fire they started 'streams of gold, silver, and other metal, molten, ran into the sea'. One Robert Chamberlain, the leader of this little group of 'bovver' boys, was caught and hanged.

In the fifteenth century Boston suffered the same decline that afterwards overtook the great ports of the Netherlands. Ships were getting bigger and there was no way of dredging the harbour. Historians generally diagnose the trouble as the silting up of the harbour. The harbour did not silt, it stayed the same but ships became of deeper and deeper draught, and therefore shallow water ports such as Boston (and Amsterdam) could not compete with places with deeper natural harbours. The Dutch saved themselves by inventing the *krabbelaar* in 1435, a tide- and sail-operated barge with rakes suspended underneath it which raked the mud at the bottom of the river on the ebb tide and enabled some of it to be carried away, and, about 1600, the *mud mill*, which was a bucket-dredger driven by a tread mill. About 1650 came the horse-driven mud mill. The Dutch ports were on the way to finding their salvation, and grass no longer grew in the streets of Amsterdam. Boston, however, had none of these devices, and in the fifteenth and sixteenth centuries suffered a severe decline. Only the draining of the Fens in the seventeenth century, which provided the town with a tremendously fertile hinterland, the two weekly markets (Wednesday and Saturday) and two yearly fairs (Feasts of St George and St James) which enabled the townspeople to cash in on this fertility, saved Boston from becoming another Wainfleet or Saltfleet. The Charter granting the fairs and incorporating the town a borough was granted by Henry VIII in 1546.

Then severe flooding in 1763 started the first serious attempt to dredge the River Witham. On 15th October 1766 the Grand Sluice was opened with enormous public rejoicing. The Witham above the Sluice was then non-tidal and could carry an enormous traffic of keels and Fen Lighters, and the improved and dredged tidal channel could bring in bigger ships from the sea. In 1820 Rennie drained the last of the Fen country, and Boston found itself the centre of one of the most productive districts in England.

Boston must have enjoyed some prosperity at least until 1450, before it fell into its period of decline, for in that year the tower of its church, known only as 'the Stump', was completed (in 1309, on the Monday after Palm Sunday, the foundations of the tower began to be 'digged by many miners'). I will not say that this is the most beautiful church tower in existence, it can indeed be faulted very seriously, and as an object to look at, from near by anyway, give me Fotheringhay. But then I have seen the old Stump standing up against the Fenland sky from every channel and sandbank in the Wash, and from many many miles away over the flat Fens, and the sight of it, thus in the distance, is like the sight of an old friend. When the Wash sailor can see the Stump he needs no compass, and, out in that loneliest of all places, he does not feel alone.

St Botolph's church is the greatest parish church in England. It is a sumptuous and superb and beautiful building. The view westward, through that mighty tower arch into the soaring base of the tower itself, and through to the towering west window, is spectacular. It is a breathtaking building. There are said to be 365 steps up the tower, which is just 272½ feet high – and climb up it by all means: the experience is most rewarding. Go to Boston, if you can possibly contrive to, in the first weekend in May, which is when one of the two annual fairs granted to the town by Henry VIII takes place. Then the streets of the town are packed with one of the most rumbustious pleasure fairs in England: roundabouts (one of them a real steam-driven one) and pleasure machines of every kind turn and whirl and compete for the attention with the Smallest Man in the World and a dozen other 'freak' shows, the streets are packed with real English country people, and to climb to the top of the Stump then, if the day be fine, is to experience a great sensation, for the music of half a dozen extremely loud machines floats up from below to blend together into a magical salad of sound, we look down at Boston as though it were a toy town, with toy chair-a-planes and steam gallopers flying round and round, a brilliantly coloured stream of gay dresses flowing past the machines, and the wide, hazy, Fens and blue waters of the Wash beyond the town's outskirts. This is what I would call a psychedelic experience.

More about St Botolph's I shall not say, because the study of this church cannot be a superficial one, and there is a table-load of booklets about it inside, to suit every purse or extent of interest. Americans visit it in large numbers because of its strong associations with their country, and the people of that other Boston over the sea have most generously given several hefty gifts of money for various restorations.

One of the vicars of this church was John Cotton, born in Derby in 1585, vicar here in 1612, forced to resign in 1625 owing to his opinions, and landed in America in 1633, where he exercised great influence on the new colonists. Richard Bellington, Recorder of Boston from 1625 to 1633 became Governor of Massachusetts. Atherton Hough, Thomas Leverett, Isaac Johnson, Thomas Dudley, William Coddington, were all Boston men who achieved distinction in America. Foxe, of the *Book of Martyrs* fame, was a Boston man.

As for the Pilgrim Fathers, they *tried* to sail from Boston, as we have seen, but were apprehended (the captain of their vessel basely gave them away), and locked up in Boston Guildhall. They were, it is pleasant to relate, 'used courteously' by the magistrates, and later allowed to sail for Holland. From there they sailed to Southampton, in the *Mayflower*, rendezvous'd with the pinnace *Speedwell*, and sailed for America on 5th August 1620. They sighted Plymouth Rock on 9th November.

We should go to the Guildhall, where we can see the very cells the Pilgrims were locked up in, and the court room in which their case was heard. There is a mighty kitchen here, still more or less as it was three hundred years ago, with ingenious smoke-fans up the great chimneys to turn the spits. The place has been made into a museum, and even has dummies dressed up like Pilgrim Fathers (and Mothers). We should see Shodfriar's Hall, an exuberant piece of fifteenth-century timber-frame building, if only because it was actually put up in 1874. We should even more see Fydell House, prime (and genuine) Queen Anne, owned by the Boston Preservation Trust, and Blackfriars, leased by them, now an art centre, and Maud Foster Mill, a magnificent five-sailed tower mill, preserved but alas not turning. But the best building in Boston for my money is the warehouse of Lincolnshire Seed Stores. This is what Boston used to be like, and the sort of building on which the prosperity of the old town was founded. Boston Preservation Trust is doing fine work preserving good things. Boston council, like every other council in the country, is apt to be busy pulling them down. The principle of ripping down old streets and just leaving 'buildings of special interest' is disastrous: it is the total *ensemble* of old buildings which gives a town like Boston its unique character. Enough has already been destroyed, not one more old building should be pulled down, on any pretext whatever. There is plenty of room round about, and two or three small cottages can always be knocked into one.

Boston has always had close links with the Low Countries. The fish packing and processing firm of Van Smirren's has practically taken over the fishing industry in Boston and is an important element of the industry of the town. Geest Industries Limited, which has its headquarters in Spalding, on the next river, is also part of the Dutch invasion.

Now south of Boston we find **Frampton**, a delicious village among trees, **Kirton** said to have been the seat of Anglian kings, great acres of tulip fields take us to the medieval sea wall again, and over it into Frampton Marsh, over the newer wall several square miles of fascinating saltings country, much cut by tidal creeks, best explored in the traditional gun punt of East Anglia, but not on foot. Even at low tide most of the creeks, being soft mud, are impassable. At a house called Marine Villa, at the end of a lane and just behind the sea wall, we have a glimpse of the insanity of the world we live in. Here is one of the choicest places to live anywhere along the shores of the Wash: a splendid farm house, up to recently in good condition, with a winding river just by it, some pleasant trees and rows of poplars, and a big greenhouse. It is empty, the windows are boarded up, and the place is being allowed to fall down. It would be wrong to leave this part of the Lincolnshire Fen country without noting the current trend of agriculture here.

In 1895 a man named Wilson Fox made a report on the farming of this part of England for the Royal Commission on Agriculture. He remarked on the great number of smallholders and small farmers who made a prosperous living in the Fens. He gave as an example one who: 'began life as a farm labourer and, having saved money out of his wages, he hired six acres of land at 66s an acre. About twenty years ago (1875) he bought twelve acres at £106 an acre. He put up all the sheds, built a good stable and made all the fences which are well kept. He grows early potatoes, bulbs of all sorts, tree and bush fruit, mustard, wheat, mangold, flowers. He also keeps pigs, poultry and bees. His land is kept clean and as neat as it is possible to be. He sells everything to buyers who come round, and only goes to market once a year. His profits for 1893 and 1894 were respectively £86 and £111, besides which bacon, eggs and vegetables were consumed in the house. The largest items of profit in 1894 were mustard £45, early potatoes £55, potatoes £32, bulbs £27, pigs £20'.

Now such men are becoming rarer and rarer. In the name of the modern gospel of 'economy of scale' the small farmers are being ruthlessly pushed out – the Government will even pay them to get out – and their holdings bulldozed together into enormous farms, where *agri-businessmen* as they call themselves, practise a husbandry tending more and more towards monoculture.

The Welland, the smallest of the four rivers that discharge into the Wash, has the village of **Fosdyke** a little way up it, with a good pub much used by fishermen, and eight small shrimpers. These boats go mostly for the small brown shrimps which are caught in shallow water, and not the (*Crangon vulgaris*) 'prawns' sought after by the Boston smacks. The Lineham family is the chief fishing family here, and any one of its members will put the stranger right about the Wash.

We cross the Welland by a delightful steel bridge built in 1910 and 1911, and make our way downstream to the Wash again. A strange phenomenon has been noticed here of late. Dead baby seals have been found in the fresh water drainage dykes *behind* the sea walls. How did they get there? They could never have climbed the high grass sea walls, and the dykes are cut off from the sea by sluices which only open to let water out, and not in. Well, the answer is a simple one (although it might go on baffling serious naturalists who do not read this book for many a year). The employees of the River Authority (one or two of whom have been known to have a drink in the very good pub at Fosdyke) have the job of clearing the fresh-water weed out of the drainage dykes. Weary of doing this by hand they have developed the (unofficial) habit of propping open the sluice gates – so as to let the salt water come in at high tide and do the job for them. The baby seals have been washed in with the salt water.

Now as we work east along the southern shore of the Wash, and arrive inland of that sand actually called the Thornback (but mis-called the Puff for some reason on Ordnance Survey maps – no local man has ever heard it called that), we turn a right-angle of the seawall and see before us, moored out on the wide saltings, a little house-boat. This is the home-from-home of Mr Kenzie Thorpe, who is perhaps the most famous wildfowler in England. That is, he does not now kill many wildfowl (only a very few geese every winter for the pot) but has lived for most of his life by either shooting wildfowl or by taking parties out shooting them. He still does this, he also goes all over the country lecturing, and paints very good pictures of the marshes and the birds that live there. He lives, most incongruously, when not out on the Wash, in a council house in Sutton Bridge. He also keeps an aviary of water birds. Mr Thorpe certainly knows more about the wildfowl in the Wash than any other living man. He estimated that in the winter of 1969–70 there were about 6,000 pinkfoot geese, 450 brent geese, 35,000 wigeon, a few bean geese and some 60 whitefront geese (the latter chiefly to be found inland on Welney Wash). The geese are much shot *at* by amateur wildfowlers, but very few of them are actually brought down. The average bag of the average amateur wildfowler is – *nil*. Many a goose that is shot, however, has lead in her, having been peppered at various times from various distances. In the winter time the sea-walls of the Wash are *lined* with wildfowlers – in places they resemble the front line trenches of the Western Front in the 1914–18 War. The shore of the Wash has been carved up by various 'Wildfowlers Associations' – here we are on the territory of the *Gedney Drove End and District Wildfowl Association*, and the banks are lined with the admonitory notice boards of this organisation.

The strange tower in front of us is one of the signal towers of the United States Air Force, which has a very large bombing range here. When the flags are up I would advise against strolling out over the mud or sand, but the sea-wall is safe enough until you get to the

Fleet Haven Outfall. You can then cut inland by road, or else stick to the Old Sea Wall, there having been a new bite of land here recently.

Gedney Drove End is as far-away and remote as its name. A mile south-east of it is (or *was* alas) a noble little pub called The Ship, crouching down behind the sea-wall. I last visited this in early 1970, and by then the landlord had had notice that his licence was to be taken away. The pub was formerly owned by Soames's Brewery, of Spalding. This brewery has been bought up by Watneys, with all the pubs belonging to it, and the policy apparently is to close down all the smaller country pubs and concentrate on main road pubs with more trade. Thus the people of this remote corner of England are to lose their only social centre, and the lamented drift to the towns will be, no doubt, accelerated.

At low tide here we can walk out along the dried-out sands to the mouth of the Nene, where that river takes a right turn at a large beacon named Big Annie. Going upstream the marks are called: Dale Beacon, Double Brush, and Big Tom. The two pretty eighteenth-century lighthouses near the *dry-land mouth* of the Nene were once right at the dry-land mouth but are now inland because a bite of saltings has been 'inned' here recently. The one on the west side is at present unoccupied, the one on the east is lived in by the warden of the Wildfowl Association. It was once the home of Mr Peter Scott when that naturalist was a young man, and when Mr Kenzie Thorpe lived there too, and worked for him, and taught him much of what he knows about birds.

And so we head upstream along the dead straight artificial cut of the Nene to **Sutton Bridge**. Here is the jetty mostly occupied by Mr Tom Lineham and his son and young helper, and from which he operates a small fleet of boats, shrimping, taking out pilots, salvaging American practice bombs, and painting and repairing bombing targets. Tom Lineham Senior knows the Wash better than any other living man. Another of his activities during the last six or seven years has been sealing. He and a small group of Scottish sealers go out every summer and take a controlled cropping from the baby seals of the Wash. The seals are killed mostly from high-powered speed boats with very big outboard engines that rush them while they are on the sands, and they are either clubbed or shot with rifles. They are skinned on the deck of a smack which accompanies the speed boats, and the skins treated and sold. This is only a revival of an age-old industry, for seals were always a crop in the Wash just as shrimps and other shellfish were. There are at present an estimated

3,000 seals in the Wash: all Common Seals (excepting for a few Grey Seals found on the Long Sands only). The seals bask on the dried-out sands at low tide, and swim away to fish at high water. In June they come high up on the saltings to pup. At this time one can often walk out on the sands, or land on them from a boat, and pick a young seal up. However sad we may feel that young seals are killed, it is incontrovertible that, in too great numbers, they do enormous harm to the fisheries around these islands. They have no natural enemies here except Man, and they directly compete with him for food. The Linehams have no intention of reducing their numbers further than they have been reduced already, and look upon them simply as a crop, to be protected and conserved as are other crops. Besides a modern Leigh-on-Sea-built 'sand topper', the Linehams have a noble old smack, the *Mermaid*, built in 1904 in Boston as a sailing smack, and sound today as the day she was built, in spite of the fact that she has worked as hard as any vessel in the world.

A strange thing just upstream from the Linehams' wharf is the old Sutton Bridge Dock – now a golf course. This was the result of a grandiose scheme of 1881, for building a huge wet dock here which was to put Wisbech out of business, and Boston too, and King's Lynn also. The huge dock, with an entrance eighteen yards wide, was opened in May 1881 and in June the lock gates collapsed – owing, it was said, to a spring of water underneath which had not been allowed for. Money had by then run out and the whole thing was abandoned.

The swing bridge at Sutton Bridge was built in 1894–97 to replace an older one. Hilaire Belloc once wrote a very good essay about it. The Bridge Inn, next to it, is a fine place to stay.

Wisbech, up-river, is not on the coast (although it once was), and therefore not in the scope of this book.

The Norfolk border is about two miles east of the mouth of the Nene.

Index